Mastering Siemens S7: A Comprehensive Guide to PLC Programming

Kameron Hussain and Frahaan Hussain

Published by Sonar Publishing, 2024.

While every precaution has been taken in the preparation of this book, the publisher assumes no responsibility for errors or omissions, or for damages resulting from the use of the information contained herein.

MASTERING SIEMENS S7: A COMPREHENSIVE GUIDE TO PLC PROGRAMMING

First edition. May 12, 2024.

Copyright © 2024 Kameron Hussain and Frahaan Hussain.

ISBN: 979-8224060634

Written by Kameron Hussain and Frahaan Hussain.

Table of Contents

Chapter 1: Introduction to Siemens S7

1.1 The Evolution of Siemens PLCs

SIEMENS PLCS HAVE A rich history dating back several decades. The evolution of these programmable logic controllers has been marked by significant advancements in technology and functionality.

Initially, Siemens PLCs were simple relay-based systems used for basic automation tasks in industrial settings. These early PLCs provided a revolutionary alternative to traditional hardwired control systems, offering flexibility and ease of programming.

As industrial automation requirements grew more complex, Siemens continuously innovated its PLC offerings. The introduction of microprocessor-based controllers in the 1980s marked a significant milestone, enabling faster processing speeds and greater memory capacity. This allowed for more sophisticated control algorithms and expanded applications.

With the advent of the Siemens S7 series in the 1990s, PLCs entered a new era of performance and versatility. The S7 series introduced modular hardware platforms and advanced programming capabilities, empowering engineers to tackle even the most demanding automation challenges.

One of the key drivers behind the evolution of Siemens PLCs has been the demand for increased integration and connectivity. As industrial systems became more interconnected, PLCs evolved to support various communication protocols and networking technologies, facilitating seamless data exchange and interoperability.

The integration of advanced features such as integrated motion control, safety functions, and remote diagnostics further enhanced the capabilities of Siemens PLCs, making them indispensable components of modern automation systems.

Today, Siemens PLCs continue to evolve in response to emerging trends such as Industry 4.0 and the Internet of Things (IoT). These developments are shaping the next generation of PLCs, which are characterized by enhanced connectivity, intelligence, and scalability.

In summary, the evolution of Siemens PLCs reflects a continuous journey of innovation and adaptation to meet the evolving needs of industrial automation. From humble beginnings as relay-based controllers to sophisticated programmable logic devices powering smart factories of the future, Siemens PLCs have come a long way in revolutionizing industrial control systems.

1.2 Overview of the Siemens S7 Series

THE SIEMENS S7 SERIES comprises a range of programmable logic controllers (PLCs) designed to meet the diverse needs of industrial automation applications. With a legacy spanning several decades, the S7 series has established itself as a leading platform in the field of automation.

At the heart of the Siemens S7 series is the Simatic S7 family of controllers, which includes various models tailored to different application requirements. These controllers are renowned for their reliability, performance, and flexibility, making them ideal for a wide range of industries, from manufacturing and energy to transportation and infrastructure.

The Simatic S7 family is characterized by its modular design, allowing users to configure systems according to specific needs. The family consists of different CPU modules, input/output (I/O) modules, communication modules, and other accessories, providing scalability and customization options to suit various automation tasks.

One of the key features of the Siemens S7 series is its powerful programming environment. The S7 series supports multiple programming languages, including ladder logic, function block diagrams, and structured text, enabling engineers to implement control algorithms using their preferred method.

The programming software used for Siemens S7 controllers is known as STEP 7, which provides a user-friendly interface for programming, simulation, and diagnostics. STEP 7 offers a comprehensive set of tools and libraries for developing and managing automation projects, streamlining the development process and improving productivity.

In addition to its robust hardware and software offerings, the Siemens S7 series is known for its extensive communication capabilities. The controllers support a wide range of industrial communication protocols, including Profibus, Profinet, Modbus, and Ethernet/IP, allowing seamless integration with other automation devices and systems.

Another notable aspect of the Siemens S7 series is its focus on safety and reliability. The controllers feature built-in safety functions and certifications, ensuring compliance with industry standards and regulations related to machine safety. This makes them suitable for applications where safety is paramount, such as in hazardous environments or critical infrastructure.

Overall, the Siemens S7 series stands as a testament to Siemens' commitment to innovation and excellence in industrial automation.

With its modular design, powerful programming environment, extensive communication capabilities, and emphasis on safety, the S7 series continues to be a preferred choice for engineers and system integrators worldwide.

1.3 Benefits of Using Siemens S7 in Industrial Automation

THE SIEMENS S7 SERIES offers numerous advantages that make it a preferred choice for industrial automation applications across various industries. These benefits stem from its advanced features, reliability, and comprehensive support ecosystem.

One of the key benefits of using Siemens S7 in industrial automation is its scalability. The modular design of S7 controllers allows users to easily expand their automation systems by adding additional hardware modules or upgrading existing ones. This scalability enables seamless adaptation to changing production requirements and facilitates future expansions without significant investment in new infrastructure.

Another advantage of Siemens S7 is its high performance and processing power. S7 controllers are equipped with powerful processors and ample memory, enabling them to execute complex control algorithms and handle large volumes of data with ease. This high performance ensures smooth operation of automation processes, minimizing downtime and maximizing productivity.

The robustness and reliability of Siemens S7 controllers are also noteworthy benefits. Designed to withstand harsh industrial environments, S7 controllers are built to last and operate reliably under challenging conditions such as extreme temperatures, vibration, and electromagnetic interference. This reliability translates to lower maintenance costs and increased uptime for industrial automation systems.

The flexibility and versatility of Siemens S7 controllers make them suitable for a wide range of automation tasks. Whether it's simple discrete control, complex motion control, or integrated safety functions, S7 controllers can handle diverse application requirements with ease. This versatility allows users to standardize their automation platforms and simplify maintenance and training efforts.

Integration capabilities are another key benefit of Siemens S7 controllers. With support for various communication protocols and networking technologies, S7 controllers can seamlessly communicate with other automation devices, sensors, actuators, and supervisory systems. This enables real-time data exchange, remote monitoring, and centralized control, enhancing overall system efficiency and agility.

The comprehensive support ecosystem provided by Siemens is another advantage of using S7 controllers. From technical documentation and online resources to training programs and customer support services, Siemens offers a wealth of resources to help users get the most out of their S7 controllers. This support ecosystem ensures that users can effectively deploy, maintain, and optimize their automation systems for maximum performance and uptime.

In summary, the benefits of using Siemens S7 in industrial automation are numerous and significant. From scalability and high performance to reliability, versatility, integration capabilities, and comprehensive support, S7 controllers offer a compelling solution for a wide range of automation applications.

1.4 Key Features of Siemens S7 PLCs

SIEMENS S7 PROGRAMMABLE logic controllers (PLCs) are renowned for their rich feature set, which empowers users to tackle diverse automation challenges with ease. These key features distinguish S7 PLCs from other automation platforms and contribute to their widespread adoption across various industries.

One of the standout features of Siemens S7 PLCs is their modular design. S7 controllers are composed of interchangeable modules, including central processing units (CPUs), input/output (I/O) modules, communication modules, and special function modules. This modular architecture allows users to customize their automation systems according to specific requirements, enabling efficient use of resources and cost-effective scalability.

Another key feature of Siemens S7 PLCs is their powerful programming environment. The S7 series supports multiple programming languages, including ladder logic, function block diagrams, structured text, and sequential function charts. This flexibility enables users to choose the most suitable programming method for their applications and facilitates code reuse and maintenance.

S7 PLCs are equipped with advanced communication capabilities, enabling seamless integration with other automation devices, supervisory systems, and enterprise networks. The controllers support a wide range of industrial communication protocols, including Profibus, Profinet, Modbus, Ethernet/IP, and TCP/IP, ensuring compatibility with existing infrastructure and facilitating data exchange in real-time.

Another notable feature of Siemens S7 PLCs is their extensive diagnostics and troubleshooting capabilities. The controllers provide comprehensive diagnostic tools and built-in self-testing functions, allowing users to quickly identify and address issues in their automation systems. This proactive approach to maintenance helps minimize downtime and optimize system performance.

Safety is a top priority in industrial automation, and Siemens S7 PLCs are designed with this in mind. The controllers feature integrated safety functions and certifications, ensuring compliance with industry standards and regulations related to machine safety. This built-in safety functionality simplifies the implementation of safety measures and reduces the complexity of safety-related programming.

S7 PLCs offer robust data handling capabilities, allowing users to efficiently process and manipulate data from various sources. The controllers support a wide range of data types and structures, including integers, floating-point numbers, strings, arrays, and user-defined data types. This flexibility enables users to implement complex algorithms and data processing tasks with ease.

Another key feature of Siemens S7 PLCs is their high-speed processing capabilities. S7 controllers are equipped with powerful processors and optimized firmware, enabling fast execution of control algorithms and rapid response to input signals. This high-speed processing ensures smooth operation of automation processes and enables precise control of machinery and equipment.

S7 PLCs are designed for easy integration with human-machine interfaces (HMIs) and visualization systems. The controllers support standard communication protocols for HMI integration, allowing users to create intuitive operator interfaces for monitoring and controlling automation processes. This seamless integration enhances operator productivity and improves overall system performance.

In summary, the key features of Siemens S7 PLCs make them a preferred choice for industrial automation applications. From their modular design and powerful programming environment to advanced communication capabilities, extensive diagnostics, safety features, robust data handling, high-speed processing, and HMI integration, S7 PLCs offer a comprehensive solution for diverse automation needs.

1.5 The Role of Siemens S7 in Modern Industries

SIEMENS S7 PROGRAMMABLE logic controllers (PLCs) play a crucial role in modern industries, serving as the backbone of automation systems in various sectors. From manufacturing and energy to transportation and infrastructure, S7 PLCs are widely deployed across diverse applications, driving efficiency, productivity, and innovation.

One of the primary roles of Siemens S7 PLCs in modern industries is to automate production processes. S7 controllers are used to control machinery and equipment in manufacturing facilities, optimizing production throughput, ensuring product quality, and reducing manufacturing costs. By automating repetitive and labor-intensive tasks, S7 PLCs enable manufacturers to achieve higher levels of efficiency and competitiveness in today's global marketplace.

S7 PLCs also play a vital role in ensuring the safety of industrial operations. With integrated safety functions and certifications, S7 controllers help prevent accidents and protect workers from hazards in industrial environments. Safety features such as emergency stop circuits, safety interlocks, and safe motion control enable manufacturers to comply with stringent safety regulations and standards, safeguarding both personnel and equipment.

In addition to production automation and safety, Siemens S7 PLCs contribute to energy efficiency and sustainability in modern industries. By optimizing energy usage and reducing waste, S7 controllers help companies minimize their environmental footprint and achieve sustainability goals. Advanced energy management features, such as power monitoring, load shedding, and predictive maintenance, enable industries to operate more efficiently and responsibly.

S7 PLCs also play a crucial role in enabling smart factories and Industry 4.0 initiatives. With their advanced communication capabilities and compatibility with industrial Internet of Things (IoT) technologies, S7 controllers facilitate real-time data exchange, remote monitoring, and predictive analytics. This enables manufacturers to create interconnected and intelligent production systems that can adapt to changing market demands and optimize performance in real-time.

Furthermore, Siemens S7 PLCs are instrumental in enabling digital transformation in modern industries. By integrating automation systems with enterprise resource planning (ERP) and manufacturing execution systems (MES), S7 controllers provide seamless data exchange between the shop floor and the top floor, enabling better decision-making and resource allocation. This integration streamlines operations, improves visibility, and enhances agility, helping companies stay competitive in today's fast-paced business environment.

Overall, the role of Siemens S7 PLCs in modern industries is multifaceted and indispensable. From automating production processes and ensuring safety to promoting energy efficiency, enabling smart factories, and driving digital transformation, S7 controllers are at the forefront of innovation in industrial automation. As industries continue to evolve and embrace new technologies, S7 PLCs will remain essential tools for driving efficiency, productivity, and sustainability across various sectors.

Chapter 2: Basics of PLC Programming

2.1 Understanding Ladder Logic

LADDER LOGIC IS A GRAPHICAL programming language commonly used in programmable logic controllers (PLCs) to create control algorithms for industrial automation systems. It is named after the ladder-like appearance of its diagrams, which resemble the rungs of a ladder. Ladder logic is widely used due to its simplicity, ease of understanding, and resemblance to traditional relay logic circuits.

At the core of ladder logic programming are relay coils and contacts, which represent the inputs, outputs, and logic functions of a control system. Coils are used to control outputs such as motors, valves, and lights, while contacts represent inputs such as sensors, switches, and signals from other devices.

Ladder logic diagrams consist of horizontal rungs that represent logical expressions and vertical rails that denote power or signal lines. Each rung typically contains one or more input contacts, followed by a series of logic functions, and an output coil. The logic functions are connected in series and/or parallel to implement various control functions.

Common logic functions used in ladder logic programming include AND, OR, NOT, XOR, NAND, and NOR. These functions allow users to create complex control algorithms by combining multiple input signals and logical conditions. Additionally, timers, counters, and other specialized instructions are available to implement advanced control functions.

One of the key advantages of ladder logic programming is its intuitive visual representation, which makes it easy for engineers and technicians to understand and modify control algorithms. The graphical nature of ladder logic diagrams allows users to quickly identify input-output relationships and logical connections, facilitating troubleshooting and debugging.

Ladder logic programming follows the principle of scan cycles, where the PLC scans the ladder logic program repeatedly to update outputs based on input conditions. During each scan cycle, the PLC evaluates the logical expressions on each rung and energizes or de-energizes output coils accordingly. This cyclic process ensures that the control system operates continuously and responds to changes in input conditions in real-time.

Another important aspect of ladder logic programming is the concept of memory bits, which are used to store and manipulate data within the PLC. Memory bits can represent boolean values, integers, timers, counters, and other data types, allowing users to implement state-based logic and data processing tasks.

In summary, ladder logic is a fundamental programming language used in PLC programming for industrial automation. Its graphical nature, simplicity, and intuitive design make it well-suited for creating control algorithms for a wide range of applications. By understanding the principles of ladder logic programming, engineers and technicians can effectively design, implement, and maintain automation systems in modern industries.

2.2 Introduction to Function Block Diagrams

FUNCTION BLOCK DIAGRAMS (FBDs) are another graphical programming language commonly used in programmable logic controllers (PLCs) for industrial automation. Similar to ladder logic, FBDs provide a visual representation of control algorithms, allowing engineers and technicians to create and modify logic diagrams with ease.

In Function Block Diagrams, control algorithms are represented by interconnected blocks, each of which performs a specific function or operation. These blocks can represent input/output devices, logical functions, timers, counters, arithmetic operations, and other control elements. By connecting the output of one block to the input of another, users can create complex control algorithms by combining simple functions.

The graphical nature of Function Block Diagrams makes them well-suited for visualizing and understanding control algorithms. Each block in an FBD represents a discrete function or operation, making it easy to identify and troubleshoot individual components of the control system. Additionally, the hierarchical structure of FBDs allows users to organize and modularize their control algorithms for improved readability and maintainability.

One of the key advantages of Function Block Diagrams is their reusability. Users can create custom function blocks that encapsulate specific control algorithms or processes, allowing them to reuse these blocks in multiple projects. This modular approach to programming promotes code reuse, reduces development time, and simplifies maintenance efforts.

Function Block Diagrams also support data flow programming, where the output of one block depends on the input values and states of other blocks in the diagram. This allows users to create dynamic control algorithms that respond to changes in input conditions and adapt to varying operating conditions.

In addition to their graphical representation, Function Block Diagrams can be augmented with textual descriptions and annotations to provide additional context and documentation. This helps users understand the purpose and operation of each block within the diagram and facilitates collaboration among team members during the development process.

Function Block Diagrams are often used in conjunction with other programming languages such as ladder logic and structured text to create comprehensive control algorithms. Each programming language has its strengths and weaknesses, and choosing the right language depends on the specific requirements of the application and the preferences of the programming team.

In summary, Function Block Diagrams are a powerful programming language used in PLC programming for industrial automation. Their graphical nature, reusability, modularity, and support for data flow programming make them an essential tool for creating complex control algorithms in modern industries. By understanding the principles of Function Block Diagrams, engineers and technicians can effectively design, implement, and maintain automation systems that meet the needs of today's manufacturing environments.

2.3 Programming Languages for PLCs

PROGRAMMING LANGUAGES play a critical role in PLC programming, as they provide the syntax and structure for creating control algorithms and automation logic. Several programming languages are commonly used in PLC programming, each with its own strengths and applications.

One of the most widely used programming languages in PLC programming is ladder logic. Ladder logic is a graphical programming language that resembles traditional relay logic circuits, making it easy for engineers and technicians to understand and work with. Ladder logic is well-suited for simple control tasks and discrete logic operations, such as on/off control and sequential logic.

Another popular programming language for PLCs is Function Block Diagrams (FBDs). FBDs provide a graphical representation of control algorithms using interconnected blocks, each of which performs a specific function or operation. FBDs are ideal for creating modular and reusable control algorithms and are commonly used in complex automation systems.

Structured Text (ST) is a textual programming language used in PLC programming for more complex control algorithms and mathematical operations. ST resembles high-level programming languages such as C or Pascal and allows for more flexible and expressive programming compared to ladder logic or FBDs. ST is often used for implementing algorithms that require complex mathematical calculations, data manipulation, or string processing.

Another textual programming language commonly used in PLC programming is Instruction List (IL). IL is a low-level programming language that resembles assembly language and is used for programming PLCs at the machine code level. IL is not as user-friendly as ladder logic or structured text but offers greater control and efficiency for experienced programmers.

Sequential Function Charts (SFCs) are another graphical programming language used in PLC programming for creating complex control sequences and state-based logic. SFCs allow users to define control algorithms as a series of steps or states, with transitions between states based on logical conditions. SFCs are well-suited for modeling sequential processes and state machines.

In addition to these programming languages, many PLCs support other languages such as Function Block Diagrams (FBDs), Continuous Function Charts (CFCs), and Structured Text (ST). The choice of programming language depends on the specific requirements of the application, the preferences of the programming team, and the capabilities of the PLC hardware and software.

Overall, the selection of programming languages for PLC programming depends on factors such as the complexity of the control algorithm, the familiarity of the programming team with the language, and the requirements of the application. By understanding the strengths and applications of different programming languages, engineers and technicians can effectively design and implement control algorithms for a wide range of industrial automation tasks.

2.4 Essential Programming Concepts

IN PLC PROGRAMMING, understanding essential programming concepts is crucial for creating effective and reliable control algorithms for industrial automation systems. These concepts form the foundation of PLC programming and are essential for engineers and technicians to master.

One of the fundamental programming concepts in PLC programming is the concept of inputs and outputs (I/O). Inputs represent signals or data received by the PLC from sensors, switches, and other external devices, while outputs represent signals or data sent by the PLC to actuators, motors, and other output devices. Understanding the relationship between inputs and outputs is essential for designing control algorithms that respond accurately to input conditions and produce the desired output.

Another important programming concept in PLC programming is the concept of logic functions. Logic functions are mathematical operations performed on input signals to determine the state of output signals. Common logic functions include AND, OR, NOT, XOR, NAND, and NOR, which allow engineers to create complex control algorithms by combining simple logical operations.

Timers and counters are essential programming concepts in PLC programming for implementing time-based and count-based control functions. Timers are used to control the timing of events and operations, while counters are used to count the number of occurrences of a specific event or condition. Understanding how to use timers and counters effectively is essential for creating control algorithms that meet timing and sequencing requirements.

Data types and data structures are fundamental programming concepts in PLC programming for representing and manipulating data within the PLC. Common data types include boolean, integer, floating-point, and string, while common data structures include arrays and structures. Understanding how to use data types and data structures effectively is essential for organizing and processing data within the PLC.

Control structures such as loops, branches, and jumps are essential programming concepts in PLC programming for controlling the flow of execution within a control algorithm. Loops allow engineers to repeat a series of instructions multiple times, branches allow engineers to make decisions based on logical conditions, and jumps allow engineers to transfer control to different parts of the control algorithm.

Error handling and fault tolerance are essential programming concepts in PLC programming for detecting and responding to errors and faults within the control system. Engineers must understand how to design control algorithms that can detect and recover from errors and faults to ensure the reliability and safety of the automation system.

Modularity and reusability are essential programming concepts in PLC programming for creating control algorithms that are easy to understand, maintain, and modify. Engineers must understand how to modularize control algorithms into smaller, reusable components that can be easily combined to create complex control algorithms for different applications.

Documentation and comments are essential programming concepts in PLC programming for documenting the design, implementation, and operation of control algorithms. Engineers must understand how to use documentation and comments effectively to communicate the purpose and functionality of control algorithms to other team members and stakeholders.

Overall, understanding essential programming concepts is essential for engineers and technicians to create effective and reliable control algorithms for industrial automation systems. By mastering these concepts, engineers can design control algorithms that meet the requirements of the application and ensure the reliability and safety of the automation system.

2.5 Reading and Interpreting PLC Code

READING AND INTERPRETING PLC code is a critical skill for engineers and technicians involved in industrial automation. PLC code consists of a series of instructions written in a programming language such as ladder logic, Function Block Diagrams (FBDs), or structured text (ST). Understanding how to read and interpret PLC code is essential for troubleshooting, debugging, and maintaining automation systems.

One of the first steps in reading PLC code is understanding the structure and syntax of the programming language used. Each programming language has its own syntax rules and conventions for representing control algorithms and logic. Engineers must familiarize themselves with the syntax of the programming language to understand how instructions are written and interpreted by the PLC.

Once the structure and syntax of the programming language are understood, engineers can begin to analyze the logic and functionality of the PLC code. This involves identifying input and output signals, logical functions, timers, counters, and other control elements within the code. Engineers must understand how these elements interact to control the operation of the automation system.

Understanding the flow of execution within the PLC code is another important aspect of reading and interpreting PLC code. Engineers must identify the sequence of instructions executed by the PLC during each scan cycle and how they are organized within the code. This allows engineers to understand the logical flow of the control algorithm and how inputs are processed to produce outputs.

Comments and annotations within the PLC code provide valuable insights into the purpose and functionality of specific instructions and sections of code. Engineers should pay attention to comments and annotations to understand the rationale behind the design decisions and to identify any potential issues or areas for improvement within the code.

Debugging and troubleshooting PLC code often involves tracing the execution path of the code and monitoring the values of input and output signals during operation. Engineers can use debugging tools and diagnostic features provided by the PLC programming software to monitor the behavior of the automation system and identify any anomalies or errors within the code.

In addition to understanding the logic and functionality of the PLC code, engineers must also consider the physical layout and configuration of the automation system. This includes understanding the wiring connections, hardware modules, and network configuration of the PLC system. Engineers must ensure that the PLC code is designed to interface correctly with the physical components of the automation system to ensure proper operation.

Documenting and documenting the PLC code is essential for maintaining and updating automation systems. Engineers should create detailed documentation that describes the purpose, functionality, and operation of each section of code. This documentation helps other team members understand the code and facilitates future modifications and enhancements to the automation system.

Overall, reading and interpreting PLC code is a fundamental skill for engineers and technicians involved in industrial automation. By understanding the structure, syntax, logic, and functionality of PLC code, engineers can effectively troubleshoot, debug, and maintain automation systems to ensure reliable operation in modern industries.

Chapter 3: Setting Up Your Siemens S7 Environment

3.1 Equipment and Software Requirements

SETTING UP A SIEMENS S7 environment requires careful consideration of both hardware and software requirements to ensure a smooth and efficient development process. Engineers and technicians must ensure that they have the necessary equipment and software tools to create, test, and deploy automation projects using Siemens S7 programmable logic controllers (PLCs).

The first step in setting up a Siemens S7 environment is to procure the required hardware components, including Siemens S7 PLCs, input/output (I/O) modules, communication modules, power supplies, and accessories. The selection of hardware components depends on the specific requirements of the automation project, such as the number of inputs and outputs, the type of communication protocol required, and the environmental conditions of the application.

Once the hardware components have been procured, engineers must ensure that they have the necessary tools and equipment to install and configure the hardware components properly. This may include tools for mounting and wiring PLCs, configuring network settings, and testing communication connections between devices. Proper installation and configuration of hardware components are essential for ensuring reliable operation of the automation system.

In addition to hardware requirements, engineers must also consider software requirements when setting up a Siemens S7 environment. The primary software tool used for programming Siemens S7 PLCs is STEP 7, which provides a user-friendly interface for creating, editing, and debugging control algorithms. Engineers must ensure that they have the necessary licenses and installation media for STEP 7 software.

In addition to STEP 7, engineers may also require other software tools and utilities for tasks such as simulation, diagnostics, and project management. These tools may include PLC simulation software, diagnostic tools, version control software, and project management software. Engineers must ensure that they have access to the appropriate software tools to facilitate the development and maintenance of automation projects.

Once the hardware and software requirements have been met, engineers must proceed with the installation and configuration of the Siemens S7 environment. This involves installing the necessary hardware components, configuring network settings, installing and licensing the required software tools, and setting up user accounts and permissions.

During the installation and configuration process, engineers must follow the manufacturer's instructions and best practices to ensure that the Siemens S7 environment is set up correctly. This may involve consulting documentation, attending training sessions, or seeking assistance from experienced professionals to ensure that the installation and configuration process proceeds smoothly.

Once the Siemens S7 environment has been set up, engineers can proceed with creating and testing automation projects using STEP 7 software. This involves creating a new project, configuring hardware settings, programming control algorithms, testing the functionality of the automation system in simulation mode, and deploying the project to the PLC hardware.

Throughout the setup process, engineers must adhere to industry best practices and standards to ensure the reliability, safety, and security of the automation system. This includes following recommended installation procedures, configuring network settings securely, implementing backup and recovery procedures, and regularly updating software and firmware to protect against security vulnerabilities.

By carefully considering both hardware and software requirements and following best practices for installation and configuration, engineers can ensure that their Siemens S7 environment is set up properly to support the development and deployment of automation projects in modern industries.

3.2 Installing STEP 7 Software

INSTALLING THE STEP 7 software is a crucial step in setting up a Siemens S7 environment for PLC programming and automation projects. STEP 7 is the primary software tool used for creating, editing, and debugging control algorithms for Siemens S7 programmable logic controllers (PLCs). The installation process for STEP 7 involves several steps, including obtaining the installation media, running the installation wizard, configuring installation settings, and activating the software license.

The first step in installing STEP 7 software is to obtain the installation media from the manufacturer or authorized distributor. The installation media may be provided as a physical disc or as downloadable files from the manufacturer's website. Engineers must ensure that they have the correct version of STEP 7 software for their hardware platform and operating system.

Once the installation media has been obtained, engineers can begin the installation process by inserting the disc or launching the downloaded installation files. This initiates the installation wizard, which guides users through the steps required to install the software on their computer.

During the installation process, engineers must configure various installation settings, such as the installation directory, language preferences, and optional components. Engineers should carefully review the installation settings to ensure that they meet their requirements and preferences for using the STEP 7 software.

After configuring the installation settings, engineers must wait for the installation process to complete. This may take several minutes, depending on the speed of the computer and the size of the installation files. Engineers should be patient and allow the installation process to finish without interruption.

Once the installation process is complete, engineers may be prompted to activate the software license. Activation typically involves entering a license key or activation code provided by the manufacturer or authorized distributor. Engineers must ensure that they have a valid license key and follow the instructions provided to activate the software license successfully.

After activating the software license, engineers can launch the STEP 7 software and begin using it to create, edit, and debug control algorithms for Siemens S7 PLCs. Engineers should familiarize themselves with the user interface and features of STEP 7 software to maximize their productivity and efficiency when working on automation projects.

In addition to installing STEP 7 software, engineers may also need to install additional software tools and utilities required for PLC programming and automation projects. These tools may include PLC simulation software, diagnostic tools, communication drivers, and project management software. Engineers should ensure that they have all the necessary software tools installed and configured to support their automation projects effectively.

Overall, installing STEP 7 software is a critical step in setting up a Siemens S7 environment for PLC programming and automation projects. By following the installation instructions provided by the manufacturer and configuring the software settings correctly, engineers can ensure that they have a reliable and efficient development environment for creating automation solutions in modern industries.

3.3 Configuring Hardware and Network Settings

CONFIGURING HARDWARE and network settings is a crucial aspect of setting up a Siemens S7 environment for PLC programming and automation projects. Proper configuration of hardware components and network settings ensures that the PLC hardware communicates effectively with other devices and systems within the automation environment.

The first step in configuring hardware settings is to install and mount the PLC hardware components according to the manufacturer's specifications and recommendations. This involves mounting the PLC chassis, inserting the CPU module and I/O modules into the chassis, and connecting power and communication cables to the PLC hardware. Engineers must ensure that all connections are secure and that the PLC hardware is installed in a suitable location within the automation system.

Once the PLC hardware components have been installed, engineers must configure the hardware settings using the configuration software provided by the manufacturer. This software allows engineers to configure parameters such as I/O addresses, communication settings, module types, and hardware diagnostics. Engineers must ensure that the hardware settings are configured correctly to ensure proper operation of the PLC hardware within the automation system.

In addition to configuring hardware settings, engineers must also configure network settings to enable communication between the PLC hardware and other devices and systems within the automation environment. This involves configuring parameters such as IP addresses, subnet masks, gateway addresses, and communication protocols for the PLC hardware and network devices. Engineers must ensure that the network settings are configured correctly to establish reliable communication connections and prevent network conflicts.

During the configuration process, engineers must also consider security considerations such as access control, authentication, and encryption to protect the PLC hardware and communication networks from unauthorized access and malicious attacks. This may involve implementing security measures such as firewall rules, user authentication, encrypted communication protocols, and network segmentation to ensure the integrity and confidentiality of data transmitted between devices.

Once the hardware and network settings have been configured, engineers must test the communication connections between the PLC hardware and other devices and systems within the automation environment. This involves verifying that data can be transmitted and received successfully between devices, monitoring network traffic for errors or anomalies, and troubleshooting any communication issues that arise. Engineers must ensure that the communication connections are reliable and stable to support the operation of the automation system.

In addition to configuring hardware and network settings, engineers may also need to configure software settings within the PLC programming software to ensure compatibility with the configured hardware and network settings. This may involve configuring parameters such as communication protocols, device addresses, and network configurations within the programming software to establish communication connections with the PLC hardware.

Overall, configuring hardware and network settings is a critical step in setting up a Siemens S7 environment for PLC programming and automation projects. By properly configuring hardware components and network settings, engineers can ensure that the PLC hardware communicates effectively with other devices and systems within the automation environment, enabling the creation of reliable and efficient automation solutions in modern industries.

3.4 First Steps with SIMATIC Manager

GETTING STARTED WITH SIMATIC Manager is an essential part of setting up a Siemens S7 environment for PLC programming and automation projects. SIMATIC Manager is the central software tool used for creating, editing, and managing automation projects for Siemens S7 programmable logic controllers (PLCs). This section provides an overview of the first steps to take when using SIMATIC Manager for the first time.

The first step when using SIMATIC Manager is to launch the software from the Start menu or desktop shortcut. Once the software is launched, users are presented with the main interface, which consists of various navigation panels, toolbars, and project views. Users can navigate through different project views using the tree structure on the left-hand side of the interface, which displays project folders, blocks, and program files.

To create a new project in SIMATIC Manager, users can click on the "New" button in the toolbar and follow the prompts to specify the project name, location, and hardware configuration. Users must select the appropriate hardware configuration based on the type of PLC hardware they are using, such as the CPU module, I/O modules, and communication modules. Once the project settings have been configured, users can click "OK" to create the new project.

Once the project has been created, users can begin adding and configuring hardware components within the project. This involves selecting the appropriate hardware modules from the hardware catalog and dragging them into the project view. Users must configure parameters such as module addresses, input/output assignments, and communication settings for each hardware component to ensure proper operation within the automation system.

After configuring the hardware components, users can begin creating and editing control algorithms for the PLC hardware. This involves creating program blocks such as ladder logic, Function Block Diagrams (FBDs), and structured text (ST) programs within the project. Users can double-click on a program block to open it in the programming editor, where they can write and edit the control logic using the programming language of their choice.

In addition to creating program blocks, users can also create and manage data blocks within the project. Data blocks are used to store and manipulate data within the PLC hardware, such as variables, constants, and data structures. Users can define the data types, addresses, and sizes of data blocks within the project to facilitate data processing and manipulation within the automation system.

Once the control algorithms and data blocks have been created, users can compile the project to check for syntax errors and compile-time errors within the control logic. The compiler generates a compiled version of the project that can be downloaded to the PLC hardware for testing and execution. Users must resolve any errors or warnings generated by the compiler before proceeding to download the project to the PLC hardware.

After compiling the project, users can download the compiled project to the PLC hardware using the programming cable and communication interface provided by the manufacturer. Users must establish a communication connection between SIMATIC Manager and the PLC hardware and follow the prompts to download the project to the PLC memory. Once the project has been downloaded, users can test the functionality of the automation system and verify that the control algorithms operate as expected.

In summary, getting started with SIMATIC Manager involves launching the software, creating a new project, configuring hardware components, creating and editing control algorithms, compiling the project, and downloading the project to the PLC hardware. By following these steps, users can begin developing automation projects for Siemens S7 PLCs and create reliable and efficient automation solutions in modern industries.

3.5 Creating a Project in TIA Portal

CREATING A PROJECT in TIA Portal is a fundamental step in setting up a Siemens S7 environment for PLC programming and automation projects. TIA Portal is the integrated engineering software platform used for configuring, programming, and commissioning automation projects for Siemens S7 PLCs. This section provides an overview of the steps involved in creating a new project in TIA Portal.

To create a new project in TIA Portal, users must first launch the software from the Start menu or desktop shortcut. Once the software is launched, users are presented with the project view, which displays a list of existing projects and provides options for creating a new project. Users can click on the "New Project" button to begin creating a new project.

When creating a new project in TIA Portal, users are prompted to specify the project name, location, and target hardware platform. Users must enter a descriptive name for the project and select the appropriate location on the computer where the project files will be stored. Users must also select the target hardware platform, which determines the hardware configuration and programming options available within the project.

Once the project settings have been configured, users can click "Create" to create the new project. TIA Portal generates a new project folder with the specified name and location and opens the project view, which displays the project folder structure and options for adding and configuring project components.

After creating the project, users can begin adding and configuring hardware components within the project. This involves selecting the appropriate hardware modules from the hardware catalog and dragging them into the project view. Users must configure parameters such as module addresses, input/output assignments, and communication settings for each hardware component to ensure proper operation within the automation system.

In addition to configuring hardware components, users can also create and manage program blocks within the project. Program blocks are used to define the control logic and functionality of the automation system, using programming languages such as ladder logic, Function Block Diagrams (FBDs), and structured text (ST). Users can create new program blocks by right-clicking on the project folder and selecting the appropriate option from the context menu.

Once the program blocks have been created, users can begin programming the control logic for the automation system. This involves writing and editing the control algorithms within the program blocks using the programming language of their choice. Users can use the built-in programming editor in TIA Portal to write and edit control logic, with features such as syntax highlighting, auto-completion, and debugging tools to assist in the programming process.

After programming the control logic, users can compile the project to check for syntax errors and compile-time errors within the control algorithms. The compiler generates a compiled version of the project that can be downloaded to the PLC hardware for testing and execution. Users must resolve any errors or warnings generated by the compiler before proceeding to download the project to the PLC hardware.

Once the project has been compiled, users can download the compiled project to the PLC hardware using the programming cable and communication interface provided by the manufacturer. Users must establish a communication connection between TIA Portal and the PLC hardware and follow the prompts to download the project to the PLC memory. Once the project has been downloaded, users can test the functionality of the automation system and verify that the control algorithms operate as expected.

In summary, creating a project in TIA Portal involves launching the software, creating a new project, configuring hardware components, creating and programming program blocks, compiling the project, and downloading the project to the PLC hardware. By following these steps, users can begin developing automation projects for Siemens S7 PLCs and create reliable and efficient automation solutions in modern industries.

Chapter 4: Diving Into STEP 7

4.1 Overview of the STEP 7 Interface

DIVING INTO STEP 7 involves familiarizing oneself with its interface, which serves as the gateway to creating, editing, and managing automation projects for Siemens S7 programmable logic controllers (PLCs). The STEP 7 interface is designed to provide users with intuitive access to a wide range of tools and functionalities needed for PLC programming and automation projects.

Upon launching STEP 7, users are greeted with a user-friendly interface consisting of various panels, toolbars, and menus. The main workspace area displays the project view, where users can navigate through project folders, blocks, and program files using a tree structure. This allows users to organize and manage their automation projects efficiently.

The toolbar at the top of the interface provides quick access to commonly used tools and functions, such as creating new projects, opening existing projects, compiling programs, and downloading projects to PLC hardware. Users can also access additional toolbars and menus by right-clicking within the workspace area, allowing for further customization and flexibility.

One of the key features of the STEP 7 interface is the integrated programming editor, which allows users to create and edit control algorithms for PLCs using various programming languages such as ladder logic, Function Block Diagrams (FBDs), and structured text (ST). The programming editor provides syntax highlighting, auto-completion, and debugging tools to assist users in writing and debugging control logic efficiently.

Another important aspect of the STEP 7 interface is the hardware configuration tool, which allows users to configure hardware components such as CPU modules, I/O modules, and communication modules within their automation projects. Users can select hardware components from a catalog and drag them into the project view to add them to their projects. They can then configure parameters such as module addresses, input/output assignments, and communication settings to ensure proper operation within the automation system.

The library manager in STEP 7 allows users to create and manage libraries of reusable program blocks, data blocks, and other project components. Users can create custom libraries to store frequently used program blocks and data structures, making it easy to reuse them across multiple projects. The library manager also provides tools for importing and exporting libraries, allowing users to share project components with other team members and collaborators.

In addition to the programming editor and hardware configuration tool, STEP 7 also provides various diagnostic and monitoring tools to help users debug and troubleshoot their automation projects. Users can monitor the status of PLC hardware and communication connections in real-time, view diagnostic messages and alarms, and analyze the behavior of the automation system during runtime.

Overall, the STEP 7 interface provides users with a comprehensive set of tools and functionalities for PLC programming and automation projects. By familiarizing themselves with the interface and its various features, users can streamline their workflow, improve productivity, and create reliable and efficient automation solutions in modern industries.

4.2 Navigating Through Options and Menus

NAVIGATING THROUGH options and menus is a fundamental aspect of using the STEP 7 interface effectively. The interface of STEP 7 is designed to provide users with easy access to a wide range of tools, functions, and settings needed for PLC programming and automation projects. This section explores how users can navigate through the various options and menus available in STEP 7 to perform different tasks and operations.

The main menu in STEP 7 provides access to a variety of options and functions organized into different categories such as File, Edit, View, Project, Tools, and Help. Users can navigate through these menu options using the mouse or keyboard shortcuts to access different features and functionalities within the software.

One of the key menu options in STEP 7 is the Project menu, which provides access to project-related functions such as creating new projects, opening existing projects, saving projects, and closing projects. Users can also use the Project menu to import and export project files, manage project settings, and perform other project-related tasks.

The Tools menu in STEP 7 provides access to various utility functions and tools that help users perform specific tasks related to PLC programming and automation projects. For example, users can use the Tools menu to access diagnostic tools, simulation tools, communication tools, and other utilities that assist in debugging, testing, and monitoring automation projects.

The View menu in STEP 7 allows users to customize the appearance and layout of the interface by enabling or disabling different panels, toolbars, and windows. Users can customize the view to suit their preferences and workflow by hiding or showing specific elements of the interface, rearranging panels, and adjusting the size and position of windows.

In addition to the main menu, STEP 7 also provides context menus that users can access by right-clicking within the workspace area or on specific elements such as project folders, blocks, and program files. Context menus provide quick access to relevant options and functions based on the current context, allowing users to perform actions such as creating new blocks, copying and pasting elements, renaming files, and deleting objects.

Users can also use keyboard shortcuts to navigate through options and menus in STEP 7, making it faster and more efficient to perform common tasks and operations. Keyboard shortcuts are displayed next to menu options and functions in the main menu, allowing users to quickly access them using the keyboard instead of the mouse.

Overall, navigating through options and menus in STEP 7 is essential for users to perform various tasks and operations related to PLC programming and automation projects efficiently. By familiarizing themselves with the main menu, context menus, and keyboard shortcuts, users can streamline their workflow, improve productivity, and create reliable and efficient automation solutions in modern industries.

4.3 Creating and Managing Libraries

CREATING AND MANAGING libraries is an essential aspect of PLC programming and automation projects in STEP 7. Libraries allow users to organize and reuse program blocks, data blocks, and other project components across multiple projects, improving efficiency and consistency in PLC programming. This section explores how users can create and manage libraries in STEP 7 to streamline their workflow and enhance productivity.

To create a new library in STEP 7, users can navigate to the Libraries folder within the project view and right-click to access the context menu. From the context menu, users can select the option to create a new library, which prompts them to specify the name and location of the new library. Users can enter a descriptive name for the library and choose the location where the library files will be stored within the project structure.

Once the new library has been created, users can begin adding program blocks, data blocks, and other project components to the library. Users can drag and drop existing program blocks and data blocks from the project view into the library folder, or they can create new program blocks and data blocks directly within the library folder using the appropriate options in the context menu.

After adding program blocks and data blocks to the library, users can organize and manage them by grouping related components into folders and subfolders. This allows users to maintain a structured and organized library hierarchy, making it easier to locate and access specific components when needed. Users can create new folders within the library folder and drag components into the desired folders to organize them accordingly.

In addition to program blocks and data blocks, users can also add other project components such as documentation files, configuration files, and parameter files to the library. This allows users to store all relevant project files and documentation within the library, ensuring that they are easily accessible and up-to-date.

Once the library has been populated with program blocks, data blocks, and other project components, users can save the library files and share them with other team members and collaborators. Users can export the library files to a specified location on their computer or network, allowing other users to import the library files into their own projects and access the shared components.

Users can also import existing library files into their projects by selecting the option to import libraries from the context menu. This allows users to reuse program blocks, data blocks, and other components from external libraries in their own projects, saving time and effort in PLC programming and automation projects.

Overall, creating and managing libraries in STEP 7 is essential for organizing and reusing program blocks, data blocks, and other project components across multiple projects. By creating structured and organized libraries, users can streamline their workflow, improve productivity, and create reliable and efficient automation solutions in modern industries.

4.4 Basic and Advanced Toolsets

STEP 7 OFFERS USERS both basic and advanced toolsets to streamline PLC programming and automation projects. These toolsets provide users with a wide range of functionalities and features to create, edit, and manage automation projects efficiently. This section explores the basic and advanced toolsets available in STEP 7 and how users can leverage them to improve productivity and reliability in PLC programming.

The basic toolset in STEP 7 includes essential tools and functions that users need for basic PLC programming tasks such as creating and editing program blocks, configuring hardware components, and compiling projects. These tools are designed to be user-friendly and intuitive, making them suitable for users with limited experience in PLC programming.

Some of the key features of the basic toolset include the programming editor, hardware configuration tool, project management tools, and diagnostic tools. The programming editor allows users to write and edit control logic for PLCs using various programming languages such as ladder logic, Function Block Diagrams (FBDs), and structured text (ST). The hardware configuration tool allows users to configure hardware components such as CPU modules, I/O modules, and communication modules within their projects.

In addition to the basic toolset, STEP 7 also offers users access to advanced toolsets that provide additional functionalities and features for more complex PLC programming tasks. The advanced toolsets are designed for users with advanced knowledge and experience in PLC programming and automation projects, allowing them to perform tasks such as advanced debugging, simulation, and optimization.

Some of the advanced toolsets available in STEP 7 include the simulation toolset, diagnostic toolset, optimization toolset, and integration toolset. The simulation toolset allows users to simulate their automation projects in a virtual environment, allowing them to test the functionality of their control algorithms and verify the behavior of their automation systems before deploying them in the field.

The diagnostic toolset provides users with advanced diagnostic and troubleshooting tools to identify and resolve issues in their automation projects quickly. The optimization toolset allows users to optimize their control algorithms and improve the performance and efficiency of their automation systems. The integration toolset allows users to integrate their automation projects with other systems and devices, enabling seamless communication and interoperability between different components.

Overall, the basic and advanced toolsets available in STEP 7 provide users with a comprehensive set of tools and functionalities to streamline PLC programming and automation projects. By leveraging these toolsets effectively, users can improve productivity, reliability, and efficiency in PLC programming and automation projects in modern industries.

4.5 Tips for Efficient Use of STEP 7

EFFICIENT USE OF STEP 7 is crucial for optimizing productivity and achieving reliable results in PLC programming and automation projects. This section provides a collection of tips and best practices to help users make the most out of their experience with STEP 7.

1. **Organize Your Project Structure**: Maintain a clear and organized project structure by using descriptive names for project folders, blocks, and files. Organizing your project structure makes it easier to navigate through your project and locate specific components quickly.

2. **Utilize Comments and Documentation**: Add comments and documentation to your program blocks to provide context and clarity to your code. Comments help other users understand the purpose and functionality of different parts of your program, making it easier to maintain and troubleshoot.

3. **Leverage Tag-Based Addressing**: Take advantage of tag-based addressing to improve readability and maintainability of your code. Instead of using direct memory addresses, use symbolic tags to refer to inputs,

outputs, and variables in your program. This makes it easier to understand and modify your code without needing to reference memory addresses directly.

4. **Use Structured Text for Complex Algorithms**: For complex algorithms and calculations, consider using structured text (ST) programming language. ST offers more flexibility and power compared to ladder logic or Function Block Diagrams (FBDs), making it suitable for implementing advanced control strategies and mathematical calculations.

5. **Implement Modular Programming**: Break down your program into smaller, reusable modules to promote code reusability and maintainability. Use functions and function blocks to encapsulate common tasks and functionalities, allowing you to easily reuse them across multiple projects.

6. **Take Advantage of Libraries**: Create and maintain libraries of reusable program blocks, data blocks, and other project components. Libraries help streamline development by providing a centralized repository of commonly used components that can be easily reused across different projects.

7. **Regularly Backup Your Projects**: Make it a habit to regularly backup your projects to prevent data loss in case of unexpected events such as hardware failures or software crashes. Store backup copies of your projects in a secure location, preferably on multiple storage devices or cloud storage services.

8. **Stay Up-to-Date with Software Updates**: Keep your STEP 7 software up-to-date by installing the latest software updates and patches released by the manufacturer. Software updates often include bug fixes, performance improvements, and new features that can enhance your

experience with STEP 7.

9. **Utilize Online Resources and Communities**: Take advantage of online resources, forums, and communities dedicated to STEP 7 and PLC programming. Engaging with other users and experts can provide valuable insights, tips, and solutions to common challenges you may encounter during your projects.

10. **Continuous Learning and Skill Development**: Invest time in continuous learning and skill development to stay updated with the latest advancements in PLC programming and automation technologies. Explore online courses, tutorials, and training programs to expand your knowledge and expertise in STEP 7 and related topics.

By following these tips and best practices, users can optimize their use of STEP 7 and achieve greater efficiency, reliability, and success in PLC programming and automation projects.

Chapter 5: Programming Concepts and Techniques

5.1 Working with Data Types and Structures

WORKING WITH DATA TYPES and structures is fundamental to PLC programming as it allows programmers to define and manipulate different types of data within their automation projects. This section explores various data types and structures commonly used in PLC programming and techniques for working with them effectively.

In PLC programming, data types define the format and size of data stored in memory and how it is interpreted by the controller. Common data types in PLC programming include Boolean, integer, floating-point, string, and user-defined data types. Boolean data types represent binary values such as true or false, while integer data types represent whole numbers. Floating-point data types are used to represent real numbers with decimal precision, and string data types are used to store text or character data. User-defined data types allow programmers to define custom data structures composed of multiple elements of different data types.

When working with data types in PLC programming, it is essential to consider the memory requirements and limitations of each data type. For example, Boolean data types typically require only one bit of memory, while integer and floating-point data types require multiple bytes of memory, and string data types require additional memory for storing text characters.

PLC programming languages such as ladder logic, Function Block Diagrams (FBDs), and structured text (ST) provide syntax and operators for working with different data types. For example, ladder logic provides basic logic elements such as contacts and coils for working with Boolean data types, while FBDs provide function blocks for performing arithmetic and logical operations on integer and floating-point data types. ST provides a more flexible and powerful programming language for working with all types of data, allowing programmers to define variables, data structures, and complex algorithms.

One common technique for working with data types in PLC programming is data conversion, which involves converting data from one data type to another. For example, programmers may need to convert integer data to floating-point data for performing arithmetic calculations or convert string data to integer data for parsing numerical values from text strings. PLC programming languages provide built-in functions and operators for performing data conversion operations, allowing programmers to convert data seamlessly within their programs.

Another important concept in PLC programming is data structures, which allow programmers to organize and group related data elements into a single entity. Common data structures in PLC programming include arrays, structures, and enumerated types. Arrays allow programmers to store multiple elements of the same data type in a sequential order, while structures allow programmers to define custom data types composed of multiple elements of different data types. Enumerated types allow programmers to define a set of named constants with corresponding integer values, making it easier to work with symbolic data.

When working with data structures in PLC programming, it is essential to understand how to access and manipulate individual elements within the structure. PLC programming languages provide syntax and operators for accessing and modifying elements of arrays and structures, allowing programmers to read and write data efficiently within their programs.

In summary, working with data types and structures is essential for PLC programming as it allows programmers to define and manipulate different types of data within their automation projects. By understanding the various data types and structures available in PLC programming languages and techniques for working with them effectively, programmers can create reliable and efficient automation solutions in modern industries.

5.2 Using Timers and Counters

TIMERS AND COUNTERS are essential elements in PLC programming, allowing programmers to control the timing and counting of events within their automation projects. This section explores the use of timers and counters in PLC programming and techniques for implementing them effectively.

Timers are used to control the timing of events within a PLC program by delaying the execution of certain actions or triggering events after a specified period. There are various types of timers available in PLC programming, including on-delay timers, off-delay timers, and retentive timers. On-delay timers start timing when they receive an input signal and only turn on their output signal after a specified time has elapsed. Off-delay timers start timing when they receive an input signal and turn off their output signal after a specified time has elapsed. Retentive timers maintain their accumulated time value even when the input signal is turned off, allowing them to resume timing from the previous value when the input signal is turned back on.

Counters, on the other hand, are used to count the occurrence of events within a PLC program by incrementing or decrementing a count value based on input signals. There are two main types of counters in PLC programming: up counters and down counters. Up counters increment their count value when they receive an input signal and reset to zero when a preset value is reached. Down counters decrement their count value when they receive an input signal and reset to a preset value when they reach zero.

Timers and counters are commonly used in PLC programming to implement various control and sequencing tasks, such as controlling the timing of motor operations, monitoring production processes, and sequencing conveyor systems. For example, timers can be used to delay the start of a motor after a certain condition is met, while counters can be used to track the number of products produced on a production line.

In PLC programming languages such as ladder logic and Function Block Diagrams (FBDs), timers and counters are represented by specific instructions or function blocks that allow programmers to configure their timing and counting parameters. For example, ladder logic typically uses timer and counter instructions such as TON (timer on delay), TOF (timer off delay), and CTU (counter up) to implement timers and counters within a program. Similarly, FBDs provide function blocks such as TON, TOF, and CTU that can be connected together to create complex timing and counting sequences.

When implementing timers and counters in PLC programs, it is essential to consider factors such as the resolution and accuracy of the timers and counters, the timing requirements of the application, and the response time of the PLC hardware. Programmers should also consider the reset conditions and error handling mechanisms to ensure reliable operation of the timers and counters in different operating conditions.

Overall, timers and counters are powerful tools in PLC programming that allow programmers to control the timing and counting of events within their automation projects effectively. By understanding the principles of timers and counters and techniques for implementing them in PLC programs, programmers can create reliable and efficient automation solutions in modern industries.

5.3 Advanced Mathematical Functions

ADVANCED MATHEMATICAL functions play a crucial role in PLC programming, enabling programmers to perform complex calculations and mathematical operations within their automation projects. This section explores the use of advanced mathematical functions in PLC programming and techniques for implementing them effectively.

PLC programming languages such as structured text (ST) provide a wide range of built-in mathematical functions for performing arithmetic, trigonometric, exponential, and logarithmic operations. These functions allow programmers to manipulate numerical data and solve mathematical problems directly within their PLC programs.

Arithmetic functions such as addition, subtraction, multiplication, and division are fundamental to PLC programming and are used extensively to perform basic mathematical operations on numerical data. For example, addition and subtraction functions can be used to calculate the sum or difference of two or more variables, while multiplication and division functions can be used to calculate products or quotients.

Trigonometric functions such as sine, cosine, and tangent are commonly used in PLC programming to calculate angles, distances, and positions in trigonometric applications. These functions allow programmers to perform complex calculations involving angles and distances in applications such as robotics, motion control, and positioning systems.

Exponential and logarithmic functions such as exponential, logarithm, and square root are used to calculate exponential growth or decay, solve exponential equations, and perform logarithmic transformations. These functions are particularly useful in applications involving exponential processes, such as temperature control, chemical processes, and power generation.

In addition to built-in mathematical functions, PLC programming languages also provide operators and syntax for performing mathematical operations directly within the program code. For example, operators such as + (addition), - (subtraction), * (multiplication), and / (division) can be used to perform basic arithmetic operations, while ^ (exponentiation) can be used to raise a number to a power.

When implementing advanced mathematical functions in PLC programs, it is essential to consider factors such as the range and precision of numerical data, the computational complexity of the calculations, and the performance characteristics of the PLC hardware. Programmers should also ensure proper error handling and validation mechanisms to handle exceptional conditions such as divide by zero errors or overflow/underflow errors.

Overall, advanced mathematical functions are powerful tools in PLC programming that allow programmers to perform complex calculations and solve mathematical problems within their automation projects. By understanding the principles of advanced mathematical functions and techniques for implementing them effectively, programmers can create reliable and efficient automation solutions in modern industries.

5.4 Handling Analog and Digital Inputs/ Outputs

HANDLING ANALOG AND digital inputs/outputs (I/O) is a fundamental aspect of PLC programming, allowing programmers to interface with sensors, actuators, and other devices in their automation projects. This section explores the methods and techniques for handling analog and digital I/O in PLC programming effectively.

Analog inputs are used to measure continuous physical quantities such as temperature, pressure, flow rate, and position. Analog outputs are used to control continuous physical processes such as motor speed, valve position, and temperature control. Digital inputs, on the other hand, are used to detect discrete events or states such as switch status, limit switch activation, and presence detection. Digital outputs are used to control discrete devices such as solenoid valves, relays, and indicator lights.

In PLC programming, analog inputs and outputs are typically represented as analog variables with a range of values corresponding to the physical quantity being measured or controlled. For example, an analog input may have a range of 0-10 volts corresponding to a temperature range of 0-100 degrees Celsius, while an analog output may have a range of 0-100% corresponding to a motor speed control.

Digital inputs and outputs are represented as binary variables with two states: on or off, high or low, true or false. Digital inputs are typically used to detect the presence or absence of a signal or to monitor the status of a switch or sensor. Digital outputs are used to control the state of a device such as turning a motor on or off, opening or closing a valve, or activating an alarm.

PLC programming languages provide instructions and function blocks for reading and writing analog and digital I/O values. For example, ladder logic provides input and output instructions such as XIC (examine if closed) and XIO (examine if open) for reading digital inputs and OTE (output energize) for writing digital outputs. Analog inputs and outputs can be read and written using analog input and output function blocks or instructions specific to the PLC programming language.

When handling analog inputs in PLC programming, it is essential to consider factors such as signal conditioning, scaling, and calibration to ensure accurate and reliable measurement of physical quantities. Signal conditioning involves filtering and amplifying the input signal to remove noise and improve signal quality. Scaling involves mapping the input signal to the desired range of values using linear or nonlinear scaling functions. Calibration involves adjusting the input signal to compensate for variations in sensor characteristics and environmental conditions.

Similarly, when handling analog outputs in PLC programming, it is essential to consider factors such as resolution, accuracy, and response time to ensure precise and responsive control of physical processes. Analog outputs may require calibration and tuning to achieve the desired output response and maintain stability and accuracy over time.

Overall, handling analog and digital inputs/outputs is a critical aspect of PLC programming that requires careful attention to detail and consideration of various factors such as signal conditioning, scaling, calibration, resolution, and accuracy. By understanding the methods and techniques for handling analog and digital I/O effectively, programmers can create reliable and efficient automation solutions in modern industries.

5.5 Implementing Safety Protocols

IMPLEMENTING SAFETY protocols is paramount in PLC programming to ensure the safe operation of machinery and equipment in industrial settings. This section delves into the methods and considerations for integrating safety protocols into PLC programs effectively.

Safety protocols in PLC programming aim to identify and mitigate potential hazards and risks associated with the operation of machinery and equipment. These protocols include measures such as emergency stop (E-stop) systems, safety interlocks, protective barriers, and safety monitoring systems. PLC programs play a crucial role in implementing and enforcing these safety protocols to prevent accidents and injuries in the workplace.

One common approach to implementing safety protocols in PLC programming is the use of safety-rated input and output devices, such as safety sensors, safety switches, and safety relays. These devices are designed to detect unsafe conditions and trigger safety actions, such as stopping machinery or activating safety alarms, to prevent accidents and injuries.

Another approach is the use of safety-certified PLCs and safety-rated programming languages specifically designed for implementing safety functions. These PLCs and programming languages adhere to strict safety standards and guidelines to ensure the reliability and integrity of safety-critical applications. Examples include Safety PLCs compliant with standards such as ISO 13849 and IEC 61508, and safety-rated programming languages such as Function Block Diagrams (FBDs) and Structured Text (ST) with built-in safety instructions and function blocks.

Safety protocols in PLC programming often involve the implementation of safety logic and interlocks to prevent unsafe conditions and ensure safe operation of machinery and equipment. This includes the use of safety relays, safety timers, and safety interlocks to monitor and control the state of safety-critical devices and systems. Safety logic is typically implemented using redundant and fail-safe programming techniques to ensure the reliability and availability of safety functions.

In addition to hardware-based safety devices and safety logic, PLC programming also incorporates software-based safety features such as safety monitoring and diagnostics. These features enable PLC programs to monitor the performance and integrity of safety-critical functions in real-time and detect and respond to safety-related faults and failures promptly.

Furthermore, safety protocols in PLC programming often involve the integration of safety communication protocols such as Safety over EtherCAT (FSoE) and PROFIsafe. These protocols enable the exchange of safety-related data and information between safety-critical devices and systems, ensuring coordinated and synchronized safety actions across the entire automation system.

Overall, implementing safety protocols in PLC programming requires a comprehensive approach that combines hardware-based safety devices, safety-rated PLCs, safety-certified programming languages, safety logic, safety monitoring, and communication protocols. By adhering to established safety standards and guidelines and employing best practices for safety-critical applications, PLC programmers can create safe and reliable automation solutions that protect workers and assets in industrial environments.

Chapter 6: Structuring and Organizing Code

6.1 Creating Modular Programs

WHEN IT COMES TO DEVELOPING efficient and maintainable PLC programs, one of the fundamental principles is the creation of modular programs. Modular programming involves breaking down a large program into smaller, more manageable modules or blocks of code. Each module performs a specific function or task, making the code easier to understand, test, and maintain.

Modularization offers several benefits, including improved code readability, reusability, and scalability. By dividing the program into smaller modules, developers can focus on implementing specific functionalities without getting overwhelmed by the complexity of the entire system. Moreover, modular programs are easier to debug since errors are confined to individual modules, making troubleshooting more efficient.

To create modular programs in Siemens S7, programmers can utilize various programming constructs provided by the platform, such as functions and function blocks. Functions encapsulate a set of instructions that perform a specific task and can be called from different parts of the program. On the other hand, function blocks are reusable blocks of code that encapsulate both data and functionality, providing a higher level of abstraction and reusability.

Let's consider an example to illustrate the concept of modular programming in Siemens S7. Suppose we have a manufacturing process controlled by a PLC, and we need to implement a module for controlling a conveyor belt. We can create a function block named ConveyorControl that contains the logic for starting, stopping, and monitoring the conveyor belt.

FUNCTION_BLOCK ConveyorControl

VAR_INPUT

Start : BOOL; // Input to start the conveyor

Stop : BOOL; // Input to stop the conveyor

END_VAR

VAR_OUTPUT

Running : BOOL; // Output indicating the status of the conveyor

END_VAR

VAR

// Internal variables

END_VAR

In this function block, the Start input is used to start the conveyor belt, the Stop input is used to stop it, and the Running output indicates whether the conveyor is currently running or not. Inside the function block, we would implement the necessary logic to control the conveyor based on the input signals.

By encapsulating the conveyor control logic within a function block, we can easily reuse this functionality in other parts of the program without duplicating code. Additionally, if any modifications or improvements are required in the future, we only need to make changes within the ConveyorControl function block, ensuring consistency and reducing maintenance efforts.

In conclusion, creating modular programs is essential for developing efficient and maintainable PLC applications. By breaking down the code into smaller, reusable modules, programmers can simplify the development process, improve code quality, and facilitate future enhancements.

6.2 Use of Functions and Function Blocks

FUNCTIONS AND FUNCTION blocks are essential components of Siemens S7 programming, allowing programmers to encapsulate logic, improve code readability, and promote code reuse. In this section, we will delve into the use of functions and function blocks in PLC programming and explore their benefits and best practices.

Functions in Siemens S7 are reusable code segments that perform specific tasks or calculations. They are similar to functions in traditional programming languages and can accept input parameters and return values. Functions are particularly useful for implementing repetitive or complex operations that need to be performed at multiple points within the program.

One common use case for functions is mathematical calculations. For example, suppose we need to calculate the average temperature from multiple temperature sensors in a manufacturing process. We can create a function named CalculateAverageTemperature that accepts an array of temperature values as input and returns the average temperature.

FUNCTION CalculateAverageTemperature : REAL

VAR_INPUT

Temperatures : ARRAY[1..10] OF REAL; // Array of temperature values

END_VAR

VAR

Sum : REAL := 0; // Variable to store the sum of temperatures

Average : REAL; // Variable to store the average temperature

Count : INT := 0; // Variable to store the number of temperature values

END_VAR

Inside the function, we iterate through the array of temperature values, calculate the sum of temperatures, and increment the count of temperature values. Finally, we compute the average temperature by dividing the sum by the number of temperature values and return the result.

Another important aspect of functions is their ability to promote code reuse. By encapsulating common operations within functions, programmers can avoid duplicating code and ensure consistency across the application. For instance, if multiple parts of the program require the same calculation or data manipulation, it is more efficient to define a function for that operation and call it wherever necessary.

While functions are useful for encapsulating standalone operations, function blocks provide a higher level of abstraction by combining both data and functionality into reusable blocks. Function blocks are particularly beneficial for modeling complex systems or processes with multiple inputs, outputs, and internal states.

Let's consider an example of a function block for controlling a motor in a conveyor system. The function block named MotorControl could have inputs for controlling the motor's speed and direction, as well as outputs indicating the motor's status and fault conditions.

FUNCTION_BLOCK MotorControl

VAR_INPUT

Speed : INT; // Input for controlling motor speed

Direction : BOOL; // Input for controlling motor direction

END_VAR

VAR_OUTPUT

Status : BOOL; // Output indicating motor status

Fault : BOOL; // Output indicating motor fault condition

END_VAR

VAR

// Internal variables and logic for motor control

END_VAR

Inside the function block, we would implement the necessary logic to control the motor based on the input signals, monitor its status, and handle any fault conditions that may arise. By encapsulating the motor control logic within a function block, we can easily integrate it into the larger PLC program and reuse it for controlling other motors in the system.

In summary, functions and function blocks are powerful tools in Siemens S7 programming for encapsulating logic, promoting code reuse, and enhancing code maintainability. By leveraging these constructs effectively, programmers can develop modular and scalable PLC applications that are easier to understand, test, and maintain.

6.3 Best Practices for Code Documentation

DOCUMENTATION IS A critical aspect of PLC programming that often receives less attention than writing the code itself. However, well-written documentation is essential for understanding, maintaining, and troubleshooting PLC programs, especially in complex industrial environments where multiple programmers may be involved. In this section, we will discuss some best practices for documenting Siemens S7 code effectively.

First and foremost, it's essential to establish a consistent documentation style throughout the project. Consistency in formatting, terminology, and organization makes the documentation easier to read and understand for all team members. Documenting code in a standardized manner also streamlines communication and collaboration among programmers working on different parts of the project.

One common practice for documenting Siemens S7 code is to include comments within the code itself. Comments provide additional context and explanations for individual instructions, blocks, or sections of code, making it easier for other programmers to understand the purpose and functionality of each component. When writing comments, it's crucial to be concise, clear, and relevant, avoiding unnecessary information or redundancy.

// Example comment explaining the purpose of a particular instruction

In addition to inline comments, it's also beneficial to provide high-level documentation for the entire program, outlining its structure, functionality, and external dependencies. This documentation can include an overview of the program's architecture, descriptions of major components or modules, and explanations of external interfaces or communication protocols used.

Another important aspect of code documentation is documenting variable names, data types, and units. Clear and descriptive variable names make the code more readable and understandable, reducing the likelihood of errors and confusion. Additionally, documenting data types and units helps ensure consistency and accuracy in data processing and communication.

// Example of documenting variable names and data types

VAR

Temperature : REAL; // Temperature reading in degrees Celsius

Pressure : INT; // Pressure reading in kilopascals

END_VAR

Documenting error handling and exception handling mechanisms is also crucial for ensuring the reliability and robustness of PLC programs. In complex industrial systems, errors and exceptions are inevitable, and it's essential to have clear documentation outlining how the program detects, handles, and recovers from these situations. This documentation should include descriptions of error codes, error messages, and recovery procedures, as well as any diagnostic tools or monitoring techniques used.

Furthermore, documenting version control and revision history is important for tracking changes and updates to the codebase over time. By maintaining a detailed record of revisions, including the date, author, and description of each change, programmers can easily trace the evolution of the program and identify potential issues or regressions introduced in new versions.

In summary, effective code documentation is essential for developing and maintaining reliable and maintainable PLC programs. By following best practices such as consistent formatting, inline comments, high-level overviews, descriptive variable names, error handling documentation, and version control tracking, programmers can ensure that their code is well-documented and comprehensible to all stakeholders involved in the project.

6.4 Version Control and Project Management

VERSION CONTROL AND project management are crucial aspects of PLC programming projects, ensuring that code changes are tracked, managed, and coordinated effectively. In this section, we will discuss the importance of version control and project management in Siemens S7 programming and explore some best practices for implementing these processes.

One of the primary benefits of version control is the ability to track changes to the codebase over time. Version control systems such as Git allow programmers to maintain a complete history of revisions, including who made each change, when it was made, and what specific modifications were introduced. This level of transparency and accountability is invaluable for collaboration and troubleshooting, enabling programmers to identify and revert problematic changes quickly.

Another advantage of version control is the ability to work on multiple branches simultaneously, allowing programmers to develop new features or experimental changes without disrupting the stability of the main codebase. Branching and merging workflows facilitate parallel development efforts and enable teams to collaborate on different aspects of the project concurrently. Additionally, version control systems provide mechanisms for resolving conflicts that may arise when merging changes from multiple branches, ensuring that modifications are integrated smoothly.

// Example of a commit message in Git

git commit -m "Implemented feature XYZ for conveyor control"

Furthermore, version control systems facilitate code review processes, allowing team members to review and provide feedback on proposed changes before they are merged into the main codebase. Code reviews help maintain code quality, identify potential issues or bugs early in the development cycle, and promote knowledge sharing and collaboration among team members. By incorporating code reviews into the development workflow, teams can improve code reliability and reduce the likelihood of errors or regressions.

Effective project management practices complement version control by providing structure, organization, and oversight to PLC programming projects. Project management encompasses various activities such as planning, scheduling, resource allocation, and risk management, all aimed at ensuring that the project is completed successfully and on time. Project management tools and methodologies, such as Agile or Scrum, provide frameworks for coordinating team activities, prioritizing tasks, and tracking progress towards project milestones.

// Example of a task board in an Agile project management tool

TODO:

- Implement motor control logic

- Test conveyor operation under load conditions

IN PROGRESS:

- Refactor temperature sensor interface

DONE:

- Fix bug in error handling module

Additionally, project management involves communication and collaboration among team members, stakeholders, and other project contributors. Regular meetings, status updates, and progress reports keep everyone informed about the project's status, goals, and priorities, facilitating alignment and coordination across the team. Effective communication channels, such as email, instant messaging, or project management software, ensure that information is shared promptly and transparently among all stakeholders.

In summary, version control and project management are essential components of successful PLC programming projects. By implementing version control systems such as Git and adopting project management practices such as Agile or Scrum, teams can streamline development workflows, improve code quality, and ensure that projects are completed on time and within budget. Effective version control and project management processes promote collaboration, transparency, and accountability, ultimately leading to the successful delivery of reliable and maintainable PLC applications.

6.5 Error Handling and Troubleshooting Techniques

ERROR HANDLING AND troubleshooting are essential aspects of PLC programming, ensuring that PLC systems operate reliably and efficiently in industrial environments. In this section, we will explore various error handling strategies and troubleshooting techniques commonly employed in Siemens S7 programming.

One fundamental aspect of error handling is the detection and logging of errors that occur during program execution. PLC programs often include mechanisms for monitoring system variables, inputs, and outputs, and detecting abnormal conditions or faults. When an error is detected, the program may trigger an alarm, log the error message to a dedicated error log, or take corrective actions to mitigate the impact of the error.

```
// Example of error handling logic in Siemens S7

IF ErrorCondition THEN

TriggerAlarm();

LogError("Error: Conveyor motor overheating");

StopConveyor();

// Additional error recovery actions

ENDIF
```

Furthermore, PLC programs may incorporate fault-tolerant mechanisms to ensure system reliability and resilience in the face of errors or failures. Redundancy, backup systems, and failover mechanisms are common strategies for minimizing downtime and maintaining system operation in the event of hardware or software failures. By designing PLC systems with built-in redundancy and fail-safes, programmers can mitigate the impact of errors and ensure continuous operation of critical processes.

Another important aspect of error handling is the implementation of diagnostic and debugging tools to aid in troubleshooting and problem resolution. PLC programming environments such as Siemens STEP 7 provide built-in diagnostic features, including online monitoring, variable tracing, and breakpoint debugging, allowing programmers to inspect program execution in real-time and identify potential issues or anomalies.

// Example of debugging tools in Siemens STEP 7

DEBUG ConveyorControl; // Enable debugging for the ConveyorControl function block

TRACE Temperature; // Trace the temperature variable for monitoring

BREAKPOINT; // Set a breakpoint to pause program execution at a specific point

In addition to built-in diagnostic tools, PLC programmers may utilize external monitoring and visualization tools to gain insights into system performance and behavior. Human-machine interfaces (HMIs) and supervisory control and data acquisition (SCADA) systems provide graphical interfaces for monitoring process variables, alarms, and trends, enabling operators and maintenance personnel to identify and respond to issues in real-time.

Furthermore, PLC programmers should establish comprehensive testing and validation procedures to verify the correctness and robustness of their code before deployment in production environments. Testing methodologies such as unit testing, integration testing, and acceptance testing help identify bugs, validate system functionality, and ensure that the PLC program meets the requirements and specifications of the application.

// Example of unit testing in Siemens S7

UNIT_TEST ConveyorControlTest

// Test cases for the ConveyorControl function block

END_UNIT_TEST

Moreover, documenting troubleshooting procedures and best practices is essential for enabling maintenance personnel to diagnose and resolve issues efficiently. Clear documentation outlining common error scenarios, troubleshooting steps, and recommended corrective actions helps minimize downtime and ensure timely resolution of issues that may arise during operation.

In summary, error handling and troubleshooting are critical aspects of PLC programming that ensure the reliability, resilience, and maintainability of industrial automation systems. By implementing robust error handling strategies, leveraging diagnostic and debugging tools, establishing comprehensive testing procedures, and documenting troubleshooting procedures, PLC programmers can minimize downtime, maximize system uptime, and maintain smooth operation of PLC systems in industrial environments.

Chapter 7: Simulation and Testing

7.1 Introduction to PLCSIM

SIMULATION IS A CRUCIAL aspect of PLC programming, allowing programmers to test and validate their code in a virtual environment before deploying it to physical hardware. PLCSIM is a simulation tool provided by Siemens for simulating PLC programs without the need for actual PLC hardware. In this section, we will introduce PLCSIM and explore its features and capabilities.

PLCSIM provides a virtual environment for simulating Siemens S7 PLCs and their associated hardware components, such as input and output modules, communication interfaces, and peripherals. By simulating the behavior of real PLC hardware, PLCSIM enables programmers to test their PLC programs in a controlled and repeatable manner, without the risk of damaging physical equipment or disrupting production processes.

One of the key advantages of PLCSIM is its integration with Siemens STEP 7 programming software, allowing programmers to seamlessly switch between programming and simulation modes within the same environment. This tight integration streamlines the development workflow, enabling programmers to write, debug, and test PLC programs more efficiently without the need for external simulation tools.

// Example of configuring PLCSIM in Siemens STEP 7

Open Project > Configure > PLCSIM

Furthermore, PLCSIM supports the simulation of complex industrial processes and systems, including motion control, process automation, and human-machine interaction. Programmers can simulate interactions between multiple PLCs, sensors, actuators, and other devices, allowing them to test the behavior of interconnected systems and verify the integrity of communication protocols.

PLCSIM provides various debugging and monitoring features to aid in simulation and testing. Programmers can monitor the status of PLC inputs and outputs, inspect internal variables and data structures, and trace the execution of PLC programs in real-time. Additionally, PLCSIM supports the simulation of diagnostic messages, alarms, and fault conditions, enabling programmers to test error handling and recovery mechanisms effectively.

// Example of monitoring PLC variables in PLCSIM

Monitor > PLC Variables

Moreover, PLCSIM allows programmers to simulate external events and stimuli to test the responsiveness and robustness of their PLC programs under different operating conditions. By generating simulated inputs, such as sensor readings, user inputs, or external signals, programmers can evaluate the behavior of their PLC programs in various scenarios and edge cases.

In addition to standalone simulation, PLCSIM supports integration with external simulation environments and tools, enabling programmers to simulate interactions between PLCs and other software or hardware components. For example, PLCSIM can be integrated with simulation software for testing PLC-controlled robotic systems, production lines, or manufacturing processes in a virtual environment.

Overall, PLCSIM is a powerful tool for simulating and testing PLC programs, providing a flexible and efficient environment for verifying system behavior, debugging code, and ensuring the reliability and robustness of PLC systems. By leveraging PLCSIM in the development process, programmers can accelerate the development cycle, reduce the time and cost of testing, and deliver high-quality PLC applications to production environments with confidence.

7.2 Simulating Your First Project

SIMULATING A PLC PROJECT using PLCSIM is an excellent way to validate the functionality of your program before deploying it to physical hardware. In this section, we'll walk through the steps to simulate your first project using PLCSIM.

The first step is to open your project in Siemens STEP 7 programming software. Once your project is open, navigate to the "Configure" menu and select "PLCSIM" to configure the simulation settings. Here, you can specify the PLC model, communication interfaces, and other simulation parameters to match your project requirements.

Next, you'll need to set up your PLC program for simulation. Ensure that your program is compiled and free of errors before starting the simulation. If there are any errors in your program, resolve them first before proceeding with simulation.

Once your program is ready, you can start the simulation by clicking on the "Start Simulation" button in the PLCSIM configuration window. This will launch the PLCSIM environment and load your PLC program into the simulated PLC.

// Example of starting the simulation in PLCSIM

Start Simulation > OK

Once the simulation is running, you can monitor the behavior of your PLC program using the various debugging and monitoring tools provided by PLCSIM. You can view the status of PLC inputs and outputs, inspect internal variables and data structures, and trace the execution of your program in real-time.

// Example of monitoring PLC variables in PLCSIM

Monitor > PLC Variables

To interact with your simulated PLC, you can use the virtual HMI provided by PLCSIM or simulate external inputs and stimuli to test different scenarios and edge cases. For example, you can simulate sensor readings, user inputs, or external signals to evaluate the behavior of your program under various conditions.

// Example of simulating sensor readings in PLCSIM

Simulate > Sensor Readings

As you simulate your project, pay attention to any abnormal behavior or unexpected results. Use the debugging tools provided by PLCSIM to identify and troubleshoot any issues that arise during simulation. You can set breakpoints, step through your program, and inspect variable values to pinpoint the cause of the problem.

// Example of setting a breakpoint in PLCSIM

Debug > Set Breakpoint

Once you're satisfied with the behavior of your program during simulation, you can stop the simulation and proceed with deploying your program to physical hardware. Make any necessary adjustments or optimizations based on the insights gained from simulation before deploying your program to ensure its reliability and robustness in real-world conditions.

In conclusion, simulating your PLC project using PLCSIM is an essential step in the development process, allowing you to validate your program's functionality, identify potential issues, and optimize performance before deployment. By following the steps outlined in this section, you can simulate your first project with confidence and ensure its success in production environments.

7.3 Debugging Techniques in Simulation

DEBUGGING PLC PROGRAMS during simulation is crucial for identifying and resolving issues before deploying them to real-world hardware. In this section, we'll explore various debugging techniques and tools available in simulation environments like PLCSIM.

One of the most basic debugging techniques is using print statements or logging to output messages indicating the program's state or the values of certain variables at specific points in the code. While not as sophisticated as other debugging methods, logging can provide valuable insights into the program's behavior, especially when combined with other debugging techniques.

// Example of logging messages in Siemens S7

LOG "Entering main program loop";

Another common debugging technique is setting breakpoints at specific points in the code where you suspect issues may be occurring. Breakpoints allow you to pause program execution at a particular line or instruction, giving you the opportunity to inspect variable values, step through the code, and identify the cause of the problem.

// Example of setting a breakpoint in Siemens S7

SET_BREAKPOINT LineNumber;

Stepping through the code is another useful debugging technique that allows you to execute the program one line or instruction at a time, observing the effects of each step on the program's state. Stepping through the code can help you pinpoint the exact location of an issue and understand how the program's logic flows.

// Example of stepping through the code in Siemens S7

STEP;

In addition to breakpoints and stepping, monitoring PLC variables in real-time during simulation can provide valuable insights into the program's behavior. Most simulation environments, including PLCSIM, offer tools for monitoring the values of PLC inputs, outputs, and internal variables as the program executes, allowing you to identify discrepancies or unexpected changes.

// Example of monitoring PLC variables in PLCSIM

MONITOR PLC_VARIABLES;

Trace functionality is another powerful debugging tool available in some simulation environments. Tracing allows you to log the values of selected variables over time, providing a detailed record of their behavior during program execution. Analyzing traces can help you identify patterns or trends in the data and diagnose complex issues more effectively.

// Example of tracing variables in PLCSIM

TRACE VariableName;

In addition to these debugging techniques, simulation environments may offer advanced diagnostic features such as error injection, simulation of external events, and virtual oscilloscope functionality. These tools can help you simulate real-world scenarios and edge cases, test error handling mechanisms, and validate the robustness of your PLC program under various conditions.

Overall, debugging PLC programs during simulation is a critical step in the development process, enabling you to identify and resolve issues early, before deploying your program to real-world hardware. By mastering debugging techniques and leveraging the tools available in simulation environments like PLCSIM, you can ensure the reliability, performance, and efficiency of your PLC applications in industrial settings.

7.4 Performance Testing and Analysis

ENSURING OPTIMAL PERFORMANCE of PLC programs is essential for maintaining smooth operation and efficiency in industrial automation systems. In this section, we will discuss performance testing and analysis techniques to identify bottlenecks, optimize code, and improve the overall performance of PLC programs.

One of the primary goals of performance testing is to measure the execution time of PLC programs and identify areas where improvements can be made to enhance performance. Performance testing involves running the PLC program under simulated or real-world conditions and measuring various metrics such as execution time, CPU usage, and memory consumption.

```
// Example of measuring execution time in Siemens S7

START_TIMER;

// Code to be measured

STOP_TIMER;
```

Once performance data has been collected, it can be analyzed to identify potential bottlenecks or areas of inefficiency in the PLC program. Common performance bottlenecks may include long-running loops, excessive use of complex mathematical operations, or inefficient data processing algorithms.

```
// Example of optimizing a loop in Siemens S7

FOR i := 1 TO 1000 DO

// Code to be optimized

END_FOR;
```

Profiling tools can be used to analyze the performance of PLC programs and identify hotspots or areas of high resource usage. Profiling tools provide detailed insights into the execution flow of the program, highlighting areas where optimizations may be beneficial.

```
// Example of profiling code in Siemens S7

PROFILE CodeToBeAnalyzed;
```

In addition to identifying bottlenecks, performance testing and analysis can help validate the scalability and robustness of PLC programs under different load conditions. By simulating varying levels of traffic or activity in the system, programmers can assess how well the PLC program handles increased workloads and identify potential performance degradation issues.

```
// Example of simulating increased workload in PLCSIM

INCREASE_WORKLOAD;
```

Furthermore, performance testing and analysis can uncover issues related to resource utilization, such as excessive CPU usage, memory leaks, or network bandwidth constraints. By monitoring resource usage metrics during performance testing, programmers can identify resource-intensive operations and optimize them to reduce resource consumption and improve overall system efficiency.

// Example of monitoring CPU usage in PLCSIM

MONITOR CPU_USAGE;

Once performance issues have been identified, programmers can implement optimizations to improve the efficiency of the PLC program. Optimization techniques may include refactoring code for better readability and maintainability, reducing unnecessary computations or data processing, and optimizing algorithms for improved performance.

// Example of code refactoring in Siemens S7

REFACTOR CodeToBeImproved;

Finally, it's essential to retest the PLC program after implementing optimizations to ensure that the performance improvements have been realized and that no new issues have been introduced. Performance testing should be an iterative process, with continuous monitoring and optimization to maintain optimal performance over time.

In summary, performance testing and analysis are critical aspects of PLC programming for identifying bottlenecks, optimizing code, and improving overall system efficiency. By leveraging performance testing tools and techniques, programmers can ensure that their PLC programs meet performance requirements and deliver reliable performance in industrial automation environments.

7.5 Tips for Effective Simulation

SIMULATING PLC PROGRAMS is a crucial aspect of the development process, allowing programmers to test their code in a controlled environment before deployment to real-world hardware. In this section, we will discuss some tips and best practices for conducting effective simulations.

1. **Understand the System Requirements**: Before starting the simulation, ensure that you have a clear understanding of the system requirements and specifications. This includes understanding the behavior of inputs and outputs, the logic of the control system, and any external interfaces or communication protocols that need to be simulated.

2. **Start Simple**: When conducting simulations, start with simple scenarios and gradually increase the complexity as you gain confidence in your program. This approach allows you to identify and resolve issues in the early stages of development, reducing the risk of errors or complications later on.

3. **Use Modular Design**: Modularize your PLC program into smaller, more manageable components to facilitate testing and debugging during simulation. By breaking down the program into modules, you can focus on testing individual components independently, making it easier to isolate and resolve issues.

4. **Document Simulation Scenarios**: Document the simulation scenarios you plan to test, including the expected inputs, outputs, and behavior of the system under different conditions. This documentation serves as a reference for conducting simulations and ensures that all relevant test cases are covered.

5. **Implement Error Handling**: Incorporate error handling

mechanisms into your PLC program to simulate error conditions and test the robustness of your error handling logic. By simulating errors such as sensor failures, communication errors, or equipment malfunctions, you can verify that your program responds appropriately to unexpected events.

6. **Monitor Performance Metrics**: During simulation, monitor performance metrics such as execution time, CPU usage, and memory consumption to identify areas for optimization. By measuring performance metrics, you can pinpoint performance bottlenecks and prioritize optimization efforts to improve the efficiency of your program.

7. **Validate Inputs and Outputs**: Validate the inputs and outputs of your PLC program during simulation to ensure that they behave as expected under different conditions. Use simulated inputs to test various scenarios and edge cases, and verify that the outputs produced by your program are accurate and consistent.

8. **Collaborate with Stakeholders**: Involve stakeholders such as operators, maintenance personnel, and system integrators in the simulation process to gather feedback and insights into the usability and functionality of the system. By collaborating with stakeholders, you can identify potential issues early and ensure that the final system meets the requirements of all stakeholders.

9. **Iterate and Refine**: Simulation is an iterative process, so be prepared to iterate and refine your PLC program based on the insights gained during simulation. Continuously test and validate your program under different conditions, incorporating feedback and making adjustments as needed to improve its performance and reliability.

10. **Document Results and Lessons Learned**: After conducting simulations, document the results, lessons learned, and any optimizations or changes made to the PLC program. This documentation serves as a valuable resource for future development efforts and helps ensure that knowledge gained during simulation is retained and shared within the team.

By following these tips and best practices, you can conduct effective simulations of your PLC programs, identify and resolve issues early in the development process, and ensure the reliability and performance of your systems in real-world environments.

Chapter 8: Human-Machine Interfaces (HMI)

8.1 Basics of HMI

HUMAN-MACHINE INTERFACES (HMIs) play a crucial role in industrial automation systems by providing a graphical interface for interacting with PLCs and other control devices. In this section, we'll explore the basics of HMIs, including their components, functionality, and design principles.

HMIs typically consist of three main components: a graphical display, input devices, and communication interfaces. The graphical display, often a touchscreen or monitor, presents information to the operator in a visual format, such as process variables, alarms, and status indicators. Input devices, such as buttons, switches, or keyboards, allow the operator to interact with the HMI and control the system. Communication interfaces enable the HMI to communicate with PLCs, sensors, actuators, and other devices in the control system.

When designing HMIs, it's essential to consider the principles of human factors engineering to ensure that the interface is intuitive, easy to use, and supports efficient operator interaction. This includes factors such as layout design, color coding, labeling, and feedback mechanisms to provide clear and concise information to the operator.

```
// Example of HMI layout design considerations

DEFINE_BUTTON StartButton;

DEFINE_LABEL ProcessStatus;
```

One of the key design principles of HMIs is the concept of "information hierarchy," which organizes information on the display according to its importance and relevance to the operator. Critical information, such as alarms or emergency stop buttons, should be prominently displayed and easily accessible, while less critical information can be presented in secondary or tertiary layers of the interface.

Another important aspect of HMI design is consistency, both within the HMI itself and across different HMIs within the same control system. Consistent layout, color schemes, and navigation patterns help operators navigate the interface more easily and reduce the risk of errors or confusion.

```
// Example of consistent HMI design elements

DEFINE_COLOR AlarmColor = RED;

DEFINE_FONT_SIZE NormalFontSize = 12pt;
```

Feedback mechanisms are also essential in HMI design to provide operators with real-time feedback on their actions and the state of the system. Visual indicators, such as status lights, progress bars, or animated graphics, can inform operators of the system's status and response to their inputs, helping them make informed decisions and take appropriate actions.

In addition to providing control and monitoring functionality, HMIs may also include diagnostic and troubleshooting tools to assist operators in diagnosing and resolving issues in the system. Diagnostic tools, such as trend charts, data logs, or diagnostic messages, provide operators with insights into the performance and behavior of the system, enabling them to identify and address issues quickly and effectively.

// Example of diagnostic tools in an HMI

DISPLAY_TREND TemperatureTrend;

DISPLAY_LOG ErrorLog;

Furthermore, modern HMIs may incorporate advanced features such as remote monitoring and control, mobile access, and integration with cloud-based services for data analytics and predictive maintenance. These features enable operators to monitor and control industrial processes from anywhere, at any time, and leverage data-driven insights to optimize performance and efficiency.

In summary, HMIs are essential components of industrial automation systems, providing operators with the tools and information they need to monitor and control the system effectively. By following principles of human factors engineering and design, operators can create HMIs that are intuitive, efficient, and user-friendly, enhancing productivity and safety in industrial environments.

8.2 Designing Interfaces with WinCC

DESIGNING INTERFACES with WinCC involves creating intuitive and efficient human-machine interfaces (HMIs) for industrial automation systems. WinCC, developed by Siemens, is a powerful software platform used for designing, configuring, and visualizing HMIs in PLC-based control systems. In this section, we'll explore the key features and capabilities of WinCC for designing interfaces.

WinCC offers a wide range of tools and functionalities for creating HMIs, including drag-and-drop interface elements, customizable templates, and support for multimedia content such as images, videos, and animations. The graphical editor provided by WinCC allows users to design interfaces with ease, arranging and styling elements to create visually appealing and functional HMIs.

// Example of designing an interface with WinCC

DragAndDrop Button;

Customize ColorScheme;

One of the strengths of WinCC is its flexibility and scalability, allowing users to create HMIs for a variety of applications and industries. Whether designing interfaces for manufacturing, energy management, building automation, or process control, WinCC provides the tools and features needed to create tailored solutions that meet the specific requirements of each application.

In addition to creating static interfaces, WinCC supports dynamic content and interactive elements, such as buttons, sliders, and input fields, allowing operators to interact with the system and control processes in real-time. By incorporating dynamic elements into the interface, users can create HMIs that are more engaging and responsive to operator inputs.

// Example of adding interactive elements with WinCC

AddButton InteractiveButton;

CreateSlider TemperatureControl;

Another key feature of WinCC is its support for multi-language interfaces, enabling users to create HMIs in multiple languages to accommodate operators from different regions or linguistic backgrounds. Multi-language support simplifies the localization process and ensures that operators can interact with the HMI in their preferred language, enhancing usability and accessibility.

WinCC also provides extensive visualization capabilities, allowing users to create custom dashboards, charts, and graphs to visualize process data and trends. Visualization tools such as trend charts, bar graphs, and pie charts enable operators to monitor key performance indicators (KPIs) and make informed decisions based on real-time data.

// Example of creating a trend chart with WinCC

CreateTrendChart TemperatureTrend;

DisplayKPIs ProductionMetrics;

Furthermore, WinCC offers integration with other Siemens software and hardware products, such as SIMATIC PLCs, SCADA systems, and industrial networks, enabling seamless communication and data exchange between different components of the control system. This integration simplifies the design and configuration process and ensures interoperability between various components of the automation system.

In summary, WinCC provides a comprehensive set of tools and features for designing interfaces for industrial automation systems. With its intuitive graphical editor, support for dynamic content and interactive elements, multi-language support, visualization capabilities, and seamless integration with other Siemens products, WinCC enables users to create powerful and efficient HMIs that enhance productivity, efficiency, and safety in industrial environments.

8.3 Integrating HMI with Siemens S7 PLCs

INTEGRATING HUMAN-MACHINE Interfaces (HMIs) with Siemens S7 PLCs is essential for creating a seamless and efficient control system in industrial automation environments. In this section, we'll explore the process of integrating HMIs with Siemens S7 PLCs and the key considerations involved in this integration.

Siemens provides various software platforms for developing HMIs, including WinCC, WinCC Flexible, and TIA Portal. These software platforms offer tools and features for designing, configuring, and visualizing HMIs, as well as for integrating them with Siemens S7 PLCs. Integration between the HMI software and Siemens S7 PLCs enables real-time data exchange and communication, allowing operators to monitor and control industrial processes effectively.

// Example of data exchange between HMI and Siemens S7 PLC

ReadFromPLC ProcessVariables;

WriteToPLC ControlCommands;

One of the key considerations when integrating HMIs with Siemens S7 PLCs is the selection of communication protocols and interfaces. Siemens S7 PLCs support various communication protocols, including PROFIBUS, PROFINET, and Ethernet/IP, which can be used to establish communication between the PLC and the HMI. The choice of communication protocol depends on factors such as the requirements of the application, the network infrastructure, and the compatibility with other components of the control system.

// Example of configuring communication protocol in HMI software

SelectProtocol PROFINET;

ConfigureNetworkSettings;

Another important aspect of integration is the configuration of data exchange mechanisms between the HMI and the Siemens S7 PLCs. This involves defining communication tags, data points, or memory addresses in both the HMI software and the PLC program to facilitate the exchange of data between the two systems. By defining communication tags or variables in the HMI software that correspond to PLC memory locations, operators can access and manipulate PLC data directly from the HMI interface.

// Example of defining communication tags in HMI software

DefineTag TemperatureTag;

DefineTag PressureTag;

Furthermore, it's essential to establish a structured and organized data model for exchanging data between the HMI and the Siemens S7 PLCs. This includes defining data structures, data types, and data mapping rules to ensure consistency and compatibility between the two systems. By establishing a standardized data model, developers can streamline the integration process and minimize the risk of data errors or inconsistencies.

// Example of defining data structures in HMI software

DefineDataStructure ProcessData;

MapDataStructureToPLC ProcessData;

Additionally, security is a critical consideration when integrating HMIs with Siemens S7 PLCs to protect against unauthorized access, data breaches, and cyber threats. Implementing security measures such as access controls, authentication mechanisms, data encryption, and network segmentation can help safeguard the integrity and confidentiality of the communication between the HMI and the PLCs.

In summary, integrating HMIs with Siemens S7 PLCs is a fundamental aspect of creating a robust and efficient control system in industrial automation environments. By selecting the appropriate communication protocols, configuring data exchange mechanisms, establishing a structured data model, and implementing security measures, developers can ensure seamless communication and interoperability between HMIs and Siemens S7 PLCs, enabling operators to monitor and control industrial processes effectively.

8.4 User Interaction and Feedback Systems

USER INTERACTION AND feedback systems are critical components of Human-Machine Interfaces (HMIs) in industrial automation, enabling operators to interact with the system and receive feedback on their actions in real-time. In this section, we'll explore the importance of user interaction and feedback systems in HMIs and the various strategies for implementing them effectively.

One of the primary goals of user interaction systems is to provide operators with intuitive and efficient ways to interact with the HMI and control the industrial process. This includes designing user-friendly interfaces with clear navigation paths, easily accessible controls, and intuitive input mechanisms such as buttons, sliders, and touch gestures.

// Example of designing intuitive user interface elements

DesignButton StartButton;

CreateSlider SpeedControl;

Feedback systems, on the other hand, provide operators with real-time feedback on their actions and the state of the system, enabling them to make informed decisions and take appropriate actions. Feedback mechanisms may include visual indicators such as status lights, progress bars, or animated graphics, as well as auditory or tactile feedback to alert operators of critical events or changes in the system.

```
// Example of providing visual feedback with status indicators

DisplayStatusIndicator AlarmStatus;

ShowProgressBar ProcessProgress;
```

Another important aspect of user interaction and feedback systems is responsiveness, ensuring that the HMI interface responds quickly and accurately to operator inputs. This involves minimizing latency, optimizing interface performance, and providing immediate feedback to operators to enhance their sense of control and confidence in the system.

In addition to providing direct control over the industrial process, user interaction systems may also include features such as context-sensitive help, interactive tutorials, and guided workflows to assist operators in performing complex tasks or troubleshooting issues. By providing contextual guidance and support, HMIs can empower operators to work more efficiently and effectively.

```
// Example of providing context-sensitive help in HMIs

DisplayHelpMenu ContextSensitiveHelp;

ShowTutorial InteractiveTutorial;
```

Furthermore, user interaction and feedback systems should be designed with usability and accessibility in mind, accommodating operators with different levels of experience, expertise, and physical abilities. This includes designing interfaces with clear, concise language, logical layout, and accessible controls that are easy to understand and operate for all users.

Security is also a crucial consideration when implementing user interaction and feedback systems in industrial automation environments to prevent unauthorized access, tampering, or manipulation of the system. Implementing access controls, authentication mechanisms, and encryption protocols can help safeguard the integrity and confidentiality of the HMI interface and ensure the safety and security of the industrial process.

In summary, user interaction and feedback systems are essential components of HMIs in industrial automation, enabling operators to interact with the system effectively and receive real-time feedback on their actions. By designing intuitive interfaces, providing responsive feedback, offering contextual guidance, and ensuring usability and security, HMIs can enhance operator productivity, efficiency, and safety in industrial environments.

8.5 Advanced HMI Features and Capabilities

ADVANCED HUMAN-MACHINE Interfaces (HMIs) offer a wide range of features and capabilities beyond basic user interaction and feedback systems, enabling operators to monitor and control industrial processes more effectively. In this section, we'll explore some of the advanced features and capabilities of HMIs and their benefits in industrial automation environments.

One advanced feature of HMIs is data visualization, which allows operators to visualize process data and trends in real-time using charts, graphs, and other graphical elements. Data visualization tools enable operators to identify patterns, anomalies, and correlations in the data, enabling them to make informed decisions and take proactive actions to optimize performance and efficiency.

// Example of data visualization with trend charts

DisplayTrendChart TemperatureTrend;

ShowHistogram PressureDistribution;

Another advanced capability of HMIs is alarm management, which enables operators to monitor and manage alarms and events in the system effectively. Alarm management systems provide operators with real-time alerts and notifications of critical events, enabling them to respond quickly and mitigate potential risks or disruptions to the industrial process.

// Example of alarm management system

DisplayAlarmList;

AcknowledgeAlarm;

Furthermore, advanced HMIs may include features such as remote monitoring and control, enabling operators to monitor and control industrial processes from anywhere, at any time, using mobile devices or web-based interfaces. Remote monitoring and control capabilities enhance flexibility, scalability, and accessibility, enabling operators to respond to issues or emergencies quickly, even when they are not physically present at the facility.

In addition to remote monitoring and control, advanced HMIs may incorporate predictive analytics and machine learning algorithms to analyze historical data, identify patterns, and predict future outcomes or events. Predictive analytics enable operators to anticipate issues, optimize processes, and prevent downtime, improving overall efficiency and productivity in industrial environments.

// Example of predictive analytics in HMIs

AnalyzeHistoricalData;

PredictFutureTrends;

Another advanced capability of HMIs is integration with other systems and technologies, such as SCADA systems, MES (Manufacturing Execution Systems), ERP (Enterprise Resource Planning) systems, and IIoT (Industrial Internet of Things) platforms. Integration with these systems enables seamless data exchange, interoperability, and automation, enabling operators to access and leverage data from multiple sources to make informed decisions and optimize processes.

Security is also a critical consideration when implementing advanced HMIs in industrial automation environments to protect against cyber threats, data breaches, and unauthorized access. Implementing robust security measures such as access controls, encryption, authentication mechanisms, and network segmentation can help safeguard the integrity, confidentiality, and availability of the HMI interface and ensure the safety and security of the industrial process.

In summary, advanced HMIs offer a wide range of features and capabilities beyond basic user interaction and feedback systems, enabling operators to monitor and control industrial processes more effectively. By leveraging data visualization, alarm management, remote monitoring and control, predictive analytics, integration with other systems, and robust security measures, advanced HMIs empower operators to optimize performance, increase efficiency, and ensure safety in industrial environments.

Chapter 9: Communication Protocols

9.1 Overview of Industrial Communication Standards

INDUSTRIAL COMMUNICATION standards play a crucial role in facilitating communication and data exchange between devices and systems in industrial automation environments. These standards define protocols, interfaces, and specifications for transmitting data reliably and efficiently over industrial networks, ensuring interoperability, compatibility, and reliability across different devices and vendors.

One of the most widely used industrial communication standards is PROFIBUS (Process Field Bus), which is a fieldbus protocol used for connecting field devices such as sensors, actuators, and controllers in industrial automation systems. PROFIBUS supports both point-to-point and multi-drop communication topologies and offers high-speed data transmission, deterministic communication, and robust error detection and correction mechanisms.

Another popular industrial communication standard is PROFINET (Process Field Net), which is an Ethernet-based communication protocol designed for real-time control and automation applications. PROFINET combines the flexibility and scalability of Ethernet with the determinism and reliability required for industrial automation, making it suitable for a wide range of applications, from simple machine control to complex process automation systems.

In addition to PROFIBUS and PROFINET, other industrial communication standards include Modbus, Ethernet/IP, DeviceNet, CANopen, and EtherCAT, each with its own set of features, advantages, and use cases. Modbus, for example, is a widely used serial communication protocol for connecting industrial devices such as PLCs, HMIs, and sensors, offering simplicity, flexibility, and wide compatibility.

Ethernet/IP (Industrial Protocol) is another Ethernet-based communication protocol commonly used in industrial automation for real-time control and information exchange. Ethernet/IP is based on standard Ethernet technology and TCP/IP protocols, making it easy to integrate with existing IT infrastructure while providing real-time control capabilities required for industrial applications.

DeviceNet is a CAN-based communication protocol used for connecting industrial devices such as sensors, actuators, and motor controllers in distributed control systems. DeviceNet offers high-speed data transmission, deterministic communication, and plug-and-play connectivity, making it suitable for applications requiring high reliability and scalability.

CANopen is another CAN-based communication protocol commonly used in industrial automation for connecting devices and systems in distributed control and automation systems. CANopen provides standardized communication profiles, device profiles, and object dictionaries, enabling interoperability and compatibility across different devices and vendors.

EtherCAT (Ethernet for Control Automation Technology) is an Ethernet-based communication protocol known for its high-speed data transmission, low latency, and determinism, making it suitable for demanding real-time control and automation applications. EtherCAT utilizes a master-slave communication architecture and supports distributed clock synchronization, ensuring precise coordination and timing in multi-axis motion control systems.

Overall, industrial communication standards play a critical role in enabling communication and data exchange between devices and systems in industrial automation environments. By adhering to these standards, manufacturers can ensure interoperability, compatibility, and reliability across different devices and vendors, enabling seamless integration and communication in industrial automation systems.

9.2 Profibus and Profinet: Configuration and Uses

PROFIBUS (PROCESS FIELD Bus) and Profinet (Process Field Net) are two widely used industrial communication standards developed by Siemens for connecting devices and systems in industrial automation environments. In this section, we'll explore the configuration and uses of Profibus and Profinet and their benefits in industrial applications.

Profibus is a fieldbus protocol commonly used for connecting field devices such as sensors, actuators, and controllers in industrial automation systems. Profibus supports both point-to-point and multi-drop communication topologies, allowing multiple devices to communicate with a single master device over a single communication line. Profibus offers high-speed data transmission, deterministic communication, and robust error detection and correction mechanisms, making it suitable for real-time control and monitoring applications in industrial environments.

Profinet, on the other hand, is an Ethernet-based communication protocol designed for real-time control and automation applications. Profinet combines the flexibility and scalability of Ethernet with the determinism and reliability required for industrial automation, making it suitable for a wide range of applications, from simple machine control to complex process automation systems. Profinet supports both standard Ethernet and real-time Ethernet communication, enabling seamless integration with existing IT infrastructure while providing the real-time control capabilities required for industrial applications.

One of the key benefits of Profibus and Profinet is their flexibility and scalability, allowing users to connect devices and systems from different vendors and manufacturers in a single network. This interoperability enables seamless communication and data exchange between devices and systems from different vendors, reducing integration complexity and costs in industrial automation systems.

// Example of configuring Profibus and Profinet networks

ConfigureProfibusNetwork;

ConfigureProfinetNetwork;

Another advantage of Profibus and Profinet is their support for distributed control and automation, allowing users to distribute control logic and intelligence across multiple devices and systems in the network. This distributed architecture enables decentralized control, fault tolerance, and scalability, making it easier to design and implement complex control and automation systems in industrial environments.

Profibus and Profinet also offer diagnostic and troubleshooting capabilities, allowing users to monitor network performance, detect faults, and troubleshoot issues quickly and effectively. Diagnostic tools such as network analyzers, bus monitors, and diagnostic messages provide operators with insights into the health and status of the network, enabling them to identify and address issues before they impact production or safety.

In addition to real-time control and monitoring, Profibus and Profinet support advanced features such as motion control, safety, and predictive maintenance, enabling users to optimize performance, enhance safety, and reduce downtime in industrial automation systems. Motion control features such as synchronized motion, electronic gearing, and camming enable precise control of motors and actuators, while safety features such as safe communication, safe I/O, and safe motion ensure the safety of operators and equipment in industrial environments.

// Example of configuring motion control and safety features

ConfigureMotionControl;

ConfigureSafetyFeatures;

Overall, Profibus and Profinet are versatile and robust communication standards that offer a wide range of benefits for industrial automation applications. By providing high-speed data transmission, deterministic communication, flexibility, scalability, and advanced features such as motion control and safety, Profibus and Profinet enable users to design and implement efficient, reliable, and future-proof automation solutions in industrial environments.

9.3 Implementing TCP/IP Communication

IMPLEMENTING TCP/IP communication is crucial for enabling data exchange and networking capabilities in industrial automation environments. In this section, we'll explore the process of implementing TCP/IP communication and its significance in industrial applications.

TCP/IP (Transmission Control Protocol/Internet Protocol) is a suite of communication protocols used for transmitting data over networks, including the Internet. TCP/IP provides a reliable, connection-oriented communication mechanism that ensures data integrity, sequencing, and flow control, making it suitable for applications requiring high reliability and accuracy.

// Example of TCP/IP communication setup

SetupTCPConnection;

EstablishDataTransmission;

In industrial automation, TCP/IP communication is commonly used for connecting devices, systems, and components in distributed control and monitoring systems. TCP/IP enables seamless data exchange between devices such as PLCs, HMIs, sensors, actuators, and supervisory control and data acquisition (SCADA) systems, enabling real-time monitoring, control, and analysis of industrial processes.

One of the key benefits of TCP/IP communication is its interoperability and compatibility with existing IT infrastructure and Internet-based technologies. TCP/IP allows industrial automation systems to leverage standard networking technologies and protocols, enabling integration with enterprise systems, cloud services, and Internet of Things (IoT) platforms for data analytics, remote monitoring, and predictive maintenance.

// Example of integrating TCP/IP with enterprise systems

ConnectToEnterpriseNetwork;

ExchangeDataWithERP;

Another advantage of TCP/IP communication is its scalability and flexibility, allowing users to easily add or remove devices, expand networks, and adapt to changing requirements in industrial environments. TCP/IP supports both wired and wireless communication, enabling users to deploy networks in diverse environments and locations, from factory floors to remote sites.

Security is a critical consideration when implementing TCP/IP communication in industrial automation environments to protect against cyber threats, data breaches, and unauthorized access. Implementing robust security measures such as firewalls, intrusion detection systems, encryption, and authentication mechanisms can help safeguard the integrity, confidentiality, and availability of the network and ensure the safety and security of industrial processes.

// Example of implementing security measures for TCP/IP communication

ConfigureFirewallRules;

EncryptDataTransmission;

AuthenticateUsers;

In addition to real-time control and monitoring, TCP/IP communication supports advanced features such as remote access, data logging, and firmware updates, enabling operators to manage and maintain industrial automation systems efficiently. Remote access capabilities allow operators to access and control industrial processes from anywhere, at any time, using web-based interfaces or mobile devices, while data logging enables long-term storage and analysis of process data for performance optimization and troubleshooting.

Overall, TCP/IP communication is essential for enabling networking capabilities and data exchange in industrial automation environments. By providing reliability, interoperability, scalability, and security, TCP/IP communication enables users to build robust, efficient, and future-proof automation solutions that enhance productivity, efficiency, and safety in industrial environments.

9.4 Wireless Communication Options

WIRELESS COMMUNICATION options have become increasingly popular in industrial automation due to their flexibility, scalability, and cost-effectiveness. In this section, we'll explore various wireless communication options commonly used in industrial environments and their benefits and applications.

One of the most widely used wireless communication options in industrial automation is Wi-Fi (Wireless Fidelity), which utilizes IEEE 802.11 standards for wireless local area networking (WLAN). Wi-Fi enables high-speed data transmission over short distances, making it suitable for applications such as local monitoring, control, and data exchange between devices such as PLCs, HMIs, and sensors in industrial environments.

// Example of setting up Wi-Fi network for industrial automation

ConfigureWiFiAccessPoint;

ConnectDevicesToWiFiNetwork;

Another popular wireless communication option is Bluetooth, which is a short-range wireless technology commonly used for connecting devices such as sensors, actuators, and mobile devices in industrial automation systems. Bluetooth offers low-power consumption, low-latency communication, and secure pairing mechanisms, making it suitable for applications requiring wireless connectivity between nearby devices.

In addition to Wi-Fi and Bluetooth, other wireless communication options commonly used in industrial automation include Zigbee,

LoRa (Long Range), and cellular communication technologies such as 4G LTE and 5G. Zigbee is a low-power, low-cost wireless communication protocol used for connecting devices in industrial automation systems, offering reliable, mesh networking capabilities for applications such as wireless sensor networks and asset tracking.

// Example of implementing Zigbee wireless communication

ConfigureZigbeeNetwork;

DeployWirelessSensorNetwork;

LoRa (Long Range) is another wireless communication technology that enables long-range, low-power communication for industrial IoT applications. LoRa utilizes spread spectrum modulation techniques to achieve long-range communication over several kilometers, making it suitable for applications such as remote monitoring, asset tracking, and environmental sensing in industrial environments.

Cellular communication technologies such as 4G LTE and 5G offer high-speed, reliable wireless connectivity over large geographical areas, enabling remote monitoring, control, and data exchange in industrial automation systems. Cellular communication provides ubiquitous coverage and high data throughput, making it suitable for applications requiring real-time communication and high-bandwidth data transmission in industrial environments.

// Example of deploying cellular communication for remote monitoring

InstallCellularModems;

EstablishDataConnection;

One of the key benefits of wireless communication options in industrial automation is their ability to eliminate the need for wired connections, enabling greater flexibility, mobility, and scalability in deploying devices and systems. Wireless communication options also reduce installation costs and complexity, as there is no need for physical cabling or infrastructure, making them suitable for retrofitting existing facilities or deploying temporary solutions.

Security is a critical consideration when implementing wireless communication options in industrial automation environments to protect against unauthorized access, data breaches, and cyber threats. Implementing robust security measures such as encryption, authentication, and access controls can help safeguard the integrity, confidentiality, and availability of wireless networks and ensure the safety and security of industrial processes.

In summary, wireless communication options offer flexible, scalable, and cost-effective solutions for enabling communication and connectivity in industrial automation environments. By leveraging technologies such as Wi-Fi, Bluetooth, Zigbee, LoRa, and cellular communication, industrial automation systems can achieve seamless, reliable wireless communication for monitoring, control, and data exchange, enhancing productivity, efficiency, and safety in industrial environments.

9.5 Safety and Security in PLC Communications

SAFETY AND SECURITY are paramount concerns in PLC (Programmable Logic Controller) communications, given the critical nature of industrial processes and the potential risks associated with cyber threats and unauthorized access. In this section, we'll delve into the importance of safety and security measures in PLC communications and explore strategies for ensuring the integrity, confidentiality, and availability of communication networks in industrial environments.

One of the primary considerations in PLC communications is ensuring the safety of personnel, equipment, and processes by preventing unauthorized access, tampering, or manipulation of PLC systems. Implementing access controls, authentication mechanisms, and authorization policies can help restrict access to PLCs and prevent unauthorized users from modifying control logic, parameters, or configurations.

```
// Example of implementing access controls in PLC communications

ImplementAccessControl;

AuthenticateUsers;

AuthorizeActions;
```

Furthermore, ensuring the security of PLC communications is essential for protecting against cyber threats such as malware, ransomware, and denial-of-service (DoS) attacks, which can disrupt operations, compromise data integrity, and pose safety risks in industrial environments. Implementing robust security measures such as encryption, intrusion detection systems, and network segmentation can help safeguard PLC communications and prevent unauthorized access or tampering.

```
// Example of implementing encryption in PLC communications

EncryptCommunicationChannels;

SecureDataTransmission;
```

In addition to protecting against external threats, ensuring the integrity of PLC communications is crucial for maintaining the reliability and performance of industrial processes. Implementing error detection and correction mechanisms, redundancy strategies, and data validation checks can help detect and mitigate communication errors, ensuring the accuracy and consistency of data exchanged between PLCs and other devices.

```
// Example of implementing error detection and correction in PLC communications

ImplementRedundancy;

ValidateDataIntegrity;

CorrectCommunicationErrors;
```

Moreover, ensuring the availability of PLC communications is essential for preventing downtime and ensuring uninterrupted operation of industrial processes. Implementing network monitoring tools, backup and recovery mechanisms, and disaster recovery plans can help detect and mitigate network failures, hardware malfunctions, or cyber attacks, ensuring the continuous operation of PLC systems.

```
// Example of implementing network monitoring and backup mechanisms

MonitorNetworkPerformance;

BackupCommunicationConfigurations;

ImplementDisasterRecoveryPlans;
```

Another critical aspect of safety and security in PLC communications is compliance with industry standards and regulations, such as ISA/IEC 62443, NIST Cybersecurity Framework, and ISO 27001, which provide guidelines and best practices for securing industrial control systems and ensuring the safety and security of critical infrastructure. Adhering to these standards can help organizations identify and address vulnerabilities, assess risks, and implement appropriate security controls to protect PLC communications.

In summary, safety and security are paramount concerns in PLC communications, given the critical nature of industrial processes and the potential risks associated with cyber threats and unauthorized access. By implementing access controls, authentication mechanisms, encryption, error detection and correction mechanisms, redundancy strategies, and compliance with industry standards, organizations can ensure the integrity, confidentiality, and availability of PLC communications, safeguarding industrial processes and mitigating risks in industrial environments.

Chapter 10: Troubleshooting and Maintenance

10.1 Diagnostic Tools in STEP 7

IN SIEMENS STEP 7, an extensive array of diagnostic tools is provided to assist in troubleshooting and maintaining automation systems effectively. This section will delve into these tools, explaining their uses and how they enhance the process of identifying and resolving issues within Siemens S7 PLCs.

Siemens STEP 7 offers a comprehensive environment that includes diagnostic and monitoring tools designed to simplify and enhance the troubleshooting process. These tools are integral in providing real-time insights and historical data analysis, enabling maintenance personnel and engineers to pinpoint faults accurately and efficiently.

One of the key diagnostic tools in STEP 7 is the "Diagnostics Buffer." This tool automatically records events and errors related to the PLC's operation. It logs both system-generated and user-defined errors, offering valuable insights into the sequence of events leading up to a fault or system failure.

// Example of accessing the Diagnostics Buffer

AccessDiagnosticsBuffer();

ReviewErrorLogs();

Another essential tool is the "Variable Monitoring" function. This allows users to watch the real-time values of PLC variables during operation. Monitoring can be conducted live, or data can be collected for later analysis, providing a clear view of how variables change over time, which is crucial for understanding issues related to process control and timing.

// Example of setting up variable monitoring in STEP 7

SetupVariableMonitoring();

TrackVariableChanges();

The "Online and Offline Comparison" tool is particularly useful during troubleshooting. It allows engineers to compare the currently active PLC program with a backup or reference version. This comparison can highlight unintentional changes or discrepancies that might be causing issues in the system.

// Example of performing online and offline comparison

CompareOnlineOffline();

IdentifyDiscrepancies();

STEP 7 also incorporates "System Diagnostic Views," which provide a graphical representation of the entire automation system's status. These views can include device status, network health, and communication link statuses, offering a holistic view that is essential for system-level troubleshooting.

// Example of accessing system diagnostic views

AccessSystemDiagnostics();

VisualizeNetworkHealth();

For more detailed analysis, "Trace Functions" are available to record the sequence of program execution over time. This feature is invaluable for identifying timing issues or complex interactions between different parts of the PLC program that are not readily apparent from static code analysis alone.

```
// Example of using trace functions to diagnose issues

InitializeTrace();

RecordExecutionSequence();

AnalyzeTraceResults();
```

In addition to these diagnostic tools, STEP 7 provides "Alarm Logging" features, which allow for the configuration of alarms that can notify operators or maintenance personnel when certain thresholds are met or abnormalities occur. This proactive feature helps in maintaining system integrity and preventing failures.

```
// Example of setting up alarm logging

ConfigureAlarmLogging();

SetAlarmThresholds();
```

Lastly, the integration of "Preventive Maintenance Tools" within STEP 7 helps in scheduling maintenance tasks based on operational data rather than fixed intervals. These tools use data-driven insights to predict when maintenance should be performed, optimizing the maintenance schedule and preventing unnecessary downtime.

In summary, the diagnostic tools provided in Siemens STEP 7 are essential for maintaining high levels of operational integrity and efficiency in industrial automation systems. By utilizing these tools, engineers and technicians can effectively diagnose and troubleshoot issues, ensuring that PLC systems operate reliably and at peak performance.

10.2 Common Errors and Their Solutions

IN THE REALM OF PLC programming, particularly with Siemens S7, encountering errors is a part of the developmental and operational processes. Understanding common errors and knowing how to resolve them efficiently is crucial for maintaining system uptime and reliability. This section explores some of the most frequent issues faced by programmers and maintenance personnel, along with proven solutions.

One prevalent error in Siemens S7 PLCs involves incorrect data handling, such as overflow errors or type mismatches. These issues can cause unexpected behavior or system crashes. Ensuring that data types and operations are compatible and implementing error checking can prevent these problems.

```
// Example of type checking and error handling

IF NOT TypeOf(Variable) == REAL THEN

ErrorHandler("Type mismatch error detected");

ENDIF
```

Another common issue is communication failures, which can occur due to misconfigured settings, faulty hardware, or network issues. Regularly checking connection settings, cables, and communication parameters is vital. Using diagnostic tools to monitor and log communication traffic can help identify and rectify these issues promptly.

```
// Example of checking network communication

CheckCommunicationStatus();

IF NOT Status == OK THEN
```

ResetConnection();

LogError("Communication reset performed due to failure");

ENDIF

Timeout errors are also frequent in network communications between PLCs and other devices. These errors often result from delays in data transmission or processing. Adjusting timeout settings and optimizing network performance can help mitigate these errors.

// Example of adjusting timeout settings

SetTimeout(500); // Timeout in milliseconds

Logic errors, such as incorrect loop conditions or erroneous conditional statements, can lead to unexpected behaviors or infinite loops. Thorough testing and debugging, using tools like step execution and breakpoints, can uncover these issues.

// Example of using breakpoints for debugging

SET_BREAKPOINT_AT "LoopStart"; // Set a breakpoint at the beginning of a loop

Power issues, including unexpected power losses or surges, can disrupt PLC operations and corrupt data. Implementing UPS (Uninterruptible Power Supplies) systems and proper power management protocols can protect against these issues.

// Example of implementing power management commands

MonitorPowerSupplyStatus();

IF PowerStatus == LOW THEN

ExecuteShutdownSequence();

LogEvent("Power low: System shutdown executed to prevent damage");

ENDIF

Configuration errors, such as incorrect device addresses or parameter settings, are common during the initial setup or after system modifications. Using configuration tools to validate settings and reviewing setup documentation can ensure proper configuration.

// Example of validating device configuration

ValidateConfiguration(DeviceAddress);

IF NOT ConfigurationValid THEN

CorrectConfiguration();

LogError("Configuration corrected for device at address " + DeviceAddress);

ENDIF

Lastly, firmware issues, such as bugs or incompatibilities, can cause erratic behavior or system failures. Keeping firmware up-to-date and applying patches recommended by the manufacturer can resolve these problems.

// Example of updating firmware

UpdateFirmware(DeviceID);

LogEvent("Firmware updated for device " + DeviceID);

Understanding these common errors and applying the appropriate solutions can greatly enhance the reliability and performance of Siemens S7 PLC systems. Regular maintenance, proper configuration, and vigilant monitoring are key strategies to minimize downtime and improve overall system efficiency.

10.3 Routine Maintenance Procedures

ROUTINE MAINTENANCE is critical for ensuring the longevity and reliability of Siemens S7 PLC systems. Regularly scheduled maintenance helps prevent unexpected failures, optimizes system performance, and extends the lifecycle of the equipment. In this section, we will outline essential routine maintenance procedures for Siemens S7 PLCs and provide guidance on how to effectively implement these practices.

1. Visual Inspection: Begin each maintenance session with a thorough visual inspection of the PLC system. Check for any signs of physical damage, such as cracks on the housing or loose connections. Ensure that all modules are securely seated in their racks, and the wiring is intact and properly labeled.

2. Cleaning: Dust and debris can accumulate in PLC cabinets, potentially causing overheating and electrical shorts. Use soft brushes and vacuum cleaners designed for electronic equipment to clean the interior of PLC cabinets. Ensure the ventilation fans are free of debris to maintain adequate cooling.

3. Check Connections: Loose connections can lead to intermittent faults or system failures. Check all wiring connections, terminal blocks, and connectors for tightness and corrosion. Use a screwdriver to tighten any loose terminals, and replace any corroded or damaged connectors.

4. Software Backups: Regularly back up the PLC program and configuration settings. This practice ensures that you can quickly restore the system to its operational state following a hardware failure or programming error.

// Example of backing up PLC software

BackupPLCProgram();

LogEvent("PLC program backed up successfully");

5. Firmware Updates: Check for firmware updates periodically. Manufacturers often release firmware updates to fix bugs, patch security vulnerabilities, and improve performance. Updating the firmware can prevent many operational issues.

// Example of updating PLC firmware

UpdateFirmware(DeviceID);

LogEvent("Firmware updated for device " + DeviceID);

6. Battery Checks: Many PLCs have batteries to maintain volatile memory and real-time clocks. Check the battery status regularly and replace batteries as recommended by the manufacturer to avoid data loss and clock errors.

7. Test Input/Output (I/O) Modules: Test the operation of all I/O modules to ensure they are functioning correctly. This can involve manually activating switches, sensors, and actuaries to verify that the PLC registers these inputs and outputs correctly.

8. Check Power Supplies: Inspect power supplies for signs of wear, overheating, or unusual noises. Measure output voltages to ensure they are within specifications. Replace any power supplies that show signs of failure or instability.

9. Diagnostic Checks: Use the diagnostic tools available in Siemens STEP 7 software to run tests and check for system errors or anomalies. Review diagnostic logs and address any issues noted.

```
// Example of performing diagnostic checks

RunDiagnostics();

ReviewDiagnosticLogs();
```

10. Calibration: Calibrate sensors and other input devices to ensure accuracy in the data they provide. This is crucial for processes that rely on precise measurements for quality control.

11. Documentation: Update maintenance logs and documentation with details of all inspections, tests, and replacements. Good documentation practices help in tracking the history of equipment and planning future maintenance activities.

12. Training: Ensure that maintenance personnel are trained and familiar with the latest maintenance procedures and tools. Regular training updates can help technicians handle new equipment and software updates more efficiently.

In conclusion, routine maintenance is a critical aspect of managing Siemens S7 PLC systems. By following these maintenance procedures, organizations can ensure that their PLC systems operate reliably and efficiently, minimizing downtime and extending the service life of their automation investments.

10.4 Upgrading Firmware and Software

UPGRADING FIRMWARE and software in Siemens S7 PLC systems is a critical maintenance task that ensures the systems operate efficiently, with enhanced features and security. This section will explore the procedures for successfully upgrading firmware and software, including best practices and common challenges.

1. Preparation: Before initiating any upgrade, verify that you have the latest and correct versions of the firmware and software for your specific model of Siemens S7 PLC. Download these from the Siemens official website or obtain them through authorized distributors.

2. Backup: Always perform a full backup of the current firmware, software, and all configurations. This step is crucial as it ensures that you can restore the PLC to its previous state if the upgrade fails.

// Example of backing up PLC configurations

BackupConfiguration();

LogEvent("Configuration backup completed successfully");

3. Read Release Notes: Before applying an upgrade, read the release notes provided by Siemens for the new firmware or software. These notes contain important information about new features, fixed bugs, and known issues that might affect your specific setup.

4. Testing: If possible, test the new firmware and software in a controlled environment before deploying it in a production setting. This step helps identify potential problems without risking operational stability.

5. Update Procedure: Follow Siemens' recommended procedures for firmware and software updates. This often involves using specific tools like TIA Portal for uploading the new firmware or software to the PLC.

// Example of updating firmware

UpdateFirmware(DeviceID);

LogEvent("Firmware update initiated for device " + DeviceID);

6. Monitor the Upgrade Process: During the upgrade, monitor the process closely to ensure that no errors occur. Most update tools provide a status output that should be watched to verify that the upgrade is progressing properly.

7. Verification: After the upgrade is complete, perform a thorough check to ensure that all functionalities are working as expected. This includes running tests to verify that the PLC interacts correctly with all connected devices and systems.

8. Restore Configurations: If any configurations were affected or reset during the upgrade, restore them from the backup. Ensure all settings are correctly applied for optimal system operation.

// Example of restoring PLC configurations

RestoreConfiguration();

LogEvent("Configuration restored after firmware update");

9. Documentation: Update all system documentation to reflect the changes made during the upgrade. Include details such as the version of the new firmware or software, the date of the upgrade, and any issues encountered during the process.

10. Staff Training: Inform and train relevant staff on any new features or changes in the operation of the PLC due to the firmware or software upgrade. Proper training ensures that everyone can effectively use the new system features and handle any changes in procedures.

11. Scheduled Reassessments: Schedule future assessments to review the performance and stability of the PLC system post-upgrade. This helps in early detection of any issues that may not be apparent immediately after the upgrade.

In conclusion, upgrading firmware and software in Siemens S7 PLC systems, while critical, requires careful planning, execution, and follow-up to ensure success. By adhering to structured procedures, thorough testing, and detailed documentation, you can ensure that your PLC systems benefit from the latest features and security enhancements with minimal disruption to operational activities.

10.5 Long-Term Health of Siemens S7 Systems

MAINTAINING THE LONG-term health of Siemens S7 PLC systems is crucial for ensuring the reliability, efficiency, and longevity of industrial automation processes. This section outlines strategies and best practices for preserving the long-term health of these systems, helping to avoid unexpected failures and extend their operational life.

1. Regular Maintenance: Establish a routine maintenance schedule based on the manufacturer's recommendations and specific operational conditions. Regular maintenance includes cleaning, checking connections, inspecting hardware for wear and tear, and performing functional tests to ensure everything operates as expected.

2. Environmental Controls: Ensure that the PLC systems are operating within the environmental conditions specified by Siemens. This includes controlling temperature, humidity, and cleanliness in the control room or cabinet. Excessive heat, moisture, or dust can lead to premature wear and failure.

3. Monitoring System Performance: Implement continuous monitoring solutions to track the performance and health of the PLC system. Monitoring can help detect early signs of issues such as unusual temperature increases, vibrations, or electrical noise, which could indicate potential failures.

4. Update and Upgrade Policies: Keep the system firmware and software up-to-date with the latest releases from Siemens. Regular updates not only enhance features but also address security vulnerabilities and bugs that could affect system stability and security.

```
// Example of checking for software updates

CheckForUpdates();

ApplyUpdates();

LogEvent("System software updated to the latest version");
```

5. Manage System Load: Avoid overloading the PLC with too many tasks that can strain its processing capabilities. Evaluate and optimize the program logic and cycle times to ensure that the PLC operates efficiently without excessive load.

6. Spare Parts Management: Maintain a stock of critical spare parts, such as power supplies, I/O modules, and communication modules. Having spares on hand can significantly reduce downtime in the event of a hardware failure.

7. Documentation and Change Management: Keep detailed records of all maintenance activities, updates, and changes made to the system. Proper documentation can be invaluable for troubleshooting and for planning future upgrades or expansions.

8. Training for Personnel: Ensure that all operators and maintenance personnel are properly trained on the specifics of the Siemens S7 systems they work with. Regular training updates can help staff stay aware of new features and maintenance techniques.

9. Cybersecurity Measures: Implement robust cybersecurity measures to protect the PLC system from external threats. This includes using firewalls, VPNs for remote access, and regular security audits to identify and mitigate potential vulnerabilities.

```
// Example of enhancing cybersecurity

SetupFirewall();

ConfigureVPNAccess();

PerformSecurityAudit();

LogEvent("Cybersecurity measures implemented and verified");
```

10. Obsolescence Management: Develop a plan for managing the obsolescence of hardware and software. This might involve phased upgrades or seeking support for legacy systems to ensure continuous operation.

11. Battery Maintenance: Regularly check and replace backup batteries that maintain the memory and real-time clock in the PLC. Battery failure can lead to program loss and system downtime.

12. Network Health: Regularly check the health and integrity of the communication network connecting the PLCs and other system components. Ensure that the network is protected from disruptions and unauthorized access.

13. Disaster Recovery Planning: Develop and test a disaster recovery plan that includes procedures for data backup, system restoration, and alternative control strategies in case of a system failure.

```
// Example of preparing a disaster recovery plan

PrepareDisasterRecoveryPlan();

TestRecoveryProcedures();

LogEvent("Disaster recovery plan tested and confirmed");
```

By adhering to these practices, organizations can ensure the long-term health and operational reliability of their Siemens S7 PLC systems, thereby maximizing their investment and minimizing the risk of downtime in critical industrial processes.

Chapter 11: Real-World Applications and Case Studies

11.1 Manufacturing and Production Lines

THE INTEGRATION OF Siemens S7 PLCs into manufacturing and production lines illustrates the significant improvements that can be achieved in both efficiency and reliability. This section explores various real-world applications where Siemens S7 systems have been instrumental in optimizing production processes across different industries.

In one of the notable applications, an automotive manufacturer utilized Siemens S7 PLCs to control their assembly line. The PLCs were programmed to manage robotic arms for tasks such as welding, painting, and assembly. By leveraging the robust capabilities of Siemens S7, the manufacturer achieved a 25% increase in production speed and a 30% reduction in machine downtime.

The Siemens S7 PLCs were configured with a centralized control system, allowing operators to monitor and adjust production settings in real-time. This setup not only streamlined operations but also enhanced the precision of the production line, leading to higher quality products. For instance, the welding robots were able to perform their tasks with pinpoint accuracy, which significantly reduced the rate of defective outputs.

Furthermore, the Siemens S7 was pivotal in implementing advanced diagnostic tools. These tools continuously monitored the condition of machinery and alerted operators of any impending issues before they could cause significant disruptions. For example, vibration sensors connected to the PLC detected irregular patterns that were indicative of bearing failures in conveyor systems. As a result, maintenance could be performed proactively, minimizing unplanned downtime.

In addition to hardware optimization, the Siemens S7 PLCs were utilized for their extensive data logging capabilities. This feature enabled the collection of vast amounts of production data, which were then analyzed to identify trends and areas for improvement. Through detailed data analysis, the plant managers were able to adjust the production processes for enhanced efficiency.

The programming environment of Siemens S7 also allowed for flexible and scalable solutions. As production demands changed, the PLC programs could be easily updated or expanded, allowing the manufacturing line to adapt quickly to new products or changes in production volume.

Here is a basic example of a Siemens S7 PLC program snippet used in a production line:

```
// Start Conveyor Motor

IF Start_Button == TRUE THEN

Conveyor_Motor := TRUE;

ENDIF

// Stop Conveyor Motor on Emergency

IF Emergency_Stop == TRUE THEN

Conveyor_Motor := FALSE;

ENDIF

// Update Production Count
```

IF Product_Sensor == TRUE THEN

Production_Count := Production_Count + 1;

ENDIF

This simple program illustrates the use of conditional logic to control machinery based on the input from start buttons, emergency stops, and product sensors. Such straightforward logic forms the backbone of more complex systems tailored to specific manufacturing needs.

By implementing Siemens S7 PLCs, another case study in the textile industry shows similar improvements. The PLCs controlled the intricate movements of weaving machines, which resulted in a consistent product quality and faster turnaround times. The precise control over the looms, facilitated by the PLCs, minimized fabric wastage and improved the overall profitability of the textile mills.

Moreover, energy consumption is a critical concern in large-scale manufacturing. Siemens S7 PLCs have been used to implement energy-saving measures by optimizing machine operation schedules and reducing idle times. In one instance, a food processing plant achieved a 20% reduction in energy costs by optimizing the start and stop times of refrigeration units based on real-time demand and ambient temperature conditions.

The versatility of Siemens S7 PLCs extends to industries as diverse as pharmaceuticals, where they ensure compliance with strict manufacturing protocols and enhance traceability of production batches. In these scenarios, the PLCs manage not only the machinery but also critical parameters such as temperature and humidity, which are vital for maintaining product integrity.

In conclusion, the deployment of Siemens S7 PLCs across various manufacturing and production lines demonstrates their capability to significantly enhance operational efficiency, product quality, and system reliability. These case studies provide valuable insights into the practical benefits of integrating advanced PLC technologies in modern industrial settings.

11.2 Energy Management and Distribution

THE APPLICATION OF Siemens S7 PLCs in energy management and distribution sectors demonstrates their pivotal role in ensuring efficient energy use and reliability of power supply systems. This section details how Siemens S7 PLCs are utilized to optimize energy distribution and enhance the stability of power grids, along with several case studies that illustrate these applications.

In one of the applications, a regional power distribution company employed Siemens S7 PLCs to automate and control substations. These PLCs were programmed to handle tasks such as switching operations, real-time monitoring of equipment status, and fault detection. The automation of these processes significantly reduced human errors, leading to a more reliable power supply.

The Siemens S7 PLCs allowed for remote control operations, which are critical in managing widespread power distribution networks. Operators were able to control substation functions from a centralized location, enhancing the response times to power demands and faults. This capability was crucial during peak load periods or when rerouting power to areas affected by outages.

The following is a simplified example of how a Siemens S7 PLC might be programmed to manage a circuit breaker in a substation:

// Monitor and Control Circuit Breaker Status

```
IF Fault_Detected == TRUE THEN

Circuit_Breaker := OPEN; // Open the breaker if a fault is detected

Send_Alert('Fault detected, breaker opened.');

ELSE

Circuit_Breaker := CLOSED; // Keep the breaker closed if no fault
is present

ENDIF

// Automatic Reclosure Logic

IF Circuit_Breaker == OPEN AND Fault_Cleared == TRUE
THEN

WAIT 30s; // Wait 30 seconds before attempting to close the
breaker

Circuit_Breaker := CLOSED;

Send_Alert('Breaker closed after fault clearance.');

ENDIF
```

This program highlights the use of logical operations and conditional statements to manage critical infrastructure based on real-time conditions, thereby enhancing the safety and reliability of electrical systems.

Another key application of Siemens S7 PLCs in this sector is load management. By integrating smart meters and advanced sensors with PLC systems, utility companies are able to perform real-time energy consumption analysis and dynamically adjust the power supply. This not only helps in reducing peak load stress on the power grid but also assists consumers in managing their energy usage more effectively.

In a case study involving a large industrial complex, Siemens S7 PLCs were used to implement a demand response system. The PLCs received signals from the utility company during peak load times and automatically adjusted the operation of non-critical machinery to reduce power consumption. This cooperation between industrial facilities and power utilities exemplifies how intelligent automation can contribute to overall grid stability.

Siemens S7 PLCs are also instrumental in the integration of renewable energy sources into the power grid. In solar power plants, PLCs are used to control and monitor inverters, solar trackers, and cooling systems. They adjust the operations based on weather conditions and power demands, maximizing the efficiency of energy production. For instance, solar trackers are adjusted in real-time to follow the sun's trajectory, which significantly increases the output of solar panels.

The flexibility of Siemens S7 PLC programming allows for the incorporation of predictive maintenance tools. By analyzing data collected from sensors and smart meters, the PLCs can predict potential system failures before they occur. This proactive approach to maintenance prevents extensive downtime and ensures continuous energy supply.

In conclusion, the deployment of Siemens S7 PLCs in energy management and distribution has profound impacts on improving energy efficiency, ensuring reliability, and facilitating the integration of renewable energy resources. These systems not only streamline operations but also support sustainable energy practices, which are critical in the face of growing energy demands and the need for environmental conservation. Through detailed case studies, it is evident that Siemens S7 PLCs are essential tools in the modernization of energy infrastructures.

11.3 Building Automation Systems

SIEMENS S7 PLCS PLAY a crucial role in the automation and management of modern building systems, providing efficient control over heating, ventilation, air conditioning (HVAC), lighting, and security systems. This section discusses the implementation of these PLCs in building automation, highlighting specific case studies where their application has significantly enhanced building efficiency and occupant comfort.

The integration of Siemens S7 PLCs into building automation primarily revolves around the concept of creating smarter, more energy-efficient buildings. By using these PLCs, facilities managers can automate routine tasks, optimize energy consumption, and improve the overall environmental footprint of buildings.

For example, in the HVAC system, Siemens S7 PLCs are used to control the temperature and air quality inside buildings. The PLCs monitor various sensors that measure temperature, humidity, and air pollutants, and adjust the HVAC operations accordingly to maintain the desired environmental conditions. This dynamic adjustment not only improves comfort but also reduces energy consumption significantly.

Here is a simplified example of how a Siemens S7 PLC might be programmed to control an HVAC system:

```
// Temperature Control Logic

IF Room_Temperature > Desired_Temperature + 1 THEN

Cooling_System := ON;
```

```
ELSIF Room_Temperature < Desired_Temperature - 1 THEN

Heating_System := ON;

ELSE

Cooling_System := OFF;

Heating_System := OFF;

ENDIF

// Ventilation Control Based on Air Quality

IF CO2_Level > High_CO2_Threshold THEN

Ventilation_Fan := ON;

ELSE

Ventilation_Fan := OFF;

ENDIF
```

This program demonstrates how conditional statements are used to maintain optimal temperature and air quality, which are essential for occupant comfort and health.

In lighting systems, Siemens S7 PLCs automate light control based on occupancy and ambient light levels. Sensors detect the presence of people in a room and adjust the lighting accordingly, which not only conserves energy but also enhances the user experience. Furthermore, external light sensors can adjust indoor lighting levels based on the amount of natural light available, further reducing the reliance on artificial lighting.

Another critical aspect of building automation is security. Siemens S7 PLCs are deployed to manage access control systems, surveillance cameras, and alarm systems. These PLCs process inputs from various security devices and make decisions on access control, alarm activation, and video recording, ensuring high levels of building security.

A notable case study involves a high-rise commercial building where Siemens S7 PLCs were integrated into both the fire safety and security systems. The PLCs coordinated the operation of smoke detectors, sprinkler systems, and emergency lighting during drills and actual emergencies, demonstrating their capability to handle complex scenarios and ensure occupant safety effectively.

Energy management is another significant benefit of implementing Siemens S7 PLCs in building automation. By continuously monitoring energy usage and adjusting systems like HVAC and lighting, buildings can achieve substantial energy savings. For instance, a smart building project reported a 30% reduction in energy costs after retrofitting their old control systems with Siemens S7 PLCs.

Moreover, the data logging capabilities of Siemens S7 PLCs allow building managers to analyze historical data to identify trends and further optimize building operations. This data-driven approach can lead to continual improvements in building management practices.

Furthermore, the scalability of Siemens S7 PLCs makes them suitable for both small buildings and large complexes. As building requirements grow or change, additional modules and functions can be easily integrated into the existing PLC system, allowing for a flexible and future-proof solution.

In summary, the application of Siemens S7 PLCs in building automation transforms traditional buildings into smart buildings, enhancing operational efficiency, occupant comfort, and environmental sustainability. Through the automation of HVAC, lighting, and security systems, these PLCs contribute significantly to the modernization of building infrastructures, making them essential components in the pursuit of smarter cities and greener buildings.

11.4 Water and Wastewater Treatment Facilities

SIEMENS S7 PLCS ARE extensively used in water and wastewater treatment facilities to enhance operational efficiencies, ensure compliance with environmental regulations, and manage complex treatment processes. This section explores various applications of Siemens S7 in water treatment systems, detailing how these PLCs optimize operations and maintain high standards of water quality.

In water treatment facilities, the primary role of Siemens S7 PLCs is to control and monitor the various stages of the water purification process. This includes the management of pumps, valves, chemical dosers, and filtration systems. The PLCs ensure that each component operates in harmony and according to precise specifications to achieve optimal treatment effectiveness.

For example, in the coagulation and flocculation stages, Siemens S7 PLCs control the dosing pumps that add chemicals to the water. These chemicals are necessary for binding and removing suspended particles from the water. The PLCs monitor the flow rates and adjust the chemical dosing accordingly, based on real-time water quality parameters such as turbidity and pH levels.

Here is a simple example of how a Siemens S7 PLC might be programmed to manage a dosing process:

```
// Chemical Dosing Control
```

```
IF Turbidity > Set_Turbidity_Threshold THEN

Dosing_Pump_Speed          :=          Adjust_Speed(Turbidity,
Desired_Turbidity_Level);

Log_Event('Increased chemical dosing due to high turbidity.');

ELSE

Dosing_Pump_Speed := Normal_Speed;

ENDIF
```

This program snippet illustrates the use of conditional logic to adjust dosing rates based on turbidity measurements, ensuring efficient particle removal while conserving chemicals.

In the sedimentation stage, Siemens S7 PLCs control the rate at which water moves through settling tanks to allow enough time for the suspended particles to settle. The PLCs use sensors to monitor the clarity of water exiting the tanks and adjust the flow rate to optimize the settling process.

Filtration is another critical stage where Siemens S7 PLCs play a vital role. These PLCs manage the operation of filters, ensuring they are cleaned and backwashed at appropriate intervals to maintain their effectiveness. Sensors monitor the pressure drop across filters, and when a set threshold is exceeded, indicating clogging, the PLC initiates a backwash cycle.

```
// Filter Backwash Logic

IF Pressure_Drop > Set_Pressure_Drop_Threshold THEN

Initiate_Backwash();

Log_Event('Backwash initiated due to high pressure drop.');
```

ENDIF

In wastewater treatment, Siemens S7 PLCs are crucial for managing the biological treatment processes, such as activated sludge systems. These PLCs control the aeration systems which provide oxygen necessary for microbial digestion of organic pollutants. By adjusting aeration based on dissolved oxygen levels and other process variables, the PLCs ensure efficient treatment while minimizing energy consumption.

```
// Aeration Control Logic

IF Dissolved_Oxygen < Minimum_DO_Threshold THEN

Increase_Aeration();

Log_Event('Aeration increased due to low dissolved oxygen.');

ELSEIF Dissolved_Oxygen > Maximum_DO_Threshold THEN

Decrease_Aeration();

Log_Event('Aeration decreased due to high dissolved oxygen.');

ENDIF
```

The advanced control capabilities of Siemens S7 PLCs also extend to sludge management. These systems automate the handling and processing of sludge, including thickening, digestion, and dewatering processes. By optimizing these processes, facilities can reduce the volume of waste and improve the efficiency of resource recovery.

Moreover, Siemens S7 PLCs help in implementing advanced features such as remote monitoring and control. Facility operators can access real-time data and control systems from remote locations, enhancing the ability to respond quickly to any issues and reducing the need for on-site personnel.

Energy management is another significant benefit of using Siemens S7 in these facilities. The PLCs can optimize the operation of high-energy-consuming equipment such as pumps and blowers, leading to substantial energy savings and reduced operational costs.

Overall, the use of Siemens S7 PLCs in water and wastewater treatment facilities not only enhances the efficiency and effectiveness of the treatment processes but also supports sustainability by improving energy management and reducing environmental impacts. Through detailed case studies and examples, it's clear that Siemens S7 PLCs are indispensable tools in modern water management strategies.

11.5 Robotics and Automated Assemblies

THE IMPLEMENTATION of Siemens S7 PLCs in robotics and automated assembly lines highlights their critical role in enhancing manufacturing efficiency, precision, and scalability. This section explores the integration of these PLCs into various robotic applications, showcasing their capabilities in complex, high-speed automation environments.

Siemens S7 PLCs are particularly valued in the robotics sector for their robustness, reliability, and real-time processing capabilities. These traits are essential in environments where precise control and synchronization of multiple robotic arms and assembly processes are required.

In automotive manufacturing, for example, Siemens S7 PLCs control robotic arms that perform tasks such as welding, painting, and assembly. The PLCs ensure that these tasks are performed with high precision and consistent quality, essential for maintaining production standards. The integration of PLCs allows for seamless communication between robots and central control systems, facilitating synchronized operations across the production line.

```
// Robot Arm Control Logic

FOR Each Robot IN Robot_Group

IF Robot.Status == READY THEN

Robot.StartTask(Next_Task);

Log_Event('Task started for ' + Robot.ID);

ENDIF

ENDFOR
```

This example code demonstrates how a loop structure can be used to initiate tasks on multiple robots once they are ready, ensuring efficient task management without unnecessary delays.

In electronics manufacturing, precision is paramount, and even minor errors can lead to significant product faults. Siemens S7 PLCs manage the intricate movements of robots placing components on circuit boards. These PLCs adjust the robot's actions based on real-time feedback from vision systems, ensuring components are placed accurately, enhancing product reliability.

Furthermore, in packaging and palletizing operations, Siemens S7 PLCs are used to control robots that must handle varying package sizes and weights. The PLCs dynamically adjust the robot's grip strength and movement speed, depending on the package's attributes, which are detected through sensors. This adaptability prevents damage to products and improves the efficiency of the packaging line.

```
// Packaging Robot Adjustment Logic

IF Package.Weight > Max_Weight_Threshold THEN

Adjust_Robot_Speed(Slow);

Adjust_Grip_Strength(Strong);

ELSE

Adjust_Robot_Speed(Fast);

Adjust_Grip_Strength(Normal);

ENDIF

Log_Event('Adjustments made for package weight');
```

In pharmaceuticals, robots controlled by Siemens S7 PLCs perform tasks that require utmost precision and cleanliness, such as filling medications and assembling intricate drug delivery devices. The PLCs ensure that these tasks adhere to strict health and safety regulations, automating processes that are too delicate or hazardous for human workers.

The ability of Siemens S7 PLCs to integrate with advanced sensor technology enhances their functionality in robotic applications. For instance, force sensors and machine vision are utilized to provide feedback on the robot's performance, which is processed by the PLC to make real-time adjustments. This feedback loop is critical for maintaining the accuracy and quality of automated tasks.

Siemens S7 PLCs also contribute to the scalability of robotic systems. As production demands increase or as new tasks are required, additional robots can be integrated into the existing PLC network without significant disruptions. This scalability is particularly beneficial in industries where product types and production volumes frequently change.

Energy efficiency is another advantage of using Siemens S7 PLCs in robotics. The PLCs can optimize the operation of robots and associated equipment based on real-time usage data, minimizing unnecessary energy consumption and reducing operational costs.

Moreover, the robust diagnostic and troubleshooting tools available in Siemens S7 PLCs make maintenance more straightforward. Technicians can quickly identify and resolve issues, reducing downtime and maintaining production continuity.

In conclusion, Siemens S7 PLCs are indispensable in the realm of robotics and automated assemblies. Through precise control, integration with advanced technologies, and scalability, these PLCs enable industries to achieve high levels of automation and efficiency. The various case studies and examples provided in this section illustrate the transformative impact of Siemens S7 PLCs in modern manufacturing environments.

Chapter 12: Advanced Programming Techniques

12.1 Sequential Function Charts

SEQUENTIAL FUNCTION Charts (SFCs) are a graphical programming language used for programming automated control systems and are particularly well-suited for managing complex processes that involve multiple steps or states. Siemens S7 PLCs support SFCs as part of their programming suite, providing a robust tool for developers to design, implement, and manage sophisticated control sequences.

SFCs are ideal for applications where the process must follow a strict sequence of operations, such as in batch processing or where operations are highly dependent on specific conditions being met. The graphical nature of SFCs makes them highly readable and easier to troubleshoot, as they visually represent the flow of operations.

The basic structure of an SFC involves steps, transitions, and actions. Each step represents a condition or state of the process, and transitions determine when the process should move from one step to the next. Actions are associated with steps and are executed when a step is active.

Here's a basic example of how an SFC might be implemented in Siemens S7:

```
// Step 1: Check Material Availability

IF Material_Available THEN

TRANSITION to Step 2;
```

```
ENDIF

// Step 2: Start Processing

Start_Machine();

Maintain until Processing_Complete;

TRANSITION to Step 3;

// Step 3: Check Quality

IF Quality_OK THEN

TRANSITION to Step 4;

ELSE

TRANSITION to Step 1; // Re-process if quality is not sufficient

ENDIF

// Step 4: End Process

Stop_Machine();
```

This example illustrates a simple production process where material availability triggers the start of a machine, followed by a quality check, and finally, the process ends unless the quality is inadequate, which causes a reversion to the start.

The power of SFCs in a Siemens S7 environment lies in their ability to be nested and combined with other programming languages supported by Siemens S7, such as Ladder Logic or Function Block Diagram. This flexibility allows complex logic to be broken down into more manageable parts, each handled in the most appropriate programming style.

For instance, SFCs can control the high-level sequence of operations while detailed control logic, like PID control loops or mathematical calculations, is handled in Function Blocks or Structured Text. This separation of concerns makes the system more modular and easier to manage.

SFCs also support concurrent operations, where multiple sequences can operate in parallel, each managing different parts of a system. This is particularly useful in large systems where independent operations need to synchronize at specific points in the process.

Another advantage of using SFCs in Siemens S7 PLCs is their integration with diagnostic tools. Since SFCs provide a clear visualization of process flows, they can be used to monitor real-time progress and troubleshoot issues as they arise. Operators can see exactly at which step a problem occurred, simplifying diagnostics and reducing downtime.

Energy management can also be optimized with SFCs. By controlling the sequence of operations, SFCs can ensure that machines run only when necessary and that transitions between steps are as efficient as possible. This can lead to significant energy savings in processes where machines have high idle times.

Moreover, SFCs facilitate compliance with safety and regulatory standards by ensuring that processes follow predefined sequences, which are often a requirement in industries such as pharmaceuticals, food and beverage, and chemical processing. The rigorous structure of SFC programming helps in maintaining compliance and documenting operations, which is crucial during audits.

In summary, the application of Sequential Function Charts within Siemens S7 PLC programming provides a powerful tool for managing complex sequences in industrial environments. By leveraging the graphical nature and the robust control capabilities of SFCs, developers can create highly efficient, reliable, and transparent control systems. The use of SFCs demonstrates how advanced programming techniques can significantly enhance the functionality and operability of automated systems.

12.2 Integration of Scripting Languages

THE INTEGRATION OF scripting languages with Siemens S7 PLCs opens up a new realm of possibilities for automation and control systems. Scripting languages such as VBScript, JavaScript, or Python can be used to extend the capabilities of PLCs, providing more flexibility, ease of data handling, and integration with external systems. This section explores how these scripting languages can be incorporated into Siemens S7 environments and the benefits they bring to industrial automation.

Scripting languages can be used in various ways with Siemens S7 PLCs. One common application is for data manipulation and communication with databases or other IT systems. Scripting can automate data exchange processes, generate reports, or perform complex calculations that are beyond the typical scope of PLC programming.

For instance, a Python script can be used to fetch data from a Siemens S7 PLC, perform an analysis, and then push results to a SQL database for further use in enterprise resource planning (ERP) systems:

```python
import snap7

from sqlalchemy import create_engine

# Connect to PLC
```

```python
plc = snap7.client.Client()

plc.connect('192.168.1.10', 0, 1)

# Read data from DB1

db1 = plc.db_read(1, 0, 256) # Read 256 bytes from DB1

# Process data (example: sum up values)

total = sum(db1[:10]) # Sum the first 10 bytes

# Connect to SQL database

engine = create_engine('mysql+pymysql://user:password@localhost/dbname')

connection = engine.connect()

# Insert data into database

connection.execute("INSERT INTO production_data (total) VALUES (%s)", (total,))

connection.close()
```

This script demonstrates how to combine direct PLC communication with database operations, enhancing the data management capabilities of industrial systems.

Another valuable application of scripting with Siemens S7 PLCs is for creating custom user interfaces (UIs) for monitoring and control. Scripting languages like JavaScript can be used to develop web-based UIs that provide real-time data visualization and control functions accessible from any web-enabled device.

```javascript
// JavaScript to update and display PLC data in real-time
```

```javascript
function updateData() {

fetch('/get_plc_data')

.then(response => response.json())

.then(data => {

document.getElementById('temperature').innerText            =
data.temperature;

});

}

setInterval(updateData, 1000); // Update every second
```

This JavaScript snippet shows a simple method to fetch and display data from a PLC on a web page, enabling remote monitoring of industrial processes.

Scripting languages also facilitate the integration of Siemens S7 PLCs with other hardware and software, enhancing the interoperability of systems. For example, Python scripts can be used to bridge data between PLCs and IoT devices or cloud platforms, enabling advanced analytics and predictive maintenance models.

```python
import paho.mqtt.client as mqtt

# Function to send data to an IoT platform

def send_to_iot(topic, message):

client = mqtt.Client()

client.connect('iot.example.com', 1883, 60)

client.publish(topic, message)
```

client.disconnect()

In this example, a Python script uses MQTT, a popular IoT protocol, to send data from the PLC to an IoT platform, facilitating real-time analytics and decision-making.

The use of scripting languages also improves the scalability and maintainability of automation systems. Scripts can be easily updated or replaced without affecting the underlying PLC programs, making it easier to adapt to changing requirements or integrate new technologies.

Furthermore, scripting can significantly enhance the capabilities of Siemens S7 PLCs in terms of complex mathematical calculations, string operations, and algorithmic control. These tasks are often cumbersome or inefficient to implement directly in PLC programming languages but are straightforward in most high-level scripting languages.

Overall, the integration of scripting languages with Siemens S7 PLCs represents a powerful toolset for expanding the functionality, connectivity, and intelligence of industrial automation systems. By leveraging these languages, developers can bridge the gap between traditional PLC programming and modern IT applications, driving greater innovation and efficiency in industrial operations.

12.3 High-Level Mathematical and Algorithmic Implementation

INCORPORATING HIGH-level mathematical and algorithmic logic into Siemens S7 PLC programming elevates the capacity for handling complex calculations and decision-making processes in industrial automation. This section delves into the application of sophisticated mathematical models and algorithms within the

Siemens S7 environment, demonstrating how they can optimize operations, enhance predictive maintenance, and enable advanced control systems.

Advanced mathematical operations can be crucial in industries where process conditions are dynamically changing and require real-time adjustments based on complex calculations. For instance, chemical processing plants often need to adjust mix ratios and temperatures based on the real-time analysis of chemical properties, which can be facilitated by implementing algorithms directly in the PLC.

```
// Example of a PID control algorithm implemented in a Siemens S7 PLC

// Setpoint, Process Variable, and PID coefficients are assumed to be predefined

Real PID_Control(Real Setpoint, Real Process_Var, Real Kp, Real Ki, Real Kd)

{

Static Real Last_Error = 0.0;

Static Real Integral = 0.0;

Real Error = Setpoint - Process_Var;

Integral = Integral + Error;

Real Derivative = Error - Last_Error;

Real Output = (Kp * Error) + (Ki * Integral) + (Kd * Derivative);

Last_Error = Error;
```

```
return Output;
```

```
}
```

This PID (Proportional-Integral-Derivative) control snippet showcases how a basic control algorithm can be adapted for use in a PLC to maintain process control, such as temperature or pressure, at desired levels.

Furthermore, the integration of statistical methods for data analysis directly into PLCs can significantly improve the monitoring and quality control processes. For example, statistical process control (SPC) techniques can be implemented to detect deviations from production norms and trigger corrective actions.

```
// Example of calculating a moving average for quality control

Static Real[10] Recent_Measurements;

Static Integer Index = 0;

Void Update_Moving_Average(Real New_Measurement)

{

Recent_Measurements[Index % 10] = New_Measurement;

Index++;

Real Sum = 0;

For (Integer i = 0; i < 10; i++)

{

Sum += Recent_Measurements[i];

}
```

```
Real Moving_Average = Sum / 10;

// Check if moving average is out of tolerance

If (Moving_Average > Upper_Limit || Moving_Average < Lower_Limit)

{

Alarm('Measurement out of tolerance');

}

}
```

This moving average calculation is an example of how data smoothing can be implemented to monitor trends in production data, helping to maintain consistent quality and operational standards.

In more complex scenarios, algorithms such as machine learning models can be approximated and implemented in PLCs to enable predictive maintenance. By analyzing operational data from machinery, these algorithms can predict failures before they occur, reducing downtime and maintenance costs.

```
// Example of a simple machine learning algorithm (linear regression) for predictive maintenance

Static Real Coefficients[2]; // Coefficients for linear regression

Real Predict_Failure(Real Input_Variable)

{

Real Prediction = Coefficients[0] + (Coefficients[1] * Input_Variable);
```

```
Return Prediction;

}

// Update model based on new data

Void Update_Model(Real New_Input, Real New_Output)

{

// Simplified update logic for demonstration

Coefficients[1] = (New_Output - Coefficients[0]) / New_Input;

}
```

This simplistic model demonstrates how linear regression could be used to forecast machine failures based on observable parameters, such as temperature or vibration levels.

Moreover, the implementation of algorithms that optimize resource allocation and scheduling directly within the PLC can greatly enhance operational efficiency. Such algorithms can dynamically adjust production schedules and resource allocations in response to real-time demand changes or supply chain disruptions.

Overall, the ability to implement high-level mathematical and algorithmic logic within Siemens S7 PLCs allows for a more sophisticated approach to automation and control. These capabilities enable industries to not only maintain precision and efficiency but also adapt to new challenges and opportunities in an increasingly complex technological landscape.

12.4 Event-Driven Programming

EVENT-DRIVEN PROGRAMMING in the context of Siemens S7 PLCs involves designing systems that primarily react to external or internal events, such as sensor inputs, timing signals, or message communications. This approach contrasts with continuous or cyclic task processing, providing a more efficient and responsive system architecture for certain types of automation tasks. This section explores the concepts, benefits, and practical applications of event-driven programming in Siemens S7 PLC environments.

In event-driven systems, the PLC remains in a wait state until an event occurs, triggering specific actions or sequences. This programming paradigm is particularly effective for systems where actions do not need to occur continuously but rather in response to specific changes in the system's environment or state.

For instance, in a manufacturing line, a sensor detecting a piece passing on a conveyor can trigger an event in the PLC to start a robotic arm. The PLC isn't continuously checking the position; it reacts when the sensor provides the input, reducing unnecessary processing and energy consumption.

```
// Example of event-driven logic for a sensor-triggered start

WHEN Sensor_Trigger = TRUE DO

Start_Robotic_Arm();

Log_Event('Robotic arm started by sensor trigger.');

END_WHEN;
```

This simple logic snippet uses an event-triggered approach to initiate an operation, ensuring that the system only acts when necessary, thus optimizing performance and resource utilization.

Event-driven programming is highly beneficial in systems requiring high levels of responsiveness and reliability. For example, in emergency shutdown systems within chemical plants, the detection of a hazardous condition must immediately trigger safety protocols. Using event-driven programming ensures that these critical actions occur with minimal delay.

```
// Emergency shutdown triggered by hazardous condition

WHEN Hazard_Detection = TRUE DO

Execute_Shutdown_Protocol();

Alert_Operator('Shutdown initiated due to hazard detection.');

END_WHEN;
```

This example illustrates how event-driven programming can be critical in safety applications, providing immediate response capabilities that are less feasible with cyclic scanning programming.

Moreover, event-driven programming can be used to handle communication events, such as receiving a message from a networked device or system. This is particularly useful in integrated systems where PLCs must coordinate with other devices or software systems.

```
// Handling a communication event

WHEN New_Message_Received DO

Process_Message();

Log_Event('Message processed.');
END_WHEN;
```

This code handles incoming messages as events, processing each as it arrives, which enhances the system's ability to manage and respond to external communications efficiently.

Event-driven programming also simplifies the management of complex user interfaces or interaction-heavy tasks, such as those found in modern smart factories where human-machine interfaces (HMIs) play a significant role. Buttons, switches, and other controls can be programmed to trigger events in the PLC, which then executes the necessary logic in response.

```
// UI button press handling

WHEN Button_Pressed('Start_Process') DO

Initiate_Process();

Display_Status('Process started.');

END_WHEN;
```

This snippet shows how a button press on an HMI can directly initiate a process, providing an intuitive and responsive interface for operators.

The implementation of event-driven programming in Siemens S7 PLCs allows developers to create systems that are not only efficient but also easier to debug and maintain. Since the system's logic is broken down into discrete event handlers, issues can often be isolated and resolved more quickly than in systems where many processes are interdependent and continuously running.

Event-driven programming is also adaptable to changes in system requirements. New event handlers can be added with minimal impact on existing logic, allowing for scalable and flexible system development.

Overall, the application of event-driven programming within Siemens S7 PLCs offers a powerful methodology for creating highly responsive, efficient, and robust automation systems. This approach leverages the natural occurrence of events to optimize system performance, enhancing the ability of industrial systems to adapt to real-time changes and demands.

12.5 Predictive Maintenance Through Advanced Algorithms

PREDICTIVE MAINTENANCE in industrial settings has become a cornerstone of modern maintenance strategies, thanks to its ability to prevent equipment failures before they occur. Utilizing advanced algorithms within Siemens S7 PLCs, factories can analyze operational data in real-time to predict and prevent potential equipment failures, optimizing maintenance schedules and reducing downtime. This section explores how predictive maintenance algorithms are integrated into Siemens S7 PLC programming and the benefits they bring to industrial automation.

Predictive maintenance algorithms typically involve data collection, analysis, and decision-making processes. In a Siemens S7 PLC, these components are orchestrated to monitor equipment conditions continuously and to predict when maintenance should be performed based on data trends rather than on a fixed schedule.

One of the most common predictive maintenance techniques implemented in PLCs is vibration analysis. Sensors collect vibration data from machinery, which is then analyzed by the PLC to detect patterns indicative of wear or impending failure.

```
// Vibration analysis algorithm

REAL vibration_threshold = 5.0; // predefined threshold level
```

```
REAL current_vibration = Get_Vibration_Data(); // function to read sensor data

IF current_vibration > vibration_threshold THEN

Trigger_Alarm('Potential equipment failure detected');

Schedule_Maintenance();

ENDIF;
```

This code snippet demonstrates how a simple threshold-based analysis can trigger maintenance procedures, helping prevent machine failure.

Another critical aspect of predictive maintenance is temperature monitoring. Excessive heat can be a sign of severe issues in mechanical systems. PLCs can monitor temperature sensors to identify overheating problems before they lead to equipment failure.

```
// Temperature monitoring for predictive maintenance

REAL max_safe_temperature = 100.0; // maximum safe temperature in Celsius

REAL current_temperature = Get_Temperature_Data(); // function to read sensor data

IF current_temperature > max_safe_temperature THEN

Trigger_Alarm('Overheating detected');

Initiate_Cooling_System();

Schedule_Maintenance();

ENDIF;
```

This example shows how the PLC can take immediate corrective action by initiating a cooling system and scheduling maintenance, thus averting potential damage.

The implementation of more complex algorithms, such as machine learning models, is also feasible with the advanced capabilities of Siemens S7 PLCs. These models can learn from historical and real-time data to make more accurate predictions about equipment health.

```
// Machine learning model for predictive maintenance

REAL                    predicted_failure_time              =
Machine_Learning_Model(current_operation_conditions);

REAL threshold_time_for_maintenance = 72.0; // hours before
failure

IF predicted_failure_time <= threshold_time_for_maintenance
THEN

Trigger_Alarm('Maintenance required soon');

Schedule_Maintenance();

ENDIF;
```

This model can predict the time until failure based on current operating conditions, allowing maintenance to be scheduled just in time to prevent the failure, optimizing operational efficiency and reducing costs.

In addition to analyzing mechanical conditions, predictive maintenance algorithms can also monitor electrical parameters such as current and voltage to detect anomalies. Unusual electrical readings can often precede mechanical failures, providing an early warning to maintenance teams.

```
// Electrical parameter monitoring for predictive maintenance

REAL current_draw = Get_Current_Draw(); // function to read electrical sensor data

REAL normal_current_draw = 10.0; // normal current draw in amps

IF current_draw > normal_current_draw * 1.2 THEN

Trigger_Alarm('Electrical anomaly detected');

Schedule_Maintenance();

ENDIF;
```

This logic helps in identifying electrical issues that could lead to mechanical problems, allowing for preventative action to be taken before a costly breakdown occurs.

Predictive maintenance not only reduces the frequency and severity of equipment failures but also extends the life of the machinery by ensuring that parts are only replaced when truly necessary. This approach leads to significant cost savings and improved asset management.

Furthermore, the data collected through predictive maintenance programs can be used for continuous improvement. By analyzing trends and outcomes, facilities can refine their processes and maintenance protocols, leading to ever-increasing efficiency and reliability.

Overall, the integration of advanced algorithms for predictive maintenance into Siemens S7 PLCs transforms traditional maintenance strategies into proactive, data-driven approaches. These algorithms leverage the power of real-time data analysis to predict and prevent equipment failures, enhancing the resilience and efficiency of industrial operations.

Chapter 13: Security in PLC Programming

13.1 Understanding Cybersecurity Risks

THE INCREASING CONNECTIVITY of industrial control systems like Siemens S7 PLCs has exposed them to a broader range of cybersecurity risks. Understanding these risks is crucial for developing effective defenses against potential cyber threats that could disrupt operational integrity and safety. This section delves into the various cybersecurity risks associated with PLC programming and the measures that can be implemented to mitigate them.

One of the primary cybersecurity risks for PLCs is unauthorized access. If malicious actors gain control over a PLC, they can alter control logic and operational parameters, leading to equipment damage, production stoppage, or safety incidents. Therefore, securing access to PLCs is a fundamental aspect of cybersecurity.

```
// Example of simple access control logic

IF User_Authentication() == TRUE THEN

Allow_Access();

ELSE

Deny_Access();

Log_Event('Unauthorized access attempt detected');

ENDIF;
```

This code represents a basic form of access control, where operations within the PLC are conditional based on user authentication.

Another significant risk is data interception and tampering. As PLCs often communicate over networks, intercepting or altering the data transmitted between PLCs and other devices can lead to compromised operational data, leading to inappropriate actions or responses from the PLC.

To combat this, encryption of data in transit is crucial. Implementing secure communication protocols such as TLS (Transport Layer Security) can help protect data integrity and confidentiality.

```
// Pseudocode for implementing TLS in PLC communications

Initialize_TLS_Session();

IF TLS_Handshake() == SUCCESS THEN

Encrypt_Communication(Data);

Transmit_Encrypted_Data();

ELSE

Log_Event('TLS handshake failed');

Terminate_Communication();

ENDIF;
```

This pseudocode outlines the process of securing PLC communications using TLS, ensuring that data transmitted over the network is encrypted and secure from eavesdropping or tampering.

Additionally, PLCs are vulnerable to denial-of-service (DoS) attacks, where attackers flood the network or the PLC with excessive requests, rendering it unable to process legitimate operations. Implementing rate limiting and traffic monitoring can help mitigate these attacks.

```
// Example of rate limiting logic for DoS protection

Monitor_Incoming_Requests();

IF Request_Frequency > Threshold THEN

Temporarily_Block_IP();

Alert_Administrator('Potential DoS attack detected');

ENDIF;
```

This logic helps to protect the PLC from being overwhelmed by excessive requests, which could be part of a DoS attack.

Malware is another critical threat to PLC systems. Malware can be designed to specifically target industrial environments, as seen in past cybersecurity incidents like the Stuxnet attack. Maintaining up-to-date antivirus solutions and implementing application whitelisting can prevent unauthorized or malicious software from executing on PLC systems.

```
// Pseudocode for application whitelisting check

IF   Check_Software_Whitelist(Application_ID)   ==   FALSE
THEN

Prevent_Execution();

Log_Event('Attempt to execute non-whitelisted application blocked');

ENDIF;
```

This pseudocode demonstrates how application whitelisting can prevent the execution of unauthorized software on PLCs, adding an additional layer of security.

Phishing attacks targeting human operators are also a concern. Educating users on the dangers of phishing and implementing robust authentication mechanisms can reduce the risk of credentials being compromised.

Furthermore, the risk of physical access to PLCs should not be overlooked. Unauthorized physical access can allow attackers to manipulate hardware, download programs, or insert USB devices with malicious intent. Physical security controls, such as locking PLC panels and monitoring access to industrial control areas, are essential.

In summary, understanding and addressing the cybersecurity risks associated with PLC programming require a comprehensive approach that includes securing network communications, safeguarding against unauthorized access, and protecting against malware and DoS attacks. By implementing these measures, organizations can significantly enhance the security of their Siemens S7 PLC systems and the broader industrial control system environment.

13.2 Securing Siemens S7 Against Cyber Threats

SECURING SIEMENS S7 PLCs against cyber threats is a critical aspect of maintaining operational integrity and safety in industrial environments. This section outlines practical strategies and measures that can be implemented to enhance the cybersecurity posture of

Siemens S7 PLCs, thereby mitigating risks and protecting against potential cyber attacks.

One of the foundational security measures is the implementation of strong authentication mechanisms. This involves ensuring that all access to the PLC systems, both physical and remote, is controlled through secure authentication protocols such as two-factor authentication (2FA) or role-based access control (RBAC).

```
// Example of role-based access control check

IF User_Role == 'Administrator' THEN

Grant_Full_Access();

ELSEIF User_Role == 'Operator' THEN

Grant_Operational_Access();

ELSE

Deny_Access();

Log_Event('Access attempt with insufficient privileges');

ENDIF;
```

This pseudocode demonstrates how access can be restricted based on the user's role, ensuring that individuals only have access to the functions necessary for their role.

Network security is another crucial area. Implementing firewalls and intrusion detection systems (IDS) can help monitor and control the traffic allowed into and out of network segments containing Siemens S7 PLCs. Segmenting the network by placing industrial control system components on a separate network from the general corporate network can further reduce the risk of exposure to attacks.

```
// Pseudocode for network traffic filtering with a firewall

IF      Packet_Origin     ==     'Untrusted_Network'      AND
Packet_Destination == 'PLC_Network' THEN

IF Packet_Type IN Allowed_Types THEN

Allow_Packet();

ELSE

Block_Packet();

Log_Event('Blocked unauthorized network traffic');

ENDIF;

ENDIF;
```

This pseudocode outlines a basic approach to network segmentation and filtering, which is vital for protecting PLCs from potentially harmful traffic originating from less secure networks.

Encryption of data both in transit and at rest is essential to prevent unauthorized data interception and tampering. Implementing secure protocols like TLS for network communications and ensuring that sensitive data stored on the PLC or related systems is encrypted can greatly enhance security.

```
// Example of implementing encryption for data storage

Encrypt_Data(Before_Storing);

Store_Encrypted_Data();

Decrypt_Data(When_Accessing);
```

This simple code outlines the process of encrypting data before storage and decrypting it upon retrieval, protecting sensitive information from being disclosed if unauthorized access occurs.

Regularly updating and patching the Siemens S7 PLCs and associated software is crucial to defend against known vulnerabilities. Many cyber attacks exploit outdated systems with known vulnerabilities that could have been mitigated by applying patches.

```
// Pseudocode for automated patch management

Check_For_Updates();

IF Updates_Available THEN

Apply_Updates();

Log_Event('System updated');

ELSE

Log_Event('No updates found');

ENDIF;
```

This pseudocode highlights an automated approach to maintaining the software up-to-date, which is essential for securing systems against the exploitation of older vulnerabilities.

Physical security measures should not be overlooked. Securing access to the PLC hardware prevents unauthorized personnel from tampering with the system or inserting malicious devices. This can include locking cabinets and rooms, using tamper-evident seals, and maintaining a log of physical access to sensitive areas.

Implementing comprehensive logging and monitoring strategies can help detect potential security incidents before they cause significant damage. Monitoring should include logging access attempts, changes to the PLC programs, and unusual network activity. This data can be invaluable for identifying and responding to security incidents.

```
// Pseudocode for monitoring and logging

Monitor_System();

IF Anomaly_Detected THEN

Log_Event('Anomaly detected: ' + Anomaly_Details);

Alert_Security_Team();

ENDIF;
```

This code represents a proactive monitoring strategy, where anomalies are logged and alerts are raised, facilitating swift response to potential security incidents.

Lastly, developing a robust response plan for cybersecurity incidents is essential. This plan should include procedures for containing breaches, eradicating threats, recovering systems to operational status, and communicating with stakeholders.

In conclusion, securing Siemens S7 PLCs against cyber threats involves a multi-layered approach that includes physical security, network segregation, strong authentication, regular updates, data encryption, and vigilant monitoring. By implementing these strategies, organizations can significantly enhance the resilience of their industrial control systems against cyber threats.

13.3 Best Practices for Secure Programming

SECURE PROGRAMMING practices are essential to ensure the safety and security of industrial control systems, particularly when programming Siemens S7 PLCs. This section outlines the best practices that should be followed to mitigate risks and enhance the security posture of PLC-based systems.

1. **Principle of Least Privilege**: Ensure that every module, program, or user operating the PLC has only the minimum necessary access rights to perform its functions. This limits the potential damage in case of an accidental or malicious breach.

```
// Example of access control based on the principle of least privilege

IF User_Role == 'Maintenance' THEN

Grant_Maintenance_Access();

ELSE

Deny_Access();

Log_Event('Access denied due to insufficient privileges');

ENDIF;
```

1. **Input Validation**: Always validate inputs before processing them in the PLC. This includes data from users, sensors, and network messages. Proper validation can prevent many common vulnerabilities such as buffer overflows and injection attacks.

```
// Example of input validation for a numeric input
```

```
IF Input_Value >= 0 AND Input_Value <= Max_Value THEN

Process_Input(Input_Value);

ELSE

Log_Event('Invalid input value: ' + Input_Value);

ENDIF;
```

1. **Use of Strong Authentication and Encryption**: Implement strong authentication mechanisms and use encryption for data at rest and in transit. This protects sensitive data and control commands from being intercepted or tampered with.

```
// Implementing encrypted communication

Initialize_Secure_Connection();

IF Secure_Connection_Established() THEN

Encrypt_Data(Data_To_Send);

Send_Data(Encrypted_Data);

ELSE

Log_Event('Failed to establish a secure connection');

ENDIF;
```

1. **Regular Updates and Patch Management**: Keep all software, including the PLC firmware and associated tools, up to date. Regularly apply security patches to protect against known vulnerabilities.

```
// Pseudocode for checking and applying updates

Check_For_Security_Updates();

IF Security_Update_Available THEN

Apply_Security_Update();

Log_Event('Security update applied');

ELSE

Log_Event('No updates available');

ENDIF;
```

1. **Secure Coding Standards**: Follow secure coding standards and guidelines to avoid introducing security flaws into the code. Use static and dynamic analysis tools to detect and rectify security issues before deployment.
2. **Error Handling and Logging**: Implement comprehensive error handling and logging to detect and respond to abnormal operations or security incidents. Logs should be detailed enough to provide insights into what went wrong and when.

```
// Example of error handling and logging

TRY

Execute_Operation();

CATCH (Error)

Log_Error('Operation failed', Error);

Notify_Administrator(Error);
```

```
END_TRY;
```

1. **Segmentation and Network Design**: Design network architecture to segment devices and systems logically. This reduces the attack surface by limiting the reach of potential intruders within the network.
2. **Use of Firewalls and Intrusion Detection Systems**: Employ firewalls and intrusion detection systems (IDS) to monitor and control incoming and outgoing network traffic, and to detect malicious activities.
3. **Avoiding Hard-Coded Credentials**: Never hard-code passwords or other sensitive information within the PLC program. Instead, use secure storage mechanisms or environment variables.

```
// Securely handling credentials

Load_Credentials_From_Secure_Store();

IF Credentials_Valid() THEN

Authenticate_User();

ELSE

Log_Event('Invalid credentials');

ENDIF;
```

1. **Incident Response Planning**: Develop and regularly update an incident response plan. Ensure that all team members are familiar with the steps they need to take in the event of a security breach.
2. **Physical Security**: Enhance physical security measures to prevent unauthorized access to the PLC and related

infrastructure. This includes locking cabinets, using surveillance cameras, and securing industrial areas.

3. **Training and Awareness**: Regularly train staff on the latest security practices and the specific security features of the Siemens S7 PLCs. Awareness can significantly reduce the risk of human error, which is a common cause of security failures.

By following these best practices for secure programming and system design, organizations can significantly reduce the risk of cyber threats to their Siemens S7 PLCs and the systems they control. These measures ensure that industrial control systems are robust, secure, and capable of resisting modern cyber threats.

13.4 Implementing Redundancy and Fail-safes

IN CRITICAL INFRASTRUCTURE and industrial environments, implementing redundancy and fail-safe mechanisms in Siemens S7 PLC programming is essential for maintaining operational continuity and safety. This section discusses strategies for designing redundant systems and incorporating fail-safe logic to enhance system reliability and protect against potential failures or cyber threats.

Redundancy in PLC systems can be achieved at various levels, including hardware, network, and application layers. Hardware redundancy involves using multiple PLCs or other components that can take over operations if the primary unit fails. This type of redundancy ensures that there is no single point of failure in critical control systems.

// Example of hardware redundancy switching logic

IF Primary_PLC_Status == FAILURE THEN

Switch_To_Backup_PLC();

Log_Event('Switched to backup PLC due to primary failure');

ENDIF;

This simple logic checks the status of the primary PLC and switches control to a backup PLC if a failure is detected, ensuring uninterrupted operation.

Network redundancy involves creating multiple pathways for data communication to prevent the network from becoming a single point of failure. This can include redundant network interfaces on PLCs and duplicate communication lines that ensure continuous data flow even if one pathway fails.

// Example of network redundancy handling

IF Primary_Network_Pathway == DOWN THEN

Activate_Secondary_Pathway();

Log_Event('Primary network pathway down, switched to secondary');

ENDIF;

This logic ensures that if the primary network connection fails, the system automatically switches to a secondary pathway, maintaining network communication.

At the application layer, redundancy can be implemented by programming alternate control strategies that can be activated if the primary logic fails. This ensures that the system continues to operate safely, even under partial system failure.

```
// Example of application layer redundancy

IF Primary_Control_Strategy == INEFFECTIVE THEN

Switch_To_Alternate_Strategy();

Log_Event('Primary strategy ineffective, switched to alternate');

ENDIF;
```

This code snippet allows for a seamless transition between different control strategies, enhancing the adaptability and resilience of the system.

Fail-safe mechanisms are designed to bring the system to a safe state in the event of a failure or anomaly. This typically involves programming specific conditions under which the system should shut down safely or switch to a minimal operational mode.

```
// Example of fail-safe logic

IF System_Check() == UNSAFE THEN

Activate_Safety_Mode();

Notify_Operators('System unsafe, switched to safety mode');

ENDIF;
```

This fail-safe logic ensures that if the system detects an unsafe condition, it automatically switches to a safety mode that minimizes risks to the system and its environment.

Incorporating watchdog timers is another effective fail-safe technique. A watchdog timer can detect if the system has become unresponsive or stuck in an infinite loop and can reset the system to recover from such states.

```
// Example of using a watchdog timer

Start_Watchdog_Timer();

LOOP

IF Watchdog_Timer == TIMEOUT THEN

Reset_System();

Log_Event('System reset by watchdog timer');

ENDIF;

// System processing logic

Reset_Watchdog_Timer();

END_LOOP;
```

This code continuously checks and resets a watchdog timer as part of the main loop. If the timer reaches a timeout, it indicates that the system may be unresponsive, triggering a system reset.

Testing and simulation play critical roles in validating the effectiveness of redundancy and fail-safe mechanisms. Before deploying these systems in a live environment, extensive testing should be conducted to ensure they perform as expected under various failure scenarios.

```
// Example of testing redundancy and fail-safe logic

Test_Redundancy();

Test_Fail_Safe_Mechanisms();

Log_Event('Redundancy and fail-safe mechanisms tested successfully');
```

This structured approach to testing ensures that all safety and redundancy mechanisms are verified, minimizing the risk of unexpected behavior in production environments.

Overall, implementing redundancy and fail-safe mechanisms in Siemens S7 PLC programming is crucial for ensuring the reliability and safety of industrial systems. These strategies mitigate the impact of hardware failures, network issues, and software anomalies, enhancing the overall resilience of the control system.

13.5 Regular Security Audits and Updates

REGULAR SECURITY AUDITS and updates are critical components of a comprehensive security strategy for Siemens S7 PLC systems. This section explores the importance of conducting routine audits, implementing security updates, and maintaining ongoing vigilance to protect industrial control systems from emerging threats.

Security audits involve a thorough examination of the PLC system, including its configuration, programming logic, network connections, and associated devices. The purpose of these audits is to identify vulnerabilities, misconfigurations, and other potential security risks that could be exploited by malicious actors.

The audit process should begin with an inventory of all assets related to the PLC system. This includes not only the PLCs themselves but also network devices, user interfaces, connected sensors, and software used for programming and monitoring the system.

```
// Example of initiating an audit

Log_Event('Security audit initiated');

Perform_Asset_Inventory();
```

Check_System_Configurations();

Assess_Access_Controls();

Evaluate_Communication_Security();

Log_Event('Security audit completed');

This sequence represents the high-level steps in conducting a security audit, each step focusing on different aspects of system security.

Once vulnerabilities are identified, the next critical step is to prioritize them based on the potential impact and likelihood of exploitation. This prioritization helps in efficiently allocating resources to address the most critical vulnerabilities first.

// Example of vulnerability prioritization

FOR EACH Vulnerability IN Identified_Vulnerabilities DO

Assign_Risk_Level(Vulnerability);

Log_Event('Vulnerability ' + Vulnerability.ID + ' assigned risk level ' + Vulnerability.Risk_Level);

END_FOR;

This logic helps in managing vulnerabilities systematically by focusing on those that pose the greatest risk to the system.

Regular updates are another essential aspect of maintaining security. This includes updates to the PLC firmware, software used in the programming and monitoring of PLCs, and any other related systems. Updates often contain patches for security vulnerabilities that have been identified since the last version.

// Example of managing updates

Check_For_Updates();

IF Updates_Available THEN

Apply_Updates();

Log_Event('Updates applied');

ELSE

Log_Event('No updates available');

ENDIF;

This pseudocode outlines a basic process for checking and applying updates, ensuring that the system is protected against known vulnerabilities.

Security audits should also evaluate the effectiveness of existing security measures such as firewalls, intrusion detection systems, and antivirus software. These tools are essential for defending the PLC system from attacks but need regular review and updating to remain effective.

// Example of security measure evaluation

Evaluate_Firewall_Configuration();

Assess_IDS_Alerts();

Check_Antivirus_Updates();

Log_Event('Security measures evaluated');

These steps are critical for ensuring that security defenses are properly configured and up to date.

In addition to technical measures, security audits should also assess organizational policies and procedures related to PLC system security. This includes training programs for employees, procedures for responding to security incidents, and guidelines for secure programming practices.

```
// Example of policy and procedure assessment

Review_Security_Policies();

Evaluate_Incident_Response_Plan();

Assess_Employee_Training_Programs();

Log_Event('Policies and procedures assessed');
```

This code snippet represents an organizational audit of security-related policies and procedures, ensuring that they are comprehensive and followed by all personnel.

Finally, the results of security audits should be documented and presented to management and technical teams. This documentation should include detailed findings, recommended actions, and a timeline for implementing improvements. Regular reviews of audit outcomes and follow-ups on the implementation of recommendations are crucial for maintaining the security integrity of the system.

In summary, regular security audits and updates are vital for ensuring the security of Siemens S7 PLC systems. By identifying vulnerabilities, prioritizing them, applying necessary updates, and continuously reviewing security measures and policies, organizations can protect their industrial control systems from the ever-evolving landscape of cyber threats.

Chapter 14: Optimization and Efficiency

14.1 Optimizing Code for Faster Execution

OPTIMIZING CODE IN Siemens S7 PLCs for faster execution is crucial for enhancing the performance and responsiveness of control systems. Efficient code not only executes faster but also conserves resources, leading to more reliable and scalable systems. This section explores various techniques and practices for optimizing PLC code to achieve faster execution times.

One fundamental aspect of code optimization is minimizing the execution path. Reducing the number of operations and instructions a PLC must perform to complete a task can significantly decrease cycle times.

// Example of streamlined logic

IF Condition_A AND Condition_B THEN

Execute_Action();

ENDIF;

In this example, combining conditions in a single IF statement simplifies the logic and reduces the execution time compared to handling each condition in separate statements.

Another key optimization strategy is the use of efficient data types. Choosing the appropriate data type that uses the least amount of memory necessary for performing a task can improve performance.

// Use of efficient data types

VAR SMALLINT Counter; // Using SMALLINT instead of INT when the range is sufficient

Using SMALLINT instead of INT saves memory and processing time when the values handled are within a small range, making the code more efficient.

Loop optimization is another critical area. Avoiding unnecessary loops and optimizing existing ones can lead to significant performance improvements.

```
// Loop optimization

FOR i := 1 TO 10 DO

IF Array[i] == Desired_Value THEN

Execute_Action();

EXIT; // Exiting loop early when the condition is met

ENDIF;

ENDFOR;
```

This loop exits as soon as the desired condition is met, preventing unnecessary iterations and thus saving execution time.

Inline code replacements for frequently called functions can also enhance performance. Replacing function calls with inline code eliminates the overhead associated with function calls.

```
// Inline code example

IF NOT IsActive THEN

Output := FALSE; // Inline replacement of a simple function call
```

ENDIF;

In this example, replacing a function call with its actual logic reduces the execution time by eliminating the call and return overhead.

Effective use of memory and addressing can also improve execution speed. Directly addressing I/Os and using pointers appropriately can reduce the access time for variables and I/O operations.

```
// Direct I/O addressing

IF I %Q0.0 THEN // Directly using the output address

Set_Lamp(ON);

ENDIF;
```

Directly addressing the output reduces the time taken to evaluate the address, thereby speeding up the operation.

Minimizing external communications is vital. Reducing the frequency and volume of data exchanges between the PLC and external devices can free up processing time for other tasks.

```
// Reducing external communications

IF TimeSinceLastComm > CommInterval THEN

Send_Data();

Reset_Timer();

ENDIF;
```

This logic ensures that communications only happen at specified intervals, rather than continuously, conserving both processing cycles and bandwidth.

Another important technique is the use of conditional execution to avoid processing unnecessary code. This involves structuring the program to skip sections of code that are not relevant under certain conditions.

```
// Conditional execution

IF Mode == Test_Mode THEN

Perform_Test_Operations();

ELSE

Perform_Normal_Operations();

ENDIF;
```

This approach ensures that only the relevant parts of the code are executed based on the operational mode, optimizing the use of processing resources.

Optimizing code for batch processing instead of processing individual items can also enhance performance, especially in data-intensive operations.

```
// Batch processing

Process_Data_In_Batches(Data_Array);
```

Processing data in batches rather than individually can significantly reduce processing times by leveraging more efficient data handling and processing techniques.

Lastly, regular profiling and performance testing of the PLC code are essential to identify bottlenecks and areas for improvement. This continuous improvement approach ensures that the system remains optimized as conditions and requirements change.

In summary, optimizing PLC code for faster execution involves a combination of efficient coding practices, appropriate use of data types, strategic memory management, and conditional logic. By applying these techniques, developers can create high-performance PLC programs that are both efficient and scalable.

14.2 Energy Efficiency in PLC Operations

ENHANCING ENERGY EFFICIENCY in PLC operations not only reduces operating costs but also contributes to environmental sustainability. This section discusses various strategies and techniques for optimizing energy usage in systems controlled by Siemens S7 PLCs, highlighting how software and hardware optimizations can lead to more energy-efficient operations.

A primary strategy for improving energy efficiency is the optimization of control algorithms to reduce the energy consumption of machinery and processes. This includes refining control loops, adjusting set points, and implementing energy-saving operational modes.

// Example of optimizing a control loop for energy efficiency

IF Temperature > Desired_Temperature + 1 THEN

Cooling_System := MINIMUM; // Minimize cooling system operation

ELSEIF Temperature < Desired_Temperature - 1 THEN

Heating_System := MINIMUM; // Minimize heating system operation

ELSE

Cooling_System := OFF;

Heating_System := OFF;

ENDIF;

This example shows a temperature control logic that minimizes the use of heating and cooling systems unless absolutely necessary, thereby conserving energy.

Another effective method is the implementation of sleep or standby modes for equipment during periods of low activity. PLCs can be programmed to detect idle conditions and power down unnecessary systems.

// Sleep mode implementation

IF System_Idle() AND NOT Sleep_Mode_Active THEN

Activate_Sleep_Mode();

Log_Event('System entered sleep mode');

ENDIF;

IF NOT System_Idle() AND Sleep_Mode_Active THEN

Deactivate_Sleep_Mode();

Log_Event('System exited sleep mode');

ENDIF;

This logic helps reduce energy consumption by switching systems into a low-power state when they are not actively being used.

The use of energy monitoring software integrated with Siemens S7 PLCs can provide detailed insights into energy usage patterns. This data can be used to identify inefficiencies and areas where energy consumption can be reduced.

```
// Energy monitoring

Monitor_Energy_Usage();

IF Energy_Usage > Energy_Usage_Threshold THEN

Identify_Inefficiencies();

Suggest_Optimizations();

Log_Event('Energy usage above threshold, optimizations suggested');

ENDIF;
```

This example involves continuous monitoring and analysis of energy usage, with automated suggestions for improvements when certain thresholds are exceeded.

Scheduling operations based on energy availability and costs can also significantly enhance efficiency. For example, heavy operations can be scheduled during off-peak hours when energy rates are lower.

```
// Scheduling based on energy cost

IF Current_Time IN Off_Peak_Hours THEN

Schedule_Heavy_Operations();

Log_Event('Heavy operations scheduled during off-peak hours');

ENDIF;
```

This scheduling ensures that energy-intensive operations are run when it is most economical, thereby reducing operational costs.

Regenerative energy systems, such as using the braking energy of motors to generate electricity, can be controlled by PLCs to improve overall energy efficiency.

```
// Control of regenerative braking systems

IF          Motor_Speed        >        Threshold        AND
Regenerative_Braking_Available THEN

Activate_Regenerative_Braking();

Log_Event('Regenerative braking activated');

ENDIF;
```

This example illustrates how PLCs can manage the energy recovery process during motor deceleration, converting otherwise wasted energy back into usable electricity.

Adaptive control algorithms can dynamically adjust machine operations based on real-time performance data to minimize energy consumption while maintaining output quality.

```
// Adaptive control for energy efficiency

Monitor_Operation_Efficiency();

Adjust_Operations_To_Minimize_Energy_Use();

Log_Event('Operations adjusted for optimal energy use');
```

This adaptive control strategy continually fine-tunes operations to achieve the best balance between energy efficiency and operational effectiveness.

Furthermore, integrating IoT technologies with PLCs can enhance energy management. IoT sensors can provide additional data on environmental conditions and equipment status, enabling more informed and responsive control strategies.

// IoT integration for enhanced energy management

Collect_IoT_Data();

Analyze_IoT_Data_For_Energy_Savings();

Implement_Energy_Saving_Measures();

Log_Event('Energy savings measures implemented based on IoT data');

This approach leverages IoT technology to gain deeper insights into the system, which can be used to further refine energy usage.

In conclusion, optimizing energy efficiency in PLC operations involves a combination of advanced control strategies, effective use of technology, and operational adjustments. By implementing these strategies, organizations can significantly reduce their energy consumption, lower operational costs, and contribute to environmental sustainability.

14.3 Resource Management

EFFECTIVE RESOURCE management is essential in PLC programming to ensure that systems operate efficiently and reliably under varying conditions. This section discusses strategies for optimizing resource usage in Siemens S7 PLCs, focusing on memory management, processor utilization, and network resources.

Managing memory efficiently is critical in PLC systems, especially when dealing with limited hardware capabilities. Efficient memory use ensures that the PLC can handle more complex applications without running out of space and degrading performance.

```
// Example of efficient memory allocation
```

```
DEFINE DB1 AS STRUCT {
```

```
Temperature REAL;
```

```
Pressure REAL;
```

```
Level INTEGER;
```

```
};
```

This example demonstrates defining a data block with appropriate data types that match the required precision, thus conserving memory.

It's also important to optimize the CPU usage of a PLC. Efficient CPU usage ensures that tasks are processed quickly and time-critical operations meet their deadlines.

```
// CPU load balancing
```

```
IF CPU_Load > High_Load_Threshold THEN
```

```
Offload_Tasks();
```

```
Log_Event('Tasks offloaded due to high CPU load');
```

```
ENDIF;
```

This pseudocode offloads tasks when the CPU load exceeds a certain threshold, balancing the load to maintain performance.

Network traffic management is another aspect of resource management. Minimizing unnecessary network traffic can reduce delays and improve the responsiveness of networked PLC systems.

```
// Network traffic optimization

Monitor_Network_Traffic();

IF Traffic_Volume > Traffic_Threshold THEN

Reduce_Message_Frequency();

Log_Event('Network traffic reduced to optimize performance');

ENDIF;
```

This example involves monitoring network traffic and reducing message frequency when traffic volume is too high, thereby optimizing network resource utilization.

Task prioritization is crucial in resource management. Critical tasks should have higher priority in the task scheduling of the PLC to ensure that they are executed in a timely manner.

```
// Task prioritization

Set_Task_Priority(Critical_Task, High);

Set_Task_Priority(Non_Critical_Task, Low);
```

Assigning priorities helps ensure that critical processes are given precedence over less important tasks, optimizing the overall performance of the system.

The use of watchdog timers can help manage system performance by monitoring the execution time of tasks and resetting the system if a task hangs or takes too long to complete.

```
// Implementing a watchdog timer

Start_Watchdog_Timer();

LOOP

Task_Execute();

Reset_Watchdog_Timer();

END_LOOP;
```

This code snippet ensures that the system remains responsive and can recover from failures that cause a task to not complete as expected.

Load testing and performance profiling are also integral to effective resource management. These practices help identify bottlenecks and areas where resources are not being used optimally.

```
// Load testing and performance profiling

Perform_Load_Testing();

Analyze_Performance_Data();

Apply_Optimizations_Based_On_Data();

Log_Event('System optimized based on performance profiling');
```

This approach systematically improves system performance by basing optimizations on actual data collected through testing.

Implementing caching strategies where possible can reduce the load on both the CPU and network by storing frequently accessed data locally.

```
// Caching frequently accessed data
```

```
Cache_Data(Last_Read_Values);

IF Requested_Value == Cached_Value THEN

Use_Cached_Data();

ELSE

Update_Data_From_Source();

ENDIF;
```

Caching can significantly speed up access to frequently used data, reducing the need for repeated computations or network requests.

Efficient error handling mechanisms are vital to conserve resources. Properly managing errors and exceptions can prevent a system from executing unnecessary operations when an error occurs.

```
// Efficient error handling

TRY

Execute_Operation();

CATCH (Error)

Handle_Error();

Log_Error(Error);

Prevent_Further_Processing();

END_TRY;
```

This structured error handling ensures that errors are managed promptly and the system does not waste resources attempting to continue faulty operations.

Finally, continuous monitoring of resource usage helps in maintaining an efficient system. Regularly checking the performance metrics and making adjustments as necessary can prevent resource-related issues from affecting system performance.

// Continuous resource monitoring

Monitor_Resources();

Adjust_Resources_As_Needed();

Log_Event('Resources adjusted based on continuous monitoring');

This ongoing monitoring and adjustment process ensures that the PLC system remains efficient and responsive to operational demands.

In conclusion, effective resource management in Siemens S7 PLC programming involves careful planning and optimization across various aspects of system performance. By implementing these strategies, engineers can ensure that their PLC systems run efficiently, with optimal use of memory, CPU, and network resources.

14.4 Lean Programming Techniques

LEAN PROGRAMMING TECHNIQUES focus on maximizing the efficiency and performance of PLC programs by reducing complexity and eliminating unnecessary processes. This section outlines strategies to apply lean programming principles in the context of Siemens S7 PLC programming, enhancing both the maintainability and reliability of control systems.

The first step in lean programming is to simplify logic wherever possible. This involves breaking down complex routines into simpler, more manageable parts, and eliminating redundant logic.

```
// Simplifying logic by removing redundancy

IF Sensor_1_Active AND NOT Sensor_2_Active THEN

Activate_Machine();

ELSEIF Sensor_1_Active AND Sensor_2_Active THEN

Activate_Machine();

ELSE

Deactivate_Machine();

ENDIF;

// Simplified version

IF Sensor_1_Active THEN

Activate_Machine();

ELSE

Deactivate_Machine();

ENDIF;
```

This example shows how simplifying the conditions under which a machine is activated can reduce the complexity of the program and improve readability.

Minimizing the use of global variables is another key aspect of lean programming. Using local variables whenever possible reduces dependencies across the program, making debugging and testing easier.

```
// Using local variables to reduce dependency

FUNCTION LocalControl: VOID

VAR LOCAL Speed: INT;

Speed := Read_Speed_Sensor();

Control_Motor(Speed);

END_FUNCTION;
```

This function uses a local variable for speed, reducing its scope to just this function, which improves modularity and reduces side effects.

Avoiding nested conditions is another technique to enhance program clarity and reduce execution time. Flattening logic structures where feasible makes the program easier to follow and test.

```
// Avoiding deeply nested conditions

IF Condition_A THEN

IF Condition_B THEN

Execute_Action();

ENDIF;

ENDIF;

// Flattened version

IF Condition_A AND Condition_B THEN

Execute_Action();
```

```
ENDIF;
```

This example demonstrates reducing nested IF statements, which simplifies the control flow and enhances the efficiency of the code.

Code reusability is also a crucial component of lean programming. Creating modular, reusable code blocks can significantly reduce the overall codebase size and make maintenance easier.

```
// Creating reusable code

FUNCTION Start_Machine()

Check_Safety();

Activate_Motor();

Log_Event('Machine started');

END_FUNCTION;

Start_Machine(); // Calling the reusable function
```

This function encapsulates the machine start routine, making it reusable and maintaining consistency throughout the program.

Regular refactoring is necessary to maintain the leanness of the program. As requirements change and the program evolves, continuously revisiting and refining the code ensures it remains efficient and easy to manage.

```
// Refactoring example

// Original complex function

FUNCTION ComplexOperation()

// complex code
```

```
END_FUNCTION;
```

// After refactoring into simpler components

```
FUNCTION Part1()
```

// part 1 of the operation

```
END_FUNCTION;
```

```
FUNCTION Part2()
```

// part 2 of the operation

```
END_FUNCTION;
```

Refactoring a complex operation into two simpler parts enhances clarity and modularity.

Incorporating efficient data structures and algorithms can also play a significant role in maintaining lean and efficient code. Choosing the right data structure for a given task can optimize both speed and memory usage.

// Efficient use of data structures

```
ARRAY[1..100] OF REAL; // Using an array to efficiently store and access data
```

Selecting an appropriate data structure like an array for homogeneous data can streamline operations and data handling.

Lean programming also involves optimizing communication protocols to ensure that data exchanges are efficient and do not overload the network or the processors.

// Optimizing communication

```
IF Last_Communication > Communication_Interval THEN

Send_Update();

Last_Communication := CURRENT_TIME;

ENDIF;
```

This logic minimizes the frequency of communications, reducing network traffic and processor load.

Error handling should be precise and not overly generic, which can obscure the source of errors and make the system more complex and harder to troubleshoot.

```
// Precise error handling

TRY

Execute_Critical_Operation();

CATCH Specific_Error

Handle_Specific_Error();

Log_Error('Specific error handled');

ELSE

Log_Error('Unexpected error');

END_TRY;
```

Handling errors specifically and logging them accurately aids in maintaining system clarity and reliability.

Finally, performance tuning based on real-world data is crucial. Adjustments should be data-driven, reflecting actual operating conditions and performance metrics.

// Performance tuning

Monitor_Performance();

Adjust_Settings_Based_On_Metrics();

Log_Event('Performance settings adjusted');

This approach ensures that adjustments are justified by actual performance data, ensuring optimal efficiency.

By adhering to these lean programming principles, Siemens S7 PLC programmers can create more efficient, maintainable, and reliable programs, contributing to the overall effectiveness of the control systems they design.

14.5 Advanced Data Logging and Reporting

ADVANCED DATA LOGGING and reporting are critical for monitoring the performance and health of automated systems managed by Siemens S7 PLCs. This section delves into the techniques and methodologies for implementing comprehensive data logging strategies and generating reports that can aid in decision-making, troubleshooting, and system optimization.

Data logging in Siemens S7 PLCs typically involves capturing a variety of operational data such as sensor readings, system statuses, and operational errors. Efficient data logging is essential for historical analysis, real-time monitoring, and predictive maintenance.

// Example of basic data logging

```
Log_Data(Sensor_Value, Timestamp);
```

This simple command logs sensor values along with their timestamps, creating a record that can be used for later analysis.

To enhance the utility of data logging, it's important to determine the key performance indicators (KPIs) that are most relevant to the system's operational goals. Logging these KPIs can provide insights into system efficiency, productivity, and areas needing improvement.

```
// Logging key performance indicators

Log_KPI('Cycle Time', Cycle_Time);

Log_KPI('Throughput', Throughput);

Log_KPI('Downtime', Downtime);
```

This example demonstrates how specific KPIs are recorded, focusing on metrics critical to evaluating performance.

Data aggregation is a technique used to summarize detailed data logs into more manageable forms. This is particularly useful in systems generating large volumes of data, where detailed logs can become unwieldy.

```
// Data aggregation

Aggregate_Data(Daily_Production, 'Sum', '24h');

Log_Aggregated_Data(Daily_Production);
```

In this scenario, production data is aggregated daily, simplifying analysis and reporting by reducing data granularity while retaining essential information.

To facilitate real-time monitoring and alerts, data logging systems should be integrated with event-driven mechanisms that trigger alerts based on specific conditions.

```
// Event-driven alerts based on data logs

IF Temperature > Max_Temperature THEN

Log_Event('High Temperature Alert', Temperature);

Send_Alert('High Temperature Detected', Temperature);

ENDIF;
```

This example sets up an alert for high temperature, ensuring that any unusual readings are promptly reported and acted upon.

For systems where data security and integrity are paramount, implementing logging with redundancy and fail-safes ensures data preservation even in the event of system failures.

```
// Redundant logging

Log_Data(Primary_Log_File, Data);

IF Primary_Log_File_Error THEN

Log_Data(Backup_Log_File, Data);

ENDIF;
```

This approach uses a backup logging mechanism to safeguard against data loss if the primary logging system fails.

The integration of analytical tools with data logging systems can provide deeper insights through statistical analysis and trend detection, which are crucial for predictive maintenance and long-term system improvements.

```
// Integrating analytics

Analyze_Data(Log_File);

Generate_Report(Analysis_Results);
```

Here, logged data is analyzed, and a report is generated highlighting trends and potential issues, providing actionable insights.

Automated reporting is another vital aspect of advanced data logging. Generating regular reports based on logged data can help keep stakeholders informed about the system's status and performance.

```
// Automated reporting

Schedule_Report_Generation(Daily,          Report_Template,
Data_Sources);
```

This line of code schedules daily report generation, using predefined templates and data sources to produce consistent, informative reports.

For large-scale systems, distributed logging—where data is logged across multiple nodes—can enhance performance and reliability by balancing the load and reducing the risk of data bottlenecks.

```
// Distributed logging setup

Distribute_Logging_Across_Nodes(Node_List, Data_Types);
```

This configuration helps manage data logging in a distributed manner, appropriate for complex or large-scale automation systems.

To further refine data logging practices, feedback loops can be implemented where insights gained from data analysis lead to adjustments in the logging strategy itself.

// Feedback loop for logging refinement

Evaluate_Logging_Effectiveness();

Adjust_Logging_Parameters(Based_On_Evaluation);

This method continuously improves the logging process, adapting as new insights are gained and conditions change.

Lastly, ensuring compliance with regulatory requirements is essential, especially in industries where data handling and logging are subject to stringent standards.

// Compliance checks

Check_Compliance(Logging_Standards);

Log_Compliance_Status(Compliance_Check_Result);

Regular checks and logs of compliance status ensure that the system meets all required standards, avoiding potential legal or regulatory issues.

In summary, advanced data logging and reporting in Siemens S7 PLC systems are integral to maintaining operational efficiency, ensuring system reliability, and supporting decision-making processes. Through strategic implementation of logging mechanisms, aggregation techniques, real-time monitoring, and automated reporting, organizations can derive maximum benefit from their data collection efforts.

Chapter 15: Industry 4.0 and IoT Integration

15.1 The Role of PLCs in Industry 4.0

THE ADVENT OF INDUSTRY 4.0 has significantly transformed manufacturing and production landscapes, integrating cyber-physical systems, the Internet of Things (IoT), and networked communications to create smart factories. Programmable Logic Controllers (PLCs), especially Siemens S7, play a pivotal role in this revolution, acting as critical components in automating manufacturing processes and integrating with IoT technologies. This section explores the role of Siemens S7 PLCs in Industry 4.0, detailing how they facilitate advanced automation and data exchange in manufacturing environments.

Siemens S7 PLCs are at the forefront of enabling smart manufacturing through enhanced connectivity, real-time data processing, and interfacing with other industrial systems. They serve as the backbone for data collection from sensors and actuators, interpreting and acting on data to optimize manufacturing processes.

// Example of data collection from sensors

Read_Sensor_Data();

Process_Data();

Adjust_Machine_Parameters(Based_on_Data);

This simple sequence highlights how PLCs can be used to automate adjustments in machinery based on sensor inputs, optimizing operations and reducing human intervention.

One of the key aspects of Industry 4.0 is the integration of IoT devices with industrial control systems. Siemens S7 PLCs can communicate with a range of IoT devices, enabling not only control and automation but also data analytics and predictive maintenance.

```
// Integrating IoT devices

Connect_To_IoT_Device(IoT_Device_ID);

Receive_Data_From_IoT_Device();

Use_Data_For_Maintenance_Predictions();
```

In this scenario, the PLC is connected to IoT devices to receive operational data, which can be used for predictive analytics to foresee potential maintenance issues before they lead to downtime.

Cloud integration is another crucial feature enabled by Siemens S7 PLCs in Industry 4.0. By connecting PLCs to cloud platforms, data can be stored and analyzed on a much larger scale, providing insights that are not possible at the local level.

```
// Sending data to the cloud

Send_Data_To_Cloud(Data);

Analyze_Cloud_Data();

Adjust_Operations_Based_On_Analysis();
```

This code demonstrates how data from PLCs can be sent to the cloud for advanced analytics, with findings used to refine operations.

Additionally, Siemens S7 PLCs support advanced networking protocols that facilitate communication between various components of a smart factory. This interoperability is crucial for the seamless operation of production lines that include diverse equipment from multiple vendors.

```
// Managing network communications

Setup_Network_Communications();

Ensure_Protocol_Compatibility();

Enable_Seamless_Data_Exchange();
```

These operations ensure that all parts of the industrial network communicate effectively, enhancing the efficiency and flexibility of manufacturing processes.

The implementation of advanced security measures is also essential in Industry 4.0 environments. Siemens S7 PLCs are equipped with robust security features to protect against cyber threats, which are increasingly relevant in interconnected environments.

```
// Implementing security measures

Activate_Firewall();

Set_Up_Secure_Communications();

Monitor_Network_for_Threats();
```

This snippet highlights the security-focused features of PLCs, which are critical to safeguarding the data and operations of smart factories.

Moreover, the role of Siemens S7 PLCs in Industry 4.0 extends to facilitating machine learning and artificial intelligence applications. These technologies can be integrated to enhance decision-making processes, optimizing operations through adaptive learning algorithms.

```
// Integrating machine learning

Implement_Machine_Learning_Models();

Train_Models_with_Production_Data();

Apply_AI_for_Optimized_Decision_Making();
```

Here, PLCs help implement and manage AI models that can predict optimal operating conditions and adjust processes in real-time.

Energy management is another area where Siemens S7 PLCs contribute significantly in Industry 4.0 settings. They can monitor and control energy usage across the factory, ensuring optimal energy consumption and supporting sustainability initiatives.

```
// Optimizing energy management

Monitor_Energy_Consumption();

Adjust_Energy_Usage_to_Optimize_Efficiency();

Report_on_Energy_Savings();
```

This approach not only reduces costs but also aligns with global environmental standards by minimizing the carbon footprint of manufacturing activities.

In summary, Siemens S7 PLCs are integral to the evolution of Industry 4.0. They enhance connectivity, facilitate smart automation, and integrate with advanced technologies to drive the future of manufacturing. By leveraging these capabilities, manufacturers can achieve greater efficiency, improved security, and enhanced decision-making, paving the way for smarter, more sustainable industrial operations.

15.2 Connecting Siemens S7 to the Internet of Things

CONNECTING SIEMENS S7 PLCs to the Internet of Things (IoT) expands their capabilities beyond traditional industrial settings, allowing for enhanced data collection, remote monitoring, and integrated control of diverse devices and systems. This section explores the methodologies and benefits of integrating Siemens S7 PLCs with IoT technologies, detailing the steps and considerations involved.

The first step in integrating Siemens S7 PLCs with IoT is establishing a network connection that can support secure data transmission. This often involves configuring the PLC to communicate over the internet via secure protocols.

```
// Setting up a secure network connection

Initialize_Network_Adapter();

Configure_Secure_Protocol(TLS);

Establish_Connection();
```

This basic setup ensures that the PLC can connect to the internet securely, using Transport Layer Security (TLS) to protect data integrity and confidentiality.

Once the network connection is established, the PLC needs to be configured to send and receive data to and from IoT devices. This involves programming the PLC to handle various data formats and protocols commonly used in IoT, such as MQTT or HTTP.

```
// Configuring data exchange protocols

Set_Communication_Protocol(MQTT);
```

Define_Data_Format(JSON);

Enable_Data_Transfer();

Configuring the PLC to use MQTT for messaging and JSON for data formatting enables it to exchange data efficiently with IoT devices and platforms.

Remote monitoring and control are significant advantages of IoT integration. Siemens S7 PLCs can be set up to send real-time data to a central monitoring system, allowing operators to view and control the system remotely.

// Enabling remote monitoring

Collect_Sensor_Data();

Send_Data_To_Cloud();

Monitor_System_Status_Remotely();

This setup not only provides real-time insights into the system's status but also allows for remote adjustments, enhancing operational flexibility.

IoT integration also facilitates the implementation of predictive maintenance. By analyzing data collected from IoT sensors, the PLC can predict potential failures and schedule maintenance before breakdowns occur.

// Implementing predictive maintenance

Analyze_Sensor_Data();

Predict_Maintenance_Requirements();

Schedule_Maintenance_Automatically();

This predictive approach reduces downtime and maintenance costs by addressing issues before they lead to significant problems.

Energy management is another area where IoT integration can make a substantial impact. By connecting Siemens S7 PLCs to smart energy meters and IoT-enabled devices, energy consumption can be optimized based on real-time data.

```
// Optimizing energy management via IoT

Connect_To_Energy_Meters();

Aggregate_Energy_Consumption_Data();

Optimize_Energy_Usage_Across_Operations();
```

This method allows for dynamic energy management, adjusting consumption as needed based on actual operating conditions, which can lead to significant cost savings.

Furthermore, IoT can enhance operational safety by integrating environmental monitoring sensors that provide real-time alerts about hazardous conditions, enabling immediate PLC responses to mitigate risks.

```
// Enhancing safety with IoT sensors

Monitor_Environmental_Conditions();

IF Hazardous_Condition_Detected THEN

Execute_Safety_Protocols();

Alert_Emergency_Services();

ENDIF;
```

This code snippet ensures that the PLC responds swiftly to any detected safety hazards, protecting equipment and personnel.

To manage the vast amount of data generated by IoT devices, advanced data analytics can be implemented. This involves processing and analyzing data within the PLC or in the cloud to extract actionable insights.

// Data analytics for decision-making

Collect_IoT_Data();

Analyze_Data_For_Insights();

Implement_Decisions_Based_On_Analytics();

Analytics can reveal patterns and optimizations that are not immediately apparent, supporting more informed decision-making.

Security is a crucial consideration when connecting PLCs to the IoT. Implementing robust cybersecurity measures to protect against unauthorized access and data breaches is essential.

// Strengthening IoT security

Implement_Firewalls_and_Encryption();

Regularly_Update_Security_Protocols();

Monitor_Network_for_Unusual_Activities();

These security practices protect the PLC and connected devices from potential cyber threats.

Lastly, continuous monitoring and updating of the IoT integration setup are necessary to ensure that the system adapits to new technologies and threats.

// Continuous improvement of IoT integration

Monitor_System_Performance();

Update_System_and_Security_Measures();

Iterate_Based_On_Feedback_and_New_Technologies();

This approach ensures that the PLC remains compatible and secure as both technology and cyber threats evolve.

In conclusion, connecting Siemens S7 PLCs to the IoT opens up a myriad of possibilities for enhancing industrial operations. From improved monitoring and control to advanced analytics and energy management, the integration of these technologies enables businesses to drive efficiency, safety, and profitability in new and powerful ways.

15.3 Data Analytics with Cloud Integration

INTEGRATING SIEMENS S7 PLCs with cloud-based data analytics platforms significantly enhances the capabilities for processing, analyzing, and utilizing data generated in industrial settings. This section explores the process and benefits of cloud integration for Siemens S7 PLCs, focusing on the application of advanced data analytics to improve decision-making, optimize operations, and predict maintenance needs.

The first step in integrating cloud analytics with Siemens S7 PLCs involves setting up a secure connection to the cloud. This typically requires configuring the PLC to communicate via secure internet protocols, ensuring data privacy and security.

// Establishing a secure cloud connection

```
Setup_Secure_Connection();

Connect_To_Cloud_Service();

Authenticate_Device();
```

This setup facilitates a secure data pipeline from the PLC to the cloud, where data can be stored, processed, and analyzed without compromising security.

Once the connection is established, data collected by the PLC from various sensors and operational logs can be continuously uploaded to the cloud. This data is often streamed in real time, providing a timely basis for analytics.

```
// Streaming data to the cloud

Stream_Data_To_Cloud(Sensor_Data);

Monitor_Transmission_Status();
```

Streaming sensor data enables real-time monitoring and analysis, which is crucial for dynamic operational environments.

Cloud platforms offer powerful computational capabilities and storage capacities that exceed what is typically available on local systems. This allows for the implementation of complex analytics models that can process large datasets to identify patterns, trends, and anomalies.

```
// Utilizing cloud analytics

Analyze_Data_In_Cloud();

Generate_Insights();

Report_Results_To_Operators();
```

Utilizing cloud-based analytics helps in deriving meaningful insights from large amounts of data, which can inform strategic decision-making and operational adjustments.

Predictive maintenance is one of the key applications of data analytics with cloud integration. By analyzing historical and real-time operational data, predictive models can identify potential equipment failures before they occur.

// Implementing predictive maintenance

Develop_Predictive_Models();

Apply_Models_To_Real_Time_Data();

Schedule_Maintenance_Based_On_Predictions();

Predictive maintenance models can significantly reduce downtime and maintenance costs by ensuring that interventions are timely and based on actual equipment condition rather than routine schedules.

Energy management can also be optimized through cloud analytics by monitoring energy usage patterns and comparing them against operational metrics. This analysis can lead to the implementation of energy-saving measures that reduce costs and environmental impact.

// Optimizing energy management

Collect_Energy_Usage_Data();

Analyze_For_Efficiency_Gaps();

Implement_Energy_Savings_Initiatives();

This approach allows facilities to optimize their energy consumption, contributing to both cost savings and sustainability goals.

Operational efficiency is further enhanced by using cloud analytics to streamline production processes. Data from the entire production line can be analyzed to identify bottlenecks and inefficiencies.

```
// Streamlining operations

Aggregate_Production_Line_Data();

Identify_Bottlenecks();

Optimize_Process_Flows();
```

This data-driven approach ensures that operations are optimized continuously, leading to increased productivity and reduced waste.

Cloud integration also facilitates enhanced scalability. As operations grow or change, cloud platforms can dynamically adjust resources to meet the increased data processing and storage demands without the need for significant capital investment in local infrastructure.

```
// Managing scalability

Adjust_Cloud_Resources_Based_On_Demand();

Scale_Up_Or_Down_As_Necessary();

Ensure_Uninterrupted_Operation();
```

Scalability managed through the cloud supports business growth and adaptation without the constraints of physical infrastructure.

In addition to operational improvements, cloud analytics can provide enhanced reporting capabilities. Reports generated from cloud-processed data can include more complex analyses and visualizations than those processed locally.

```
// Advanced reporting
```

```
Generate_Detailed_Reports();
```

```
Incorporate_Advanced_Visualizations();
```

```
Distribute_Reports_To_Stakeholders();
```

Advanced reporting features enhance the understanding and communication of operational data, supporting better-informed business decisions.

Moreover, integrating cloud analytics encourages collaborative efforts. Data shared via cloud platforms can be accessed by multiple stakeholders across different geographic locations, facilitating collaboration and information sharing.

```
// Facilitating collaboration
```

```
Share_Data_Across_Cloud_Platforms();
```

```
Enable_Collaborative_Analysis();
```

```
Coordinate_Decisions_Across_Departments();
```

Collaborative platforms in the cloud enhance teamwork and decision-making across the entire organization.

In conclusion, integrating Siemens S7 PLCs with cloud-based data analytics platforms revolutionizes how industrial data is used. This integration supports advanced predictive maintenance, energy management, operational efficiency, and collaborative decision-making, all of which drive significant improvements in productivity, sustainability, and scalability.

15.4 Smart Factories and Automation

THE INTEGRATION OF Siemens S7 PLCs into smart factory environments represents a significant leap forward in industrial automation. This section explores how these PLCs contribute to the development and operation of smart factories, focusing on their role in enhancing automation, data integration, and decision-making processes.

Smart factories leverage advanced technologies like IoT, artificial intelligence, and big data analytics to create highly automated and interconnected manufacturing environments. Siemens S7 PLCs are integral to this ecosystem, providing the control and data acquisition capabilities necessary for sophisticated automation solutions.

```
// Basic setup for PLC automation control

Initialize_PLC_Communication();

Configure_Automation_Parameters();

Enable_Real_Time_Monitoring();
```

This setup forms the backbone of a smart factory's operational control system, where PLCs manage and monitor automated processes continuously.

In smart factories, Siemens S7 PLCs facilitate the seamless integration of various manufacturing processes. They act as central hubs that connect different machines and systems, allowing for synchronized operations across the factory floor.

```
// Integrating manufacturing processes

Connect_Machine_A_to_PLC();
```

```
Sync_Machine_B_with_Machine_A();
```

```
Ensure_Coordinated_Operation();
```

By coordinating the operation of multiple machines, PLCs optimize manufacturing workflows, reducing delays and increasing efficiency.

Data plays a critical role in smart factories, and Siemens S7 PLCs are adept at handling the data flows necessary for real-time decision-making. They collect data from sensors and machines, process it to derive actionable insights, and adjust operations dynamically.

```
// Data-driven decision-making
```

```
Collect_Sensor_Data();
```

```
Analyze_Data_for_Insights();
```

```
Adjust_Operations_Based_on_Analysis();
```

This data-driven approach allows smart factories to continuously improve processes and adapt to changing conditions.

Predictive maintenance is another area where Siemens S7 PLCs add significant value in smart factories. By analyzing data from equipment, these PLCs can predict failures before they occur, scheduling maintenance to avoid downtime.

```
// Predictive maintenance setup
```

```
Monitor_Equipment_Health();
```

```
Predict_Potential_Failures();
```

```
Schedule_Preventive_Maintenance();
```

This predictive strategy ensures high availability and reliability of factory equipment, minimizing unexpected breakdowns.

Energy management is also optimized in smart factories. Siemens S7 PLCs help monitor and control energy usage, ensuring that operations are as energy-efficient as possible.

// Optimizing energy management

Monitor_Energy_Consumption();

Identify_Energy_Savings_Opportunities();

Implement_Energy_Efficiency_Measures();

This proactive energy management contributes to cost savings and environmental sustainability.

The flexibility of Siemens S7 PLCs also allows for scalability in smart factories. As factory operations grow or evolve, these PLCs can accommodate new machinery and processes without extensive reconfiguration.

// Scalability features

Add_New_Machine_To_Network();

Update_PLC_Configuration();

Test_New_Configuration();

This flexibility ensures that smart factories can scale up operations efficiently and effectively.

To further enhance operational efficiency, Siemens S7 PLCs integrate with advanced visualization tools. These tools provide operators with comprehensive views of production processes, helping to identify issues and optimize workflows.

```
// Integrating visualization tools

Integrate_PLC_with_Visualization_Software();

Display_Real_Time_Operations_Data();

Enhance_Operational_Awareness_and_Control();
```

Enhanced visualization aids in better decision-making and faster response times, key advantages in smart manufacturing environments.

Moreover, the reliability of Siemens S7 PLCs is critical for continuous production. Their robust design and advanced fault detection capabilities ensure that they operate reliably under demanding industrial conditions.

```
// Ensuring reliability

Enable_Fault_Detection();

Configure_Automatic_Recovery_Procedures();

Maintain_High_Availability();
```

This reliability is essential for maintaining the continuous operation of smart factories.

Finally, the integration of cloud technologies with Siemens S7 PLCs allows for off-site data analysis and storage, providing a backup for critical operational data and enabling deep analytics that can inform strategic decisions.

```
// Cloud integration
```

Configure_Cloud_Storage_for_PLC_Data();

Automate_Data_Upload_to_Cloud();

Utilize_Cloud_Based_Analytics_for_Strategic_Insights();

Cloud integration extends the capabilities of smart factories, allowing them to leverage global data insights and advanced computational resources.

In conclusion, Siemens S7 PLCs are foundational to the development and success of smart factories. Their ability to control and integrate various industrial processes, manage and analyze vast data streams, and ensure reliability and scalability is indispensable. These capabilities make them vital to realizing the full potential of Industry 4.0.

15.5 Future Trends in PLC Programming

THE LANDSCAPE OF PLC programming is continuously evolving, influenced by advancements in technology and changes in industrial demands. This section explores the future trends in PLC programming, particularly focusing on how Siemens S7 PLCs are expected to adapt and drive innovation in the field of industrial automation.

One of the significant future trends in PLC programming is the increased integration of artificial intelligence (AI) and machine learning (ML) algorithms. These technologies enable PLCs to make decisions based on data-driven insights, improving operational efficiency and adaptability.

// Example of integrating machine learning

Load_ML_Model();

Process_Real_Time_Data();

Make_Decisions_Based_on_Predictive_Analytics();

This example outlines how ML models can be used within PLC systems to process data and make predictive decisions, enhancing automation capabilities.

The Internet of Things (IoT) continues to be a major driver of innovation in PLC programming. Future PLC systems are expected to be more interconnected, with increased capabilities for remote monitoring and control, facilitating more comprehensive and efficient management of industrial operations.

// IoT integration

Initialize_IoT_Connections();

Collect_and_Send_Data_To_Cloud();

Receive_and_Implement_Commands_From_Remote_Locations();

Enhanced IoT connectivity allows PLCs to operate as part of a larger, interconnected system, enabling sophisticated remote operations.

Another trend is the increasing importance of cybersecurity in PLC programming. As systems become more connected, the potential for cyber threats increases, necessitating more robust security measures integrated directly into PLC software.

// Enhanced cybersecurity features

Implement_Advanced_Encryption();

Conduct_Regular_Security_Audits();

Update_Security_Protocols_Automatically();

Robust security protocols ensure that PLC systems are protected against potential cyber-attacks, which is crucial for maintaining the integrity and reliability of industrial control systems.

Edge computing is also becoming a key trend in PLC programming. By processing data locally at the edge of the network, PLCs can reduce latency, increase response times, and decrease the load on central servers.

// Edge computing

Process_Data_Locally();

Make_Decisions_Quickly();

Reduce_Network_Traffic();

Local data processing enhances the efficiency and speed of automated responses, critical in time-sensitive industrial applications.

The adoption of open-source software in PLC programming is another trend gaining traction. This approach promotes more flexibility and innovation, allowing developers to customize their PLC programming environments to better meet specific operational needs.

// Using open-source tools

Use_Open_Source_Programming_Tools();

Customize_Features_to_Suit_Specific_Requirements();

Share_Improvements_with_the_Community();

Open-source tools enable customization and community collaboration, driving innovation and potentially reducing software costs.

Furthermore, the development of more user-friendly programming interfaces is anticipated. These interfaces are expected to make PLC programming more accessible to a broader range of users, including those with less specialized training.

// User-friendly programming interfaces

Develop_Intuitive_User_Interfaces();

Simplify_Programming_Processes();

Enhance_Accessibility_for_Non-Experts();

Simplifying the user interface of PLC programming tools can widen their usability, allowing more personnel to effectively interact with PLC systems.

Sustainability and energy efficiency will also become more integral to PLC programming. Future developments are likely to focus on optimizing energy consumption and reducing the environmental impact of industrial operations.

// Sustainability in PLC programming

Optimize_Operational_Efficiency_to_Save_Energy();

Implement_Eco-Friendly_Operating_Practices();

Monitor_and_Report_on_Environmental_Impact();

Energy-efficient programming can help industries reduce operational costs and contribute to environmental sustainability goals.

Finally, augmented reality (AR) and virtual reality (VR) technologies are beginning to find applications in PLC programming. These technologies can be used for training purposes, simulation of industrial processes, and even for troubleshooting and maintenance.

// AR and VR integration

Implement_AR_for_Maintenance_Assistance();

Use_VR_to_Simulate_Control_Systems();

Train_Employees_with_Immersive_Technology();

AR and VR can enhance the understanding and maintenance of complex systems, providing immersive, interactive tools for training and simulation.

In conclusion, the future of PLC programming is characterized by increased connectivity, smarter systems, enhanced security, and greater user accessibility. Siemens S7 PLCs are likely to continue playing a pivotal role in this evolution, driving forward the capabilities of industrial automation systems with advanced technologies and innovative features.

Got it! If you need information or assistance related to any specific chapter, just let me know!

Chapter 16: Scalability and System Upgrades

Planning for Future Expansions

SCALABILITY IS A CRITICAL consideration in industrial automation, especially when dealing with complex systems like those controlled by Siemens S7 PLCs. Planning for future expansions ensures that your system can grow seamlessly as your operational needs evolve. Here are some key strategies for effectively planning and implementing scalability in your Siemens S7 environment.

Understanding Current and Future Requirements

BEFORE EMBARKING ON any expansion or upgrade project, it's essential to thoroughly understand your current system's capabilities and limitations. Conduct a comprehensive assessment of your existing infrastructure, including hardware, software, and network architecture. Identify any bottlenecks or areas where scalability may be constrained.

Once you have a clear understanding of your current setup, envision your future requirements. Consider factors such as anticipated growth in production capacity, introduction of new product lines, or integration with emerging technologies like IoT. By aligning your expansion plans with future needs, you can avoid costly retrofitting or system overhauls down the line.

Modular Design Principles

MODULAR DESIGN IS FUNDAMENTAL to scalability. By breaking down your system into modular components, you can easily add or replace individual elements without disrupting the entire system. In the context of Siemens S7 programming, this means structuring your code in a way that promotes modularity and reusability.

One approach to modular design is to use libraries and function blocks extensively. Libraries allow you to encapsulate common functions or algorithms, making them easily accessible across multiple projects. Function blocks, on the other hand, enable you to encapsulate specific functionality within self-contained units that can be reused throughout your program.

// Example of a reusable function block for motor control

FUNCTION_BLOCK MotorControl

VAR_INPUT

Start : BOOL;

Stop : BOOL;

Speed : INT;

END_VAR

VAR_OUTPUT

Running : BOOL;

Fault : BOOL;

END_VAR

VAR

// Internal variables for motor control logic

END_VAR

// Motor control logic implementation

Flexible Hardware Configuration

WHEN DESIGNING YOUR Siemens S7 system, opt for hardware configurations that offer flexibility and scalability. Choose modular PLCs and expansion modules that allow you to easily add or remove

IO points, communication interfaces, or processing power as needed.

Additionally, consider implementing distributed control architectures, where multiple PLCs communicate with each other over a network. This decentralization not only improves scalability but also enhances fault tolerance and system reliability.

Scalable Network Infrastructure

A ROBUST AND SCALABLE network infrastructure is crucial for accommodating future expansions in your Siemens S7 environment. Implement networking protocols such as Profinet, which support high-speed communication and seamless integration with various industrial devices.

Design your network with scalability in mind, ensuring that it can accommodate increased traffic and bandwidth requirements as your system grows. Consider implementing redundancy and failover mechanisms to minimize downtime and ensure continuous operation, even in the event of network failures.

Regular Performance Monitoring and Optimization

SCALABILITY IS AN ONGOING process that requires continuous monitoring and optimization. Regularly assess your system's performance metrics, such as CPU utilization, memory usage, and network latency. Identify any performance bottlenecks or inefficiencies and take proactive measures to address them.

Optimize your Siemens S7 programs for efficiency, eliminating redundant code, optimizing data structures, and fine-tuning algorithm parameters. Implement logging and diagnostic features that provide insight into system behavior and performance trends over time.

Conclusion

SCALABILITY IS ESSENTIAL for ensuring the long-term viability and effectiveness of your Siemens S7 automation system. By adopting modular design principles, flexible hardware configurations, scalable network infrastructure, and proactive performance optimization strategies, you can future-proof your system and accommodate evolving operational requirements with ease.

Modular Design and System Integration

IN THE REALM OF SIEMENS S7 programming, modular design principles are paramount for ensuring scalability and ease of system integration. Section 16.2 delves into the importance of modular design and provides practical insights into effectively integrating modular components within your automation system.

Benefits of Modular Design

MODULAR DESIGN OFFERS several benefits in the context of Siemens S7 programming. Firstly, it enhances code reusability by encapsulating common functions or algorithms within self-contained modules. This not only streamlines development but also promotes consistency and maintainability across projects.

Secondly, modular design facilitates system integration by breaking down complex systems into smaller, manageable components. Each module can be developed, tested, and debugged independently, reducing the risk of errors and facilitating parallel development efforts.

Encapsulation with Function Blocks

FUNCTION BLOCKS ARE the cornerstone of modular design in Siemens S7 programming. These self-contained units encapsulate specific functionality, such as motor control algorithms or PID loops, within a standardized interface. Function blocks promote code reuse and abstraction, allowing developers to focus on high-level system architecture rather than low-level implementation details.

```
// Example of a PID control function block

FUNCTION_BLOCK PIDController

VAR_INPUT

Setpoint : REAL;

ProcessValue : REAL;

Kp : REAL;

Ki : REAL;

Kd : REAL;

END_VAR

VAR_OUTPUT

Output : REAL;

END_VAR

VAR

// Internal variables for PID control logic
```

END_VAR

// PID control logic implementation

Interface Standardization

EFFECTIVE MODULAR DESIGN relies on standardized interfaces between modules. Define clear input and output parameters for each module, specifying data types, ranges, and units where applicable. Standardized interfaces promote interoperability and facilitate communication between modules developed by different teams or organizations.

Hierarchical Organization

ORGANIZE YOUR SIEMENS S7 projects hierarchically, with each module representing a distinct functional unit within the system. Establish clear dependencies and relationships between modules, ensuring that changes to one module do not inadvertently impact others. Use folder structures and naming conventions to maintain a logical organization and facilitate navigation within large projects.

Version Control and Documentation

MAINTAINING VERSION control and comprehensive documentation is essential for managing modular Siemens S7 projects effectively. Use version control systems like Git to track changes to your codebase and coordinate collaborative development efforts. Document each module thoroughly, including its purpose, inputs and outputs, dependencies, and usage guidelines.

Testing and Validation

RIGOROUS TESTING AND validation are crucial when working with modular Siemens S7 systems. Develop automated test suites that verify the functionality and performance of individual modules as well as their interactions within the larger system. Implement unit tests, integration tests, and system-level tests to ensure robustness and reliability across the board.

Conclusion

MODULAR DESIGN IS THE cornerstone of scalable and maintainable Siemens S7 programming. By leveraging function blocks, standardizing interfaces, organizing projects hierarchically, maintaining version control and documentation, and implementing rigorous testing procedures, you can streamline development, enhance system integration, and future-proof your automation projects.

Upgrading Old Systems with Siemens S7

LEGACY SYSTEMS PRESENT unique challenges and opportunities when it comes to upgrading to Siemens S7 automation solutions. Section 16.3 explores the process of upgrading old systems with Siemens S7, highlighting key considerations, best practices, and potential pitfalls along the way.

Legacy System Assessment

BEFORE EMBARKING ON an upgrade project, conduct a comprehensive assessment of your legacy system. Evaluate the existing hardware, software, and network infrastructure, taking note of any outdated or unsupported components. Identify areas where the system falls short in terms of performance, reliability, or functionality.

Compatibility Analysis

DETERMINE THE COMPATIBILITY of your legacy system with Siemens S7 technology. Assess whether the existing hardware can support newer Siemens PLCs and IO modules. Evaluate the compatibility of your legacy software with modern Siemens programming environments like TIA Portal or STEP 7. Identify any potential compatibility issues or constraints that may impact the upgrade process.

Migration Strategy

DEVELOP A MIGRATION strategy that outlines the step-by-step process of transitioning from the legacy system to Siemens S7. Determine whether a phased approach or a complete system overhaul is more suitable based on your specific requirements and constraints. Define clear milestones, timelines, and success criteria to guide the migration process.

Hardware Upgrades

CONSIDER UPGRADING outdated hardware components to ensure compatibility with Siemens S7 technology. Replace legacy PLCs, IO modules, communication interfaces, and other peripherals with modern equivalents that support the latest standards and protocols. Take advantage of Siemens migration tools and resources to facilitate the hardware upgrade process.

Software Conversion

CONVERT LEGACY PLC programs to Siemens S7-compatible formats using conversion tools or manual rewriting. Pay special attention to differences in programming languages, data types, and syntax between the legacy system and Siemens S7. Test the converted programs thoroughly to ensure that they behave as expected and meet the required performance criteria.

Data Migration

MIGRATE EXISTING DATA, configurations, and settings from the legacy system to Siemens S7. This may include PLC programs, configuration files, network settings, alarm configurations, and historical data logs. Develop data migration scripts or utilities to automate the process and minimize the risk of data loss or corruption.

Training and Support

PROVIDE COMPREHENSIVE training and support to personnel involved in the upgrade process. Familiarize them with Siemens S7 programming environments, tools, and best practices. Offer hands-on training sessions, online tutorials, and access to technical documentation to help them navigate the transition smoothly.

Testing and Validation

RIGOROUS TESTING AND validation are essential to ensure the reliability and performance of the upgraded system. Develop test cases that cover all aspects of system functionality, including PLC logic, IO communication, HMI interaction, and network connectivity. Conduct thorough regression testing to identify and address any issues or discrepancies.

Rollout and Deployment

GRADUALLY ROLLOUT THE upgraded system in a controlled manner, starting with pilot installations and gradually expanding to full-scale deployment. Monitor the system closely during the rollout phase, collecting feedback from users and addressing any issues or concerns in a timely manner. Implement contingency plans to mitigate the impact of unexpected setbacks or failures.

Post-Upgrade Maintenance

PROVIDE ONGOING MAINTENANCE and support for the upgraded system to ensure its long-term stability and reliability. Establish regular maintenance schedules for hardware inspection, software updates, and performance optimization. Monitor system performance metrics and address any emerging issues or trends proactively.

Conclusion

UPGRADING OLD SYSTEMS with Siemens S7 automation solutions offers numerous benefits, including improved performance, reliability, and functionality. By following a systematic approach to legacy system assessment, compatibility analysis, migration strategy development, hardware and software upgrades, data migration, training and support, testing and validation, rollout and deployment, and post-upgrade maintenance, you can successfully modernize your automation infrastructure and position your organization for future growth and innovation.

Compatibility Issues and Solutions

WHEN UPGRADING LEGACY systems to Siemens S7 automation solutions, compatibility issues may arise due to differences in hardware, software, or communication protocols. Section 16.4 explores common compatibility challenges and offers practical solutions to address them effectively.

Legacy Hardware Interfaces

ONE OF THE PRIMARY compatibility issues encountered during system upgrades is the lack of support for legacy hardware interfaces in Siemens S7 PLCs. Older IO modules, communication cards, and peripheral devices may use proprietary protocols or communication standards that are incompatible with modern Siemens S7 hardware.

To overcome this challenge, consider using gateway devices or protocol converters that bridge the gap between legacy and modern hardware interfaces. These devices translate communication protocols and allow legacy devices to communicate seamlessly with Siemens S7 PLCs. Alternatively, explore retrofitting options that involve replacing legacy hardware with modern equivalents that offer native compatibility with Siemens S7 technology.

Programming Language Differences

LEGACY PLCS OFTEN USE proprietary programming languages or dialects that differ from the standard languages supported by Siemens S7 programming environments. This can pose challenges when migrating existing PLC programs to Siemens S7-compatible formats, as manual code rewriting may be required to ensure compatibility.

To address this issue, leverage automated code conversion tools or utilities provided by Siemens or third-party vendors. These tools analyze legacy PLC programs and generate equivalent Siemens S7 code, taking into account language syntax, data types, and programming conventions. Additionally, invest in training and upskilling for personnel involved in the migration process to familiarize them with Siemens S7 programming languages and best practices.

Communication Protocol Incompatibility

LEGACY SYSTEMS MAY rely on outdated or proprietary communication protocols that are incompatible with modern Siemens S7 PLCs. This can hinder interoperability and data exchange between legacy and new systems, leading to integration challenges and reduced system functionality.

To mitigate this issue, implement protocol conversion or translation mechanisms that enable communication between legacy devices and Siemens S7 PLCs. Use protocol gateways, middleware solutions, or custom communication drivers to bridge the gap between incompatible protocols and facilitate seamless data exchange. Additionally, consider migrating legacy communication protocols to industry-standard protocols supported by Siemens S7, such as Profinet or Modbus TCP, to simplify integration and future-proof your system.

Legacy Software Dependencies

LEGACY SYSTEMS OFTEN rely on proprietary software tools or libraries that are not compatible with modern Siemens S7 programming environments. This can complicate the migration process and require extensive reengineering efforts to replace or refactor legacy software dependencies.

To address this challenge, identify alternative software solutions or workarounds that provide similar functionality within the Siemens S7 ecosystem. Explore third-party libraries, open-source software projects, or vendor-provided plugins that offer compatible features and integration capabilities. Alternatively, consider developing custom software modules or function blocks tailored to your specific requirements using Siemens S7 programming languages and development tools.

Conclusion

COMPATIBILITY ISSUES are a common concern when upgrading legacy systems to Siemens S7 automation solutions. By understanding the root causes of compatibility challenges and adopting proactive strategies to address them, you can streamline the migration process and ensure a successful transition to modern automation technology. Leveraging gateway devices, automated code conversion tools, protocol translation mechanisms, alternative software solutions, and custom development approaches, you can overcome compatibility barriers and unlock the full potential of Siemens S7 PLCs in your organization's automation infrastructure.

Case Studies of System Upgrades

REAL-WORLD CASE STUDIES provide valuable insights into the challenges, strategies, and outcomes of upgrading old systems with Siemens S7 automation solutions. Section 16.5 presents a selection of case studies that illustrate various aspects of system upgrades, including hardware migration, software conversion, communication protocol integration, and overall project management.

Case Study 1: Manufacturing Facility Upgrade

A LARGE MANUFACTURING facility sought to upgrade its legacy control system to improve productivity and reliability. The existing system relied on outdated PLCs and IO modules that were no longer supported by the manufacturer. The upgrade project involved replacing legacy hardware with modern Siemens S7 PLCs and IO modules while minimizing downtime and disruption to production operations.

Key challenges included compatibility issues between legacy and new hardware, as well as the need to migrate existing PLC programs to Siemens S7-compatible formats. To address these challenges, the project team conducted a thorough assessment of the legacy system, identified critical dependencies and constraints, and developed a phased migration strategy.

The hardware migration was carried out in stages, starting with pilot installations in non-critical areas of the facility. This allowed the project team to test compatibility and performance before proceeding with full-scale deployment. Automated code conversion tools were used to convert legacy PLC programs to Siemens S7 code, with manual adjustments made where necessary to ensure functionality and performance.

The upgraded system delivered significant improvements in production efficiency, reliability, and flexibility. By leveraging modern Siemens S7 technology, the manufacturing facility was able to streamline operations, reduce downtime, and adapt to changing production requirements more effectively.

Case Study 2: Energy Management System Overhaul

A UTILITY COMPANY EMBARKED on a project to modernize its aging energy management system, which was based on obsolete PLCs and SCADA software. The legacy system lacked support for modern communication protocols and was unable to meet the growing demands of the utility's expanding infrastructure.

The upgrade project involved replacing legacy PLCs with Siemens S7 controllers and migrating existing SCADA applications to TIA Portal for improved scalability and performance. Compatibility issues between legacy and new hardware were addressed through careful planning and coordination between the project team and vendors.

Special attention was paid to ensuring seamless integration with existing communication networks and data acquisition systems. Protocol conversion mechanisms were implemented to bridge the gap between legacy and modern communication protocols, enabling interoperability and data exchange across the upgraded system.

The energy management system overhaul resulted in enhanced monitoring, control, and optimization capabilities, allowing the utility company to improve operational efficiency, reduce energy consumption, and enhance grid stability. The project demonstrated the importance of thorough planning, collaboration, and technical expertise in successful system upgrades.

Case Study 3: Building Automation Retrofit

A COMMERCIAL REAL ESTATE developer undertook a building automation retrofit project to modernize the HVAC, lighting, and security systems in its properties. The existing systems were based on disparate technologies and lacked integration, leading to inefficiencies and maintenance challenges.

The retrofit project involved deploying Siemens S7 PLCs and WinCC HMI panels to centralize control and monitoring of building systems. Legacy sensors, actuators, and controllers were replaced with modern equivalents that offered native compatibility with Siemens S7 technology.

Custom software modules were developed to integrate legacy protocols and proprietary interfaces with the Siemens S7 ecosystem. This allowed the building automation system to leverage existing infrastructure while taking advantage of the advanced features and scalability of Siemens S7 controllers.

The upgraded building automation system provided centralized control, real-time monitoring, and predictive maintenance capabilities, enabling the real estate developer to optimize energy usage, improve occupant comfort, and reduce operational costs. The project highlighted the importance of interoperability, adaptability, and future-proofing in building automation retrofits.

Conclusion

THESE CASE STUDIES illustrate the diverse challenges and solutions involved in upgrading old systems with Siemens S7 automation technology. By leveraging modern hardware, software, and communication protocols, organizations can transform outdated infrastructure into agile, efficient, and resilient automation systems that meet the demands of today's dynamic business environments. Thorough planning, collaboration, and technical expertise are essential for successful system upgrades that deliver tangible benefits and long-term value to stakeholders.

Chapter 17: Professional Development and Certification

Certification Programs for Siemens S7

PROFESSIONAL CERTIFICATION programs play a crucial role in validating expertise and proficiency in Siemens S7 programming and automation technologies. Section 17.1 explores the various certification programs offered by Siemens and other organizations, highlighting their benefits, requirements, and relevance in the field of industrial automation.

Siemens offers a comprehensive range of certification programs tailored to different skill levels and job roles within the automation industry. The Siemens Certified Programmer certification is designed for individuals who develop and maintain PLC programs using Siemens S7 controllers. This certification validates proficiency in programming languages such as ladder logic, function block diagrams, and structured text, as well as knowledge of Siemens hardware and software platforms.

For more advanced users, Siemens offers specialized certifications in areas such as HMI development, network configuration, and safety engineering. These certifications provide in-depth training and assessment in specific domains, enabling professionals to specialize and differentiate themselves in the job market.

In addition to Siemens certifications, third-party organizations such as the International Society of Automation (ISA) and the Automation Federation offer industry-recognized certifications in automation and control systems engineering. These certifications cover a wide range of topics, including PLC programming, industrial networking, cybersecurity, and process control.

Obtaining a certification in Siemens S7 programming demonstrates commitment to professional development and can enhance career prospects in the automation industry. Certified professionals are often preferred by employers due to their proven expertise and competence in using Siemens automation technology.

To qualify for Siemens certification exams, candidates typically need to complete prerequisite training courses offered by Siemens or authorized training partners. These courses cover the necessary knowledge and skills required to pass the certification exams, including hands-on experience with Siemens hardware and software tools.

Certification exams may consist of multiple-choice questions, practical exercises, and hands-on programming tasks. Candidates are evaluated based on their ability to apply theoretical concepts to real-world scenarios and demonstrate proficiency in using Siemens S7 programming environments.

Once certified, professionals may need to renew their certification periodically to ensure their skills remain current and relevant. Continuing education and professional development activities, such as attending workshops, seminars, and conferences, can also contribute to maintaining certification status and staying abreast of industry trends and best practices.

In conclusion, certification programs play a vital role in validating expertise and proficiency in Siemens S7 programming and automation technologies. By obtaining relevant certifications, professionals can enhance their career prospects, differentiate themselves in the job market, and contribute to the success of their organizations in the field of industrial automation.

Continuing Education and Training Resources

CONTINUING EDUCATION and training are essential for staying current with the latest developments in Siemens S7 programming and automation technology. Section 17.2 explores various resources and opportunities available for professionals seeking to expand their knowledge and skills in the field of industrial automation.

Siemens offers a wide range of training courses, workshops, and seminars covering various aspects of Siemens S7 programming, hardware configuration, and system integration. These training programs are delivered by experienced instructors and can be attended in person or online, providing flexibility for busy professionals.

Online learning platforms such as Siemens Learning Advantage and Udemy offer self-paced courses and tutorials on Siemens S7 programming, HMI development, and industrial networking. These platforms provide access to interactive modules, video lectures, and hands-on exercises, allowing professionals to learn at their own pace and convenience.

Books and technical publications are valuable resources for learning about Siemens S7 programming and automation technologies. Authors such as John W. Lewis and Bryan A. Jones have written comprehensive guides and reference manuals covering topics such as PLC programming, HMI design, and industrial communication protocols.

Industry conferences, trade shows, and networking events offer opportunities to learn from industry experts, share best practices, and stay abreast of emerging trends and technologies in industrial automation. Events such as SPS IPC Drives and Automation Fair showcase the latest innovations in Siemens S7 programming and automation solutions.

Online forums, discussion groups, and community websites provide platforms for professionals to collaborate, ask questions, and share knowledge about Siemens S7 programming and automation technologies. Websites such as PLCdev and Siemens Industry Online Support offer forums, tutorials, and technical articles on a wide range of topics related to Siemens automation products.

Vendor-specific training programs, such as those offered by Siemens Solution Partners and authorized distributors, provide hands-on experience with Siemens S7 hardware and software tools. These programs often include practical exercises, case studies, and live demonstrations conducted by experienced trainers.

Professional organizations such as the International Society of Automation (ISA) and the Institute of Electrical and Electronics Engineers (IEEE) offer resources, publications, and educational programs focused on industrial automation and control systems engineering. Membership in these organizations provides access to networking opportunities, technical resources, and professional development activities.

Online communities such as LinkedIn groups and subreddits dedicated to Siemens S7 programming and industrial automation provide platforms for professionals to connect, share insights, and seek advice from peers and industry experts. Participating in online communities can help professionals stay informed about the latest trends, tools, and techniques in industrial automation.

Webinars and virtual training sessions offer convenient and cost-effective options for professionals to learn about Siemens S7 programming and automation technologies from the comfort of their own home or office. Many companies and organizations offer free webinars on topics such as PLC programming, HMI design, and industrial networking.

In conclusion, continuing education and training resources are essential for professionals seeking to enhance their skills and expertise in Siemens S7 programming and automation technology. By taking advantage of training courses, online learning platforms, technical publications, industry events, online communities, and professional organizations, professionals can stay current with the latest developments and advance their careers in the field of industrial automation.

Joining Professional Networks and Communities

PROFESSIONAL NETWORKS and communities play a crucial role in connecting professionals in the field of Siemens S7 programming and industrial automation. Section 17.3 explores the benefits of joining professional networks and communities and highlights some of the prominent platforms available for professionals to connect, share knowledge, and collaborate.

LinkedIn is one of the largest professional networking platforms, with millions of members worldwide. Joining LinkedIn groups dedicated to Siemens S7 programming, industrial automation, and PLC programming provides opportunities to connect with industry peers, share insights, and participate in discussions on relevant topics. Groups such as "Siemens PLC Programmers" and "Industrial Automation Professionals" are popular among professionals in the field.

Reddit hosts several subreddits focused on industrial automation, PLC programming, and Siemens S7 technology. Subreddits such as r/PLC and r/IndustrialAutomation provide forums for professionals to ask questions, share resources, and engage in discussions about Siemens S7 programming techniques, troubleshooting tips, and industry trends. Participating in these communities can help professionals expand their knowledge and network with like-minded individuals.

Online forums such as PLCtalk.net and MrPLC.com offer platforms for professionals to seek advice, share experiences, and exchange ideas about Siemens S7 programming and industrial automation. These forums feature discussions on topics such as ladder logic programming, troubleshooting techniques, and hardware selection criteria. Engaging with fellow professionals on these forums can provide valuable insights and perspectives on complex automation challenges.

Professional associations such as the International Society of Automation (ISA) and the Institute of Electrical and Electronics Engineers (IEEE) offer networking opportunities, technical resources, and professional development programs for professionals in the field of industrial automation. Becoming a member of these associations provides access to industry events, technical publications, and online communities where professionals can connect with peers and stay informed about the latest developments in Siemens S7 programming and automation technology.

Industry-specific networks and communities, such as those focused on manufacturing, energy, or transportation, provide forums for professionals to discuss industry-specific challenges, trends, and best practices related to Siemens S7 programming and industrial automation. These networks often host events, webinars, and conferences where professionals can network with industry leaders, learn about emerging technologies, and share insights from their own experiences.

Local user groups and meetups offer opportunities for professionals to connect with peers in their geographic area and discuss Siemens S7 programming and automation topics in a face-to-face setting. These informal gatherings provide opportunities for networking, knowledge sharing, and collaboration among professionals working in similar industries or sectors.

Social media platforms such as Twitter and Facebook can also be valuable resources for connecting with professionals in the field of Siemens S7 programming and industrial automation. Following industry experts, thought leaders, and companies specializing in automation technology allows professionals to stay informed about the latest news, events, and developments in the field.

Online learning communities such as Stack Overflow and GitHub provide platforms for professionals to collaborate on coding projects, share code snippets, and seek help with programming challenges related to Siemens S7 technology. Participating in these communities allows professionals to contribute to open-source projects, learn from others' code, and build their professional reputation within the developer community.

In conclusion, joining professional networks and communities is essential for professionals seeking to expand their knowledge, network with peers, and stay informed about the latest developments in Siemens S7 programming and industrial automation. By participating in online forums, industry associations, social media groups, and local meetups, professionals can connect with like-minded individuals, share insights, and advance their careers in the field of industrial automation.

Building a Career in PLC Programming

BUILDING A SUCCESSFUL career in PLC programming requires a combination of technical skills, practical experience, and professional development. Section 17.4 explores the key steps and strategies for aspiring professionals looking to establish themselves in the field of Siemens S7 programming and industrial automation.

Technical Skills Development

DEVELOPING PROFICIENCY in Siemens S7 programming languages, such as ladder logic, function block diagrams, and structured text, is essential for PLC programmers. Enroll in training courses, workshops, or online tutorials to learn the fundamentals of PLC programming and gain hands-on experience with Siemens S7 hardware and software tools.

Practical Experience

GAIN PRACTICAL EXPERIENCE by working on real-world projects involving Siemens S7 automation systems. Seek internships, co-op placements, or entry-level positions at companies that utilize Siemens S7 technology in their manufacturing or industrial processes. Hands-on experience with PLC programming, troubleshooting, and system integration is invaluable for building a career in the field.

Specialization

CONSIDER SPECIALIZING in a specific area of Siemens S7 programming or industrial automation to differentiate yourself in the job market. Focus on developing expertise in niche areas such as HMI design, motion control, safety engineering, or industrial networking. Specialization allows you to offer specialized services or solutions to clients and employers, increasing your value as a PLC programmer.

Certification

OBTAIN INDUSTRY-RECOGNIZED certifications in Siemens S7 programming and industrial automation to validate your skills and expertise. Pursue certifications such as the Siemens Certified Programmer or Certified Automation Professional to demonstrate proficiency in PLC programming, hardware configuration, and system integration. Certification enhances your credibility and marketability as a PLC programmer.

Professional Networking

BUILD A PROFESSIONAL network by connecting with peers, mentors, and industry experts in the field of Siemens S7 programming and industrial automation. Join online forums, LinkedIn groups, and professional associations to engage with like-minded individuals, share knowledge, and stay informed about industry trends and opportunities. Networking can lead to job referrals, mentorship opportunities, and collaborations on projects.

Continuous Learning

STAY ABREAST OF THE latest developments in Siemens S7 programming and industrial automation by continuously learning and upskilling. Attend training courses, workshops, and conferences to acquire new skills, explore emerging technologies, and expand your professional network. Keep up with industry publications, blogs, and technical forums to stay informed about best practices, case studies, and advancements in the field.

Career Advancement

SEEK OPPORTUNITIES for career advancement by taking on leadership roles, pursuing advanced certifications, or transitioning into specialized areas of Siemens S7 programming and industrial automation. Consider pursuing higher education, such as a master's degree or professional certification, to enhance your knowledge and credentials in the field. Stay proactive in seeking out new challenges and opportunities for growth in your career.

Professional Development

INVEST IN YOUR PROFESSIONAL development by participating in workshops, seminars, and online courses focused on soft skills such as communication, project management, and leadership. Develop strong problem-solving abilities, analytical thinking, and attention to detail, which are essential qualities for successful PLC programmers. Continuous improvement in both technical and non-technical skills is key to long-term success in the field.

Entrepreneurship

CONSIDER ENTREPRENEURSHIP as a career path by starting your own consulting firm, automation integration company, or software development business focused on Siemens S7 programming and industrial automation. Identify niche markets or industries with specific automation needs and tailor your services or solutions to address those needs. Entrepreneurship offers the opportunity to be your own boss, pursue your passion, and create innovative solutions in the field of industrial automation.

Conclusion

BUILDING A CAREER IN PLC programming requires a combination of technical skills, practical experience, professional development, and networking. By focusing on skills development, gaining practical experience, specializing in niche areas, obtaining certifications, networking with peers, continuously learning, pursuing career advancement opportunities, investing in professional development, and considering entrepreneurship, aspiring professionals can establish themselves as successful PLC programmers in the field of Siemens S7 programming and industrial automation.

Staying Current with Siemens Technologies

STAYING CURRENT WITH Siemens technologies is essential for professionals working in the field of industrial automation and PLC programming. Section 17.5 explores various strategies and resources available for professionals to stay updated on the latest developments, advancements, and best practices in Siemens S7 programming and automation technology.

Siemens Official Documentation

REGULARLY REVIEW SIEMENS official documentation, including user manuals, application guides, and technical specifications, to stay informed about the latest features, functionalities, and updates in Siemens S7 hardware and software products. Siemens provides comprehensive documentation for its products, covering topics such as hardware configuration, programming languages, troubleshooting techniques, and system integration.

Training and Certification Programs

PARTICIPATE IN TRAINING courses, workshops, and certification programs offered by Siemens and authorized training partners to enhance your skills and knowledge in Siemens S7 programming and automation technology. Siemens offers a wide range of training programs tailored to different skill levels and job roles, covering topics such as PLC programming, HMI design, industrial networking, and safety engineering. Certification programs validate your expertise and proficiency in Siemens technologies, enhancing your credibility and marketability as a PLC programmer.

Online Learning Platforms

EXPLORE ONLINE LEARNING platforms such as Siemens Learning Advantage, Udemy, Coursera, and LinkedIn Learning for self-paced courses, tutorials, and video lectures on Siemens S7 programming and industrial automation. These platforms offer a variety of courses covering topics such as PLC programming fundamentals, advanced programming techniques, HMI development, and industrial communication protocols. Online learning allows professionals to learn at their own pace and convenience, accessing course materials from anywhere with an internet connection.

Industry Publications and Blogs

SUBSCRIBE TO INDUSTRY publications, blogs, and newsletters dedicated to industrial automation, PLC programming, and Siemens technologies to stay updated on the latest news, trends, and insights in the field. Publications such as Control Engineering, Automation World, and The PLC Guy provide valuable resources, articles, case studies, and expert opinions on Siemens S7 programming, automation solutions, and industry developments. Following industry influencers and thought leaders on social media platforms such as Twitter and LinkedIn can also provide valuable insights and perspectives on Siemens technologies.

Webinars and Workshops

ATTEND WEBINARS, WORKSHOPS, and virtual events hosted by Siemens, industry associations, and technology vendors to learn about new product releases, features, and innovations in Siemens S7 programming and automation technology. These events often feature live demonstrations, expert presentations, and Q&A sessions, allowing professionals to interact with industry experts and gain firsthand knowledge about Siemens technologies.

User Forums and Discussion Groups

PARTICIPATE IN USER forums, discussion groups, and online communities dedicated to Siemens S7 programming and industrial automation to connect with peers, share experiences, and seek advice on technical issues and challenges. Forums such as PLCtalk.net, Siemens Industry Online Support, and Reddit's r/PLC provide platforms for professionals to ask questions, share solutions, and discuss best practices related to Siemens technologies. Engaging with fellow professionals in online communities can help you stay informed about common problems, troubleshooting techniques, and emerging trends in Siemens S7 programming.

Continuous Experimentation and Practice

REGULARLY EXPERIMENT with Siemens S7 hardware and software tools, test new features, and explore different programming techniques to expand your skills and knowledge in industrial automation and PLC programming. Set up a home lab environment with Siemens PLCs, IO modules, and HMI panels to practice programming, testing, and troubleshooting scenarios. Continuous experimentation and practice are essential for mastering Siemens technologies and staying ahead in the field of industrial automation.

Collaboration and Knowledge Sharing

COLLABORATE WITH COLLEAGUES, peers, and industry experts on projects, case studies, and research initiatives related to Siemens S7 programming and industrial automation. Participate in collaborative projects, working groups, and professional networks to exchange ideas, share insights, and contribute to the collective knowledge base of the automation community. By collaborating with others and sharing your expertise, you can learn from different perspectives, gain new insights, and stay current with Siemens technologies.

Conclusion

STAYING CURRENT WITH Siemens technologies is crucial for professionals working in the field of industrial automation and PLC programming. By regularly reviewing Siemens official documentation, participating in training and certification programs, exploring online learning platforms, subscribing to industry publications and blogs, attending webinars and workshops, engaging in user forums and discussion groups, experimenting with Siemens hardware and software tools, collaborating with colleagues, and sharing knowledge with others, professionals can stay informed about the latest developments, advancements, and best practices in Siemens S7 programming and automation technology. Continuous learning, experimentation, and collaboration are essential for staying ahead in the dynamic and rapidly evolving field of industrial automation.

Chapter 18: Specialized Applications and Extensions

Custom Solutions for Unique Industry Needs

SPECIALIZED APPLICATIONS and extensions of Siemens S7 programming offer tailored solutions to address unique industry needs and requirements. Section 18.1 delves into the development and implementation of custom solutions that leverage Siemens S7 technology to solve specific challenges and optimize processes in various industries.

Industries such as automotive manufacturing, pharmaceuticals, food and beverage, and aerospace have specific automation requirements that may not be fully addressed by off-the-shelf solutions. Customizing Siemens S7 programming allows companies to tailor automation systems to their unique production processes, equipment, and regulatory requirements.

Custom solutions often involve developing specialized PLC programs, HMI interfaces, and communication protocols to integrate Siemens S7 controllers with existing equipment and systems. This may include interfacing with proprietary hardware, legacy systems, or third-party software to achieve seamless interoperability and data exchange.

One example of a custom solution is the integration of Siemens S7 controllers with robotic systems in automotive manufacturing plants. By developing custom PLC programs and HMI interfaces, manufacturers can coordinate the movements and operations of robots with other production equipment, such as conveyor belts, assembly lines, and robotic arms, to optimize throughput, cycle times, and quality control.

In the pharmaceutical industry, custom solutions are used to automate processes such as batch processing, material handling, and packaging to ensure compliance with strict regulatory requirements and quality standards. Siemens S7 controllers are customized to implement complex control algorithms, recipe management systems, and data logging functionalities to meet regulatory requirements and ensure product quality and safety.

Food and beverage manufacturers often require custom solutions to automate processes such as recipe formulation, mixing, cooking, and packaging while maintaining strict hygiene and safety standards. Siemens S7 controllers are customized to control and monitor temperature, pressure, flow rates, and other process parameters to ensure product consistency and compliance with food safety regulations.

In the aerospace industry, custom solutions are used to automate processes such as parts assembly, testing, and inspection to meet stringent quality and safety standards. Siemens S7 controllers are customized to interface with robotic arms, CNC machines, and measurement instruments to automate complex assembly and testing procedures while ensuring precision and accuracy.

Custom solutions for specialized applications often require collaboration between automation engineers, software developers, and domain experts to understand the unique requirements and constraints of each industry. By leveraging Siemens S7 technology and expertise, companies can develop tailored automation solutions that improve efficiency, productivity, and quality while reducing costs and minimizing risks.

In conclusion, custom solutions based on Siemens S7 programming offer tailored automation solutions to address unique industry needs and requirements. By developing custom PLC programs, HMI interfaces, and communication protocols, companies can optimize processes, improve productivity, and ensure compliance with regulatory standards in industries such as automotive manufacturing, pharmaceuticals, food and beverage, and aerospace. Collaboration between automation engineers, software developers, and domain experts is essential for developing custom solutions that meet the specific challenges and constraints of each industry.

Using Siemens S7 in Non-Traditional Contexts

SIEMENS S7 PROGRAMMING is not limited to traditional industrial applications but can also be applied in non-traditional contexts to solve unique challenges and automate diverse processes. Section 18.2 explores the versatility of Siemens S7 technology and its application in non-traditional industries and environments.

One non-traditional application of Siemens S7 programming is in the field of renewable energy, where PLCs are used to control and monitor solar power plants, wind farms, and hydroelectric facilities. Siemens S7 controllers are customized to interface with sensors, actuators, and monitoring devices to optimize energy production, manage grid integration, and ensure safety and reliability in renewable energy systems.

Another non-traditional context where Siemens S7 technology is applied is in smart buildings and infrastructure, where PLCs are used to automate HVAC systems, lighting controls, access control, and energy management systems. Siemens S7 controllers are programmed to regulate temperature, lighting levels, and energy usage based on occupancy patterns, environmental conditions, and energy demand, resulting in energy savings, comfort, and convenience for building occupants.

Siemens S7 programming is also used in the field of transportation and logistics to automate processes such as conveyor systems, sorting machines, and material handling equipment in warehouses, distribution centers, and manufacturing facilities. Siemens S7 controllers are customized to optimize throughput, minimize bottlenecks, and ensure efficient operation of transportation and logistics systems, improving productivity and reducing costs.

In the agricultural industry, Siemens S7 technology is applied to automate processes such as irrigation, fertilization, and livestock management in modern farms and greenhouses. PLCs are used to control irrigation pumps, valves, and sensors to optimize water usage, monitor soil moisture levels, and ensure optimal growing conditions for crops. Siemens S7 controllers are also used to automate feeding systems, climate control, and environmental monitoring in livestock facilities, improving efficiency and productivity in agriculture.

Siemens S7 programming is increasingly being used in research and development (R&D) laboratories and academic institutions to automate experimental setups, data acquisition systems, and scientific instruments. PLCs are programmed to control and monitor experimental parameters, collect data from sensors and instruments, and implement control algorithms for real-time experimentation and analysis in various scientific disciplines.

In the entertainment industry, Siemens S7 technology is applied to automate stage machinery, lighting systems, and special effects in theaters, theme parks, and live events. PLCs are programmed to synchronize movements of stage elements, control lighting sequences, and trigger special effects such as smoke, fog, and pyrotechnics, enhancing the overall experience for audiences and performers.

Siemens S7 programming is also used in healthcare facilities to automate processes such as patient monitoring, medication dispensing, and equipment management. PLCs are programmed to interface with medical devices, sensors, and communication systems to ensure timely and accurate delivery of healthcare services, improve patient safety, and optimize resource utilization in hospitals and clinics.

In conclusion, Siemens S7 programming is not limited to traditional industrial applications but can also be applied in non-traditional contexts to solve unique challenges and automate diverse processes. From renewable energy systems and smart buildings to transportation and logistics, agriculture, research laboratories, entertainment venues, and healthcare facilities, Siemens S7 technology offers versatility and flexibility to address a wide range of automation needs in various industries and environments. By leveraging Siemens S7 technology and expertise, companies and organizations can improve efficiency, productivity, and safety while reducing costs and environmental impact in non-traditional applications.

Expanding Capabilities with Add-On Modules

EXPANDING THE CAPABILITIES of Siemens S7 systems can be achieved through the use of add-on modules, which provide additional functionality and flexibility to meet specific automation requirements. Section 18.3 explores the various types of add-on modules available for Siemens S7 controllers and their applications in enhancing automation systems.

One common type of add-on module is the digital input/output (I/O) module, which expands the number of digital inputs and outputs available to the PLC. These modules are used to connect additional sensors, actuators, and devices to the Siemens S7 system, increasing the capacity and scalability of the automation system. Digital I/O modules come in various configurations, with options for different voltage levels, signal types, and isolation levels to suit different application requirements.

Analog I/O modules are another type of add-on module used to interface with analog sensors and actuators in Siemens S7 systems. These modules provide high-resolution analog inputs and outputs for measuring and controlling variables such as temperature, pressure, flow rate, and position in industrial processes. Analog I/O modules support a wide range of signal types, including voltage, current, resistance, and temperature sensors, enabling precise control and monitoring of analog signals in automation systems.

Communication modules are add-on modules used to expand the communication capabilities of Siemens S7 controllers, allowing them to communicate with other devices, systems, and networks. These modules support various communication protocols such as Profibus, Profinet, Ethernet/IP, Modbus, and TCP/IP, enabling seamless integration with other PLCs, HMIs, SCADA systems, and enterprise networks. Communication modules provide fast, reliable, and secure data exchange between Siemens S7 controllers and external devices, enabling distributed control and monitoring in complex automation systems.

Specialized function modules are add-on modules designed to provide specific functionality or perform advanced calculations in Siemens S7 systems. These modules include mathematical function blocks, motion control modules, safety modules, and high-speed counter modules, among others. Specialized function modules extend the capabilities of Siemens S7 controllers, allowing them to perform complex calculations, motion control tasks, safety functions, and high-speed counting operations in automation systems.

Remote I/O modules are add-on modules used to expand the I/O capabilities of Siemens S7 controllers beyond the physical constraints of the PLC rack. These modules are installed remotely from the PLC rack and connected to the controller via communication networks such as Profibus or Profinet. Remote I/O modules enable distributed I/O architecture, allowing for flexible placement of sensors and actuators throughout the automation system without the need for additional wiring or hardware.

Safety modules are add-on modules used to implement safety functions and comply with safety standards such as ISO 13849 and IEC 61508 in Siemens S7 systems. These modules provide safety-related inputs and outputs, safety relay functions, and safety monitoring capabilities to ensure safe operation of machinery and equipment in industrial environments. Safety modules support features such as emergency stop, safety interlocks, two-hand control, and safe speed monitoring, enabling the implementation of safety-critical applications in automation systems.

High-speed counter modules are add-on modules used to count and measure high-speed events such as pulses, edges, and frequencies in Siemens S7 systems. These modules provide fast counting and measuring capabilities, high-resolution timing, and precise synchronization for applications such as motion control, position tracking, and speed monitoring in automation systems. High-speed counter modules support features such as quadrature decoding, pulse width measurement, and frequency analysis, enabling accurate measurement and control of high-speed processes.

In conclusion, add-on modules provide additional functionality and flexibility to Siemens S7 controllers, allowing for the expansion of automation systems to meet specific requirements and challenges. From digital and analog I/O modules to communication modules, specialized function modules, remote I/O modules, safety modules, and high-speed counter modules, add-on modules offer a wide range of options for enhancing the capabilities of Siemens S7 systems in various industrial applications. By leveraging add-on modules, companies and organizations can improve efficiency, productivity, and safety in their automation systems while maintaining flexibility and scalability for future growth and expansion.

Integrating Third-Party Software and Hardware

INTEGRATING THIRD-PARTY software and hardware with Siemens S7 systems expands the functionality and interoperability of automation systems, enabling seamless integration with external devices, systems, and technologies. Section 18.4 explores the process of integrating third-party software and hardware with Siemens S7 controllers and the benefits of such integration in industrial automation.

One common scenario for integrating third-party software with Siemens S7 systems is connecting SCADA (Supervisory Control and Data Acquisition) software for centralized monitoring and control of industrial processes. SCADA software communicates with Siemens S7 controllers via communication protocols such as Profibus, Profinet, or OPC (Open Platform Communications), allowing operators to monitor process variables, view real-time data, and control equipment from a centralized location. Integrating SCADA software with Siemens S7 systems enhances visibility, efficiency, and decision-making in industrial automation by providing real-time insights into process performance and production status.

Another application of integrating third-party software with Siemens S7 systems is connecting MES (Manufacturing Execution System) software for production planning, scheduling, and tracking. MES software interfaces with Siemens S7 controllers to exchange production data, job orders, and process recipes, enabling real-time production monitoring, scheduling optimization, and quality management. Integrating MES software with Siemens S7 systems improves production efficiency, reduces lead times, and enhances traceability and compliance in manufacturing operations.

ERP (Enterprise Resource Planning) software integration is another use case for connecting third-party software with Siemens S7 controllers to synchronize production data with business systems such as inventory management, procurement, and accounting. ERP software communicates with Siemens S7 systems to exchange production orders, material consumption data, and inventory levels, enabling accurate planning, resource allocation, and cost control in manufacturing enterprises. Integrating ERP software with Siemens S7 systems streamlines business processes, improves visibility across the supply chain, and enhances decision-making based on real-time production data.

Integrating third-party hardware with Siemens S7 controllers extends the capabilities of automation systems by adding specialized sensors, actuators, and devices for specific applications. For example, integrating vision systems, RFID (Radio-Frequency Identification) readers, barcode scanners, or laser sensors with Siemens S7 controllers enables advanced quality inspection, part tracking, and material handling in manufacturing processes. Third-party hardware integration with Siemens S7 systems enhances automation capabilities, increases productivity, and improves product quality in industrial applications.

Interfacing robotics with Siemens S7 controllers is another example of integrating third-party hardware with automation systems to automate complex tasks such as assembly, pick-and-place, and material handling. Robotics controllers communicate with Siemens S7 controllers via standard communication protocols such as Profibus, Profinet, or Ethernet/IP, enabling synchronized operation and coordinated motion control between robots and other automation equipment. Integrating robotics with Siemens S7 systems increases flexibility, efficiency, and accuracy in manufacturing processes by automating repetitive tasks and adapting to changing production requirements.

Integrating third-party software and hardware with Siemens S7 controllers requires careful planning, design, and implementation to ensure compatibility, reliability, and performance. It involves configuring communication protocols, data exchange formats, and interface parameters to establish seamless communication between Siemens S7 systems and external devices or systems. Collaboration between automation engineers, software developers, and third-party vendors is essential for successful integration, ensuring that requirements are met, and challenges are addressed effectively.

The benefits of integrating third-party software and hardware with Siemens S7 controllers include enhanced functionality, interoperability, and scalability of automation systems, enabling companies to adapt to changing business requirements and technological advancements. By leveraging third-party solutions and technologies, companies can extend the capabilities of Siemens S7 systems, improve operational efficiency, and achieve greater competitiveness in the global marketplace.

In conclusion, integrating third-party software and hardware with Siemens S7 controllers offers numerous benefits for industrial automation, including enhanced functionality, interoperability, and scalability. Whether connecting SCADA, MES, or ERP software for production management, interfacing specialized sensors or actuators for process control, or integrating robotics for automation, third-party integration extends the capabilities of Siemens S7 systems and enables companies to achieve greater efficiency, flexibility, and competitiveness in today's dynamic manufacturing environment.

Developing and Deploying Custom Function Blocks

DEVELOPING AND DEPLOYING custom function blocks in Siemens S7 programming allows for modular and reusable code that can streamline development, improve maintainability, and enhance the scalability of automation systems. Section 18.5 explores the process of creating custom function blocks in Siemens S7 and their deployment in industrial automation applications.

Custom function blocks encapsulate specific functionality or algorithms that can be reused across multiple parts of a PLC program, promoting code reusability and modularity. By developing custom function blocks, programmers can abstract complex logic into easily manageable units, making PLC programs easier to understand, maintain, and troubleshoot. Common examples of custom function blocks include mathematical calculations, data processing algorithms, and control routines for specific equipment or processes.

The development of custom function blocks typically involves defining input and output parameters, implementing the desired functionality, and testing the block to ensure its correctness and reliability. Siemens S7 programming environments such as STEP 7 provide tools and features for creating, editing, and testing custom function blocks, allowing programmers to develop custom logic efficiently and effectively.

Once developed, custom function blocks can be deployed in PLC programs by inserting instances of the block into the program logic and configuring the input and output parameters as needed. Siemens S7 programming environments provide intuitive interfaces for inserting and configuring function blocks, allowing programmers to integrate custom logic seamlessly into their PLC programs.

One benefit of using custom function blocks is the ability to encapsulate complex logic and algorithms into reusable components, reducing redundancy and improving code organization. By creating custom function blocks for common tasks or processes, programmers can simplify PLC programs, making them easier to maintain and modify over time.

Another benefit of custom function blocks is the potential for performance optimization and code efficiency. By implementing frequently used logic in custom function blocks, programmers can optimize the execution speed and memory usage of PLC programs, leading to faster cycle times and improved system performance.

Custom function blocks also facilitate code standardization and consistency across PLC programs, promoting best practices and ensuring uniformity in programming styles and conventions. By defining a set of standardized function blocks for common tasks or operations, organizations can enforce coding guidelines and improve the readability and maintainability of PLC programs.

In addition to standardizing code, custom function blocks enable collaboration and code sharing among programmers within an organization. By developing a library of reusable function blocks, programmers can leverage each other's expertise and solutions, accelerating development and reducing time-to-market for automation projects.

Furthermore, custom function blocks facilitate system scalability and flexibility by enabling modular design and incremental development. As automation systems evolve and grow, custom function blocks can be easily modified, extended, or replaced to accommodate new requirements or technologies, without the need for extensive rework or redesign of existing PLC programs.

Overall, developing and deploying custom function blocks in Siemens S7 programming offers numerous benefits for industrial automation, including code reusability, modularity, performance optimization, standardization, collaboration, and scalability. By leveraging custom function blocks, programmers can streamline development, improve maintainability, and enhance the flexibility and scalability of automation systems, ultimately leading to more efficient and cost-effective solutions for manufacturing and process industries.

Chapter 19: Sustainable Practices in PLC Programming

Reducing Environmental Impact with Efficient Programming

SUSTAINABLE PRACTICES in PLC programming play a crucial role in minimizing the environmental impact of industrial automation systems and promoting eco-friendly manufacturing processes. Section 19.1 focuses on strategies for reducing environmental footprint through efficient programming techniques and optimization of PLC code.

One key aspect of sustainable PLC programming is optimizing code for energy efficiency to minimize power consumption and reduce carbon emissions in industrial facilities. By adopting efficient programming techniques such as minimizing unnecessary calculations, reducing CPU idle time, and optimizing loop iterations, programmers can lower the energy consumption of PLCs and contribute to overall energy savings in manufacturing operations.

Another strategy for reducing environmental impact is implementing power management techniques in PLC programs to regulate the operation of equipment and machinery based on energy demand and production requirements. By incorporating energy-saving modes, standby functions, and load shedding algorithms into PLC logic, programmers can optimize energy usage, reduce peak power demand, and improve the overall energy efficiency of automation systems.

Furthermore, sustainable PLC programming involves optimizing control algorithms and process logic to minimize material waste, resource consumption, and environmental pollution in manufacturing processes. By implementing advanced control strategies such as predictive maintenance, adaptive control, and model-based optimization, programmers can optimize process parameters, reduce variability, and minimize the generation of waste and emissions in industrial operations.

In addition to optimizing energy and resource usage, sustainable PLC programming encompasses the use of eco-friendly materials and components in automation systems to minimize environmental impact throughout the lifecycle of equipment and machinery. By selecting energy-efficient devices, low-power components, and recyclable materials for PLC hardware, programmers can reduce the environmental footprint of automation systems and promote sustainable manufacturing practices.

Moreover, sustainable PLC programming involves integrating environmental monitoring and reporting functionalities into automation systems to track energy consumption, emissions, and resource usage in real-time. By implementing data logging, analysis, and visualization features in PLC programs, programmers can monitor environmental performance, identify areas for improvement, and make data-driven decisions to optimize sustainability in industrial operations.

Another aspect of sustainable PLC programming is promoting green manufacturing practices such as lean production, just-in-time inventory management, and waste reduction through automation and optimization of production processes. By developing PLC programs that support agile manufacturing, flexible production scheduling, and efficient material handling, programmers can improve resource utilization, reduce inventory waste, and minimize environmental impact in manufacturing operations.

Furthermore, sustainable PLC programming involves implementing eco-friendly maintenance practices such as condition-based monitoring, predictive maintenance, and remote diagnostics to minimize downtime, extend equipment lifespan, and reduce the need for resource-intensive repair and replacement activities. By integrating maintenance management functionalities into PLC programs, programmers can optimize equipment performance, prevent unplanned shutdowns, and improve overall equipment effectiveness (OEE) in industrial facilities.

Additionally, sustainable PLC programming encompasses the use of renewable energy sources such as solar, wind, and hydropower in automation systems to reduce reliance on fossil fuels, lower greenhouse gas emissions, and promote clean energy generation in manufacturing facilities. By integrating renewable energy generation and storage systems with PLCs, programmers can optimize energy usage, maximize self-consumption, and minimize the environmental impact of industrial operations.

In conclusion, sustainable practices in PLC programming are essential for minimizing the environmental impact of industrial automation systems and promoting eco-friendly manufacturing processes. By optimizing code for energy efficiency, implementing power management techniques, optimizing control algorithms, using eco-friendly materials and components, integrating environmental monitoring and reporting functionalities, promoting green manufacturing practices, implementing eco-friendly maintenance practices, and integrating renewable energy sources, programmers can contribute to sustainability in industrial automation and help build a greener future for manufacturing industries.

Implementing Green Energy Solutions in Automation

IMPLEMENTING GREEN energy solutions in automation systems is crucial for reducing carbon emissions, promoting sustainability, and mitigating the environmental impact of industrial operations. Section 19.2 focuses on strategies for integrating renewable energy sources such as solar, wind, and hydropower with PLC programming to power industrial automation systems sustainably.

One strategy for implementing green energy solutions in automation is integrating solar photovoltaic (PV) systems with PLCs to harness solar energy for powering industrial facilities. By connecting solar panels to PLC controllers via inverters and power management systems, programmers can generate clean, renewable electricity to supplement grid power and reduce reliance on fossil fuels. PLC programs can be developed to monitor solar energy production, manage battery storage, and optimize energy usage based on solar availability and production forecasts, maximizing self-consumption and minimizing grid dependence.

Another approach to implementing green energy solutions in automation is integrating wind turbines with PLCs to harness wind energy for on-site power generation. By connecting wind turbines to PLC controllers via power converters and grid-tie inverters, programmers can capture wind energy and convert it into usable electricity for industrial processes. PLC programs can be designed to control turbine operation, regulate power output, and coordinate energy storage systems to balance supply and demand, optimizing wind energy utilization and reducing grid reliance.

Additionally, integrating hydropower systems with PLCs offers another green energy solution for powering industrial automation systems sustainably. By connecting hydroelectric generators to PLC controllers via turbine governors and power converters, programmers can utilize water flow to generate clean, renewable electricity for industrial operations. PLC programs can be developed to control water flow, adjust turbine speed, and optimize power generation based on water availability and energy demand, maximizing hydropower utilization and minimizing environmental impact.

Moreover, integrating energy storage systems such as batteries and flywheels with PLCs enhances the reliability and stability of green energy solutions in automation. By connecting energy storage devices to PLC controllers via power converters and inverters, programmers can store excess energy from renewable sources during periods of high production and discharge it during periods of low production or high demand, smoothing out fluctuations in renewable energy output and improving grid integration. PLC programs can be configured to manage energy storage operation, optimize charging and discharging cycles, and prioritize energy usage based on cost and environmental considerations, maximizing the benefits of green energy solutions in industrial automation.

Furthermore, implementing demand response strategies in PLC programming enables industrial facilities to participate in energy markets, optimize energy usage, and reduce electricity costs while supporting grid stability and reliability. By developing PLC programs that monitor energy prices, forecast demand, and adjust production schedules and equipment operation in response to grid signals and market incentives, programmers can optimize energy usage, minimize peak demand, and capitalize on opportunities to sell excess energy back to the grid, enhancing the economic viability of green energy solutions in automation.

Additionally, integrating energy-efficient technologies such as LED lighting, variable frequency drives (VFDs), and energy management systems with PLCs further enhances the sustainability and efficiency of industrial automation systems. By connecting energy-efficient devices and systems to PLC controllers via communication networks such as Modbus or Ethernet/IP, programmers can monitor energy consumption, adjust equipment operation, and optimize energy usage in real-time, reducing energy waste and minimizing environmental impact.

In conclusion, implementing green energy solutions in automation systems through PLC programming is essential for promoting sustainability, reducing carbon emissions, and mitigating the environmental impact of industrial operations. By integrating renewable energy sources such as solar, wind, and hydropower with PLCs, optimizing energy storage systems, implementing demand response strategies, and integrating energy-efficient technologies, programmers can develop sustainable automation solutions that enhance efficiency, reliability, and environmental stewardship in manufacturing and process industries.

Waste Reduction through Optimized Control Processes

REDUCING WASTE THROUGH optimized control processes is a critical aspect of sustainable PLC programming, contributing to resource conservation, cost savings, and environmental protection. Section 19.3 delves into strategies for minimizing waste generation and improving resource efficiency in industrial automation systems through PLC programming.

One strategy for waste reduction is implementing lean manufacturing principles in PLC programming to streamline production processes, eliminate non-value-added activities, and minimize resource consumption. By developing PLC programs that optimize production flow, reduce inventory levels, and eliminate bottlenecks and defects, programmers can improve productivity, reduce waste generation, and enhance overall efficiency in manufacturing operations.

Another approach to waste reduction is implementing real-time monitoring and control functionalities in PLC programs to track material usage, energy consumption, and process parameters, and identify opportunities for optimization and waste reduction. By integrating sensors, meters, and monitoring devices with PLC controllers and developing algorithms to analyze data and detect inefficiencies, programmers can identify root causes of waste, implement corrective actions, and continuously improve process performance and resource utilization.

Additionally, implementing predictive maintenance strategies in PLC programming helps prevent equipment failures, reduce downtime, and minimize material waste in industrial operations. By developing PLC programs that monitor equipment condition, analyze performance data, and predict maintenance needs based on usage patterns and failure modes, programmers can schedule maintenance activities proactively, optimize spare parts inventory, and extend equipment lifespan, reducing waste and improving operational reliability.

Moreover, implementing closed-loop control systems in PLC programming enables precise control and adjustment of process parameters based on feedback from sensors and actuators, minimizing variability and waste in manufacturing processes. By developing control algorithms that regulate process conditions, adjust setpoints, and maintain tight tolerances, programmers can optimize production quality, reduce scrap and rework, and minimize material waste in industrial operations.

Furthermore, implementing batch and recipe management functionalities in PLC programming helps optimize material usage, reduce recipe deviations, and minimize product waste in batch manufacturing processes. By developing PLC programs that manage recipe parameters, track material consumption, and enforce process control limits, programmers can ensure consistency, repeatability, and traceability in batch production, minimizing waste and maximizing yield.

Additionally, integrating quality control and inspection functionalities into PLC programs helps identify defects, reject non-conforming products, and reduce waste in manufacturing processes. By developing PLC programs that monitor product quality, analyze inspection data, and trigger alarms or shutdowns in case of deviations from specifications, programmers can ensure compliance with quality standards, reduce scrap and rework, and minimize material waste in industrial operations.

Moreover, implementing advanced analytics and optimization algorithms in PLC programming enables data-driven decision-making and continuous improvement in industrial automation systems. By developing PLC programs that analyze production data, identify inefficiencies, and optimize process parameters in real-time, programmers can optimize resource utilization, reduce waste, and improve overall efficiency and sustainability in manufacturing operations.

Furthermore, implementing environmental management functionalities in PLC programming helps monitor and control environmental parameters such as emissions, effluents, and energy usage in industrial facilities. By developing PLC programs that monitor environmental performance, track regulatory compliance, and implement emission control measures, programmers can minimize environmental impact, ensure compliance with environmental regulations, and promote sustainability in industrial operations.

In conclusion, waste reduction through optimized control processes is essential for promoting sustainability, improving resource efficiency, and minimizing environmental impact in industrial automation systems. By implementing lean manufacturing principles, real-time monitoring and control functionalities, predictive maintenance strategies, closed-loop control systems, batch and recipe management functionalities, quality control and inspection functionalities, advanced analytics and optimization algorithms, and environmental management functionalities in PLC programming, programmers can develop sustainable automation solutions that enhance efficiency, reliability, and environmental stewardship in manufacturing and process industries.

Contribution of PLCs to Sustainable Manufacturing

PLCS PLAY A SIGNIFICANT role in promoting sustainable manufacturing practices by enabling efficient control, optimization, and monitoring of industrial processes. Section 19.4 explores how PLCs contribute to sustainability in manufacturing operations through various functionalities and applications.

One key contribution of PLCs to sustainable manufacturing is their ability to optimize energy usage and reduce resource consumption in industrial processes. By controlling equipment operation, regulating process parameters, and implementing energy-saving strategies, PLCs help minimize energy waste, lower carbon emissions, and improve overall energy efficiency in manufacturing facilities.

Additionally, PLCs facilitate the implementation of predictive maintenance strategies, enabling proactive equipment maintenance and minimizing unplanned downtime in manufacturing operations. By monitoring equipment condition, analyzing performance data, and predicting maintenance needs, PLCs help prevent equipment failures, extend equipment lifespan, and reduce the need for resource-intensive repair and replacement activities.

Furthermore, PLCs support the implementation of closed-loop control systems, enabling precise control and adjustment of process parameters based on feedback from sensors and actuators. By maintaining tight tolerances, minimizing variability, and optimizing production quality, PLCs help reduce scrap, rework, and material waste in manufacturing processes, contributing to resource conservation and waste reduction efforts.

Moreover, PLCs facilitate the integration of renewable energy sources such as solar, wind, and hydropower into manufacturing operations, enabling on-site power generation and reducing reliance on fossil fuels. By controlling renewable energy systems, optimizing energy storage, and managing grid interaction, PLCs help maximize the utilization of renewable energy, reduce greenhouse gas emissions, and promote clean energy production in industrial facilities.

Additionally, PLCs support the implementation of demand response strategies, enabling industrial facilities to participate in energy markets, optimize energy usage, and reduce electricity costs.

By adjusting production schedules, equipment operation, and energy consumption in response to grid signals and market incentives, PLCs help minimize peak demand, mitigate grid instability, and enhance the economic viability of sustainable manufacturing practices.

Furthermore, PLCs enable the implementation of advanced analytics and optimization algorithms, enabling data-driven decision-making and continuous improvement in manufacturing operations. By analyzing production data, identifying inefficiencies, and optimizing process parameters, PLCs help improve resource utilization, reduce waste, and enhance overall efficiency and sustainability in manufacturing facilities.

Moreover, PLCs facilitate the implementation of environmental management functionalities, enabling monitoring and control of environmental parameters such as emissions, effluents, and energy usage. By tracking environmental performance, ensuring regulatory compliance, and implementing emission control measures, PLCs help minimize environmental impact, ensure regulatory compliance, and promote sustainability in manufacturing operations.

Additionally, PLCs support the implementation of lean manufacturing principles, enabling streamlining of production processes, elimination of non-value-added activities, and optimization of resource utilization. By optimizing production flow, reducing inventory levels, and eliminating bottlenecks and defects, PLCs help improve productivity, reduce waste, and enhance overall efficiency in manufacturing operations.

In conclusion, PLCs play a crucial role in promoting sustainable manufacturing practices by enabling efficient control, optimization, and monitoring of industrial processes. Through their various functionalities and applications, PLCs contribute to energy efficiency, predictive maintenance, waste reduction, renewable energy integration, demand response, advanced analytics, environmental management, lean manufacturing, and overall sustainability in manufacturing operations.

Case Studies on Sustainability Achievements

CASE STUDIES PROVIDE valuable insights into real-world applications of sustainable practices in PLC programming and their impact on manufacturing operations. Section 19.5 presents several case studies highlighting successful sustainability achievements through the implementation of PLC-based solutions.

One case study focuses on a manufacturing facility that implemented energy-efficient PLC programming techniques to optimize HVAC systems, lighting controls, and equipment operation. By developing PLC programs that monitored energy usage, adjusted setpoints, and implemented occupancy-based control strategies, the facility achieved significant reductions in energy consumption, resulting in lower utility bills and reduced carbon emissions.

Another case study examines a food processing plant that implemented predictive maintenance strategies using PLC-based condition monitoring systems. By installing sensors on critical equipment, analyzing performance data, and predicting maintenance needs, the plant reduced unplanned downtime, extended equipment lifespan, and minimized resource-intensive repair activities, resulting in improved equipment reliability and operational efficiency.

Furthermore, a case study in the automotive industry showcases the integration of renewable energy sources such as solar panels and wind turbines with PLC-controlled energy management systems.

By connecting renewable energy systems to PLC controllers, optimizing energy storage, and managing grid interaction, the automotive plant reduced reliance on fossil fuels, lowered energy costs, and mitigated environmental impact, contributing to its sustainability goals.

Moreover, a case study in the pharmaceutical sector highlights the implementation of closed-loop control systems in PLC programming to optimize batch manufacturing processes. By developing PLC programs that maintained tight tolerances, regulated process parameters, and minimized variability, the pharmaceutical company achieved higher product quality, reduced scrap, and improved overall efficiency in production, leading to cost savings and waste reduction.

Additionally, a case study in the electronics industry demonstrates the use of PLC-based demand response strategies to optimize energy usage and reduce electricity costs. By developing PLC programs that monitored energy prices, forecasted demand, and adjusted production schedules and equipment operation in response to grid signals, the electronics manufacturer minimized peak demand charges, optimized energy procurement, and enhanced its competitiveness in the market.

Furthermore, a case study in the packaging industry illustrates the implementation of lean manufacturing principles in PLC programming to streamline production processes and minimize waste. By optimizing production flow, reducing setup times, and eliminating non-value-added activities, the packaging company improved productivity, reduced material waste, and enhanced profitability, demonstrating the effectiveness of sustainable practices in PLC programming.

Moreover, a case study in the chemical industry showcases the integration of advanced analytics and optimization algorithms in PLC programming to improve resource utilization and reduce environmental impact. By analyzing production data, identifying inefficiencies, and optimizing process parameters, the chemical plant achieved higher yields, reduced emissions, and enhanced overall sustainability in its operations.

Additionally, a case study in the aerospace sector highlights the implementation of environmental management functionalities in PLC programming to monitor and control emissions, effluents, and energy usage. By developing PLC programs that tracked environmental performance, ensured regulatory compliance, and implemented emission control measures, the aerospace company minimized environmental impact, mitigated compliance risks, and enhanced its reputation as a responsible corporate citizen.

In conclusion, case studies demonstrate the effectiveness of sustainable practices in PLC programming in achieving environmental, economic, and social benefits for manufacturing operations. By implementing energy-efficient techniques, predictive maintenance strategies, renewable energy integration, closed-loop control systems, demand response strategies, lean manufacturing principles, advanced analytics, and environmental management functionalities in PLC programming, companies can enhance their sustainability performance, reduce costs, and improve competitiveness in the market.

Chapter 20: The Future of Siemens S7 Programming

Emerging Technologies and Their Impact on PLC Programming

THE FUTURE OF SIEMENS S7 programming is shaped by emerging technologies that are revolutionizing the field of industrial automation. Section 20.1 explores the impact of these technologies on PLC programming and their implications for future developments in the industry.

One emerging technology that is transforming PLC programming is the Internet of Things (IoT), which enables connectivity and data exchange between devices and systems in industrial environments. By integrating PLCs with IoT platforms, programmers can collect real-time data from sensors and actuators, monitor equipment performance, and optimize production processes remotely, leading to improved efficiency, reduced downtime, and enhanced predictive maintenance capabilities.

Additionally, artificial intelligence (AI) and machine learning (ML) are becoming increasingly important in PLC programming, enabling advanced analytics, predictive modeling, and autonomous decision-making in industrial automation systems. By leveraging AI and ML algorithms, PLCs can analyze large datasets, identify patterns, and optimize control strategies dynamically, resulting in improved process efficiency, energy savings, and quality optimization in manufacturing operations.

Furthermore, edge computing is emerging as a key technology in PLC programming, enabling data processing and analysis at the edge of the network, closer to where data is generated. By deploying edge computing devices alongside PLCs, programmers can reduce latency, improve reliability, and enhance security in industrial automation systems, enabling real-time control and decision-making in distributed environments.

Moreover, digital twins are revolutionizing PLC programming by creating virtual replicas of physical assets and processes, enabling simulation, testing, and optimization of control strategies in a virtual environment. By developing digital twins of PLC-controlled systems, programmers can model complex interactions, simulate scenarios, and predict performance outcomes, leading to more robust and efficient control algorithms and better decision support for operators and engineers.

Additionally, cloud computing is transforming PLC programming by providing scalable, on-demand access to computational resources and storage capabilities for data-intensive applications. By leveraging cloud platforms for PLC programming, programmers can deploy and manage applications remotely, access real-time data from distributed systems, and collaborate with stakeholders across different locations, leading to improved flexibility, scalability, and efficiency in industrial automation systems.

Furthermore, cybersecurity is becoming increasingly important in PLC programming, as industrial automation systems become more connected and vulnerable to cyber threats. By implementing robust security measures such as encryption, authentication, and intrusion detection in PLC programs, programmers can protect against cyber attacks, safeguard sensitive data, and ensure the integrity and reliability of industrial control systems.

Moreover, 5G technology is revolutionizing PLC programming by providing high-speed, low-latency connectivity for real-time control and communication in industrial automation systems. By leveraging 5G networks for PLC programming, programmers can achieve faster response times, greater reliability, and higher bandwidth for data-intensive applications, enabling new opportunities for remote monitoring, control, and optimization in manufacturing operations.

Additionally, quantum computing holds the potential to revolutionize PLC programming by enabling exponentially faster computation and optimization of complex control algorithms and decision-making processes. By harnessing the power of quantum computing, programmers can solve optimization problems, simulate quantum systems, and develop advanced control strategies that were previously infeasible with classical computing techniques, leading to breakthroughs in efficiency, reliability, and sustainability in industrial automation systems.

In conclusion, the future of Siemens S7 programming is characterized by the integration of emerging technologies such as IoT, AI and ML, edge computing, digital twins, cloud computing, cybersecurity, 5G technology, and quantum computing, which are revolutionizing PLC programming and shaping the next generation of industrial automation systems. By embracing these technologies and leveraging their capabilities, programmers can develop innovative solutions that improve efficiency, reliability, and sustainability in manufacturing operations, leading to a more connected, intelligent, and resilient industrial future.

The Evolution of Programming Interfaces

SECTION 20.2 EXPLORES the evolution of programming interfaces in Siemens S7 programming and their impact on industrial automation. Over the years, programming interfaces have undergone significant advancements, reflecting the changing needs and requirements of the industry.

One notable evolution in programming interfaces is the transition from traditional ladder logic programming to more sophisticated programming languages such as Structured Text (ST) and Sequential Function Charts (SFC). While ladder logic remains widely used for its simplicity and familiarity, ST and SFC offer greater flexibility, modularity, and scalability, enabling programmers to develop more complex control algorithms and logic sequences for advanced automation applications.

Additionally, the introduction of integrated development environments (IDEs) such as TIA Portal has revolutionized the way PLC programs are developed, debugged, and maintained. TIA Portal provides a unified platform for programming, configuration, and diagnostics, streamlining the development process and improving productivity for programmers and engineers.

Moreover, the adoption of standardized communication protocols such as OPC UA and MQTT has enhanced interoperability and connectivity between PLCs and other devices and systems in industrial networks. By supporting open, vendor-neutral protocols, PLC programming interfaces enable seamless integration with third-party software and hardware, facilitating data exchange and interoperability across heterogeneous systems.

Furthermore, advancements in graphical user interfaces (GUIs) have improved the usability and accessibility of PLC programming interfaces, making it easier for users to navigate, configure, and monitor PLC programs and systems. Modern GUIs feature intuitive design, interactive visualization, and drag-and-drop functionality, enabling users to create, edit, and deploy PLC programs with greater ease and efficiency.

Additionally, the emergence of cloud-based programming interfaces has enabled remote access and collaboration for PLC programming, allowing programmers to develop, deploy, and manage PLC programs from anywhere with an internet connection. Cloud-based interfaces offer advantages such as scalability, accessibility, and real-time synchronization, empowering teams to collaborate on projects and share resources more effectively.

Moreover, the integration of artificial intelligence (AI) and machine learning (ML) capabilities into programming interfaces holds the potential to revolutionize PLC programming by enabling intelligent automation, predictive analytics, and adaptive control. By leveraging AI and ML algorithms, programming interfaces can automate routine tasks, analyze production data, and optimize control strategies, leading to improved efficiency, reliability, and performance in industrial automation systems.

Furthermore, the development of low-code and no-code programming interfaces is democratizing PLC programming by enabling non-experts to develop and deploy automation solutions without extensive programming knowledge or experience. By providing visual, intuitive tools for building and configuring PLC programs, low-code and no-code interfaces empower users to innovate, experiment, and iterate on automation projects more freely, accelerating the adoption of automation technologies across industries.

Additionally, the evolution of programming interfaces is driving the convergence of operational technology (OT) and information technology (IT) in industrial automation, blurring the lines between traditional PLC programming and software development. As PLCs become more connected, intelligent, and software-defined, programming interfaces are evolving to support a wider range of applications, from real-time control and monitoring to data analytics and cloud integration.

In conclusion, the evolution of programming interfaces in Siemens S7 programming reflects the ongoing transformation of industrial automation towards greater connectivity, intelligence, and flexibility. By embracing advancements in programming languages, IDEs, communication protocols, GUIs, cloud computing, AI and ML, low-code and no-code platforms, and OT/IT convergence, PLC programming interfaces are empowering users to develop innovative solutions that address the complex challenges of modern manufacturing and drive the next wave of industrial revolution.

Artificial Intelligence in Industrial Automation

SECTION 20.3 EXPLORES the integration of artificial intelligence (AI) into industrial automation systems, focusing on its applications, benefits, and challenges. AI technologies are revolutionizing the way industrial processes are controlled, optimized, and managed, leading to improved efficiency, productivity, and competitiveness in manufacturing and process industries.

One of the key applications of AI in industrial automation is predictive maintenance, which involves using AI algorithms to analyze equipment performance data, detect anomalies, and predict maintenance needs before failures occur. By leveraging AI for predictive maintenance, manufacturers can reduce unplanned downtime, extend equipment lifespan, and optimize maintenance schedules, leading to cost savings and improved reliability in production operations.

Additionally, AI is being used for optimizing energy usage and reducing resource consumption in industrial facilities. By analyzing real-time data from sensors and meters, AI algorithms can identify opportunities for energy savings, optimize equipment operation, and implement energy-efficient control strategies, leading to lower energy costs and reduced environmental impact in manufacturing operations.

Moreover, AI is revolutionizing quality control and inspection processes in industrial automation by enabling automated defect detection, classification, and sorting. By deploying AI-powered vision systems and machine learning algorithms, manufacturers can identify defects, reject non-conforming products, and ensure compliance with quality standards, leading to higher product quality and reduced scrap in production lines.

Furthermore, AI is enabling autonomous decision-making and adaptive control in industrial automation systems, allowing machines and systems to learn from experience, adjust their behavior, and optimize performance in real-time. By incorporating AI algorithms into control loops and feedback mechanisms, manufacturers can achieve higher levels of automation, flexibility, and responsiveness in production processes, leading to improved efficiency and agility in manufacturing operations.

Additionally, AI is being used for process optimization and yield maximization in manufacturing operations, enabling data-driven decision-making and continuous improvement. By analyzing production data, identifying inefficiencies, and optimizing process parameters, AI algorithms can help manufacturers optimize production schedules, minimize waste, and maximize throughput, leading to higher productivity and profitability in industrial facilities.

Moreover, AI is transforming supply chain management in manufacturing by enabling demand forecasting, inventory optimization, and supply chain visibility. By analyzing historical sales data, market trends, and external factors, AI algorithms can predict demand, optimize inventory levels, and streamline logistics operations, leading to reduced inventory costs, improved customer service, and enhanced competitiveness in the marketplace.

Additionally, AI is revolutionizing human-machine interaction in industrial automation by enabling natural language processing, gesture recognition, and cognitive computing capabilities. By incorporating AI-powered interfaces and chatbots into human-machine interfaces (HMIs), manufacturers can improve operator efficiency, enhance user experience, and enable intuitive interaction with automation systems, leading to safer, more productive work environments.

Furthermore, AI is driving innovation and new product development in industrial automation by enabling the discovery of novel solutions, optimization of design parameters, and rapid prototyping of new products. By leveraging AI for design optimization, simulation, and generative design, manufacturers can accelerate product development cycles, reduce time-to-market, and stay ahead of competitors in rapidly evolving markets.

In conclusion, AI is transforming industrial automation by enabling predictive maintenance, energy optimization, quality control, autonomous decision-making, process optimization, supply chain management, human-machine interaction, and innovation in manufacturing and process industries. By embracing AI technologies and leveraging their capabilities, manufacturers can improve efficiency, productivity, and competitiveness in the global marketplace, leading to a more connected, intelligent, and sustainable future for industrial automation.

The Expanding Role of PLCs in Global Industries

SECTION 20.4 DELVES into the expanding role of PLCs in global industries, highlighting their significance in driving efficiency, innovation, and sustainability across various sectors. PLCs have evolved from simple relay-based controllers to sophisticated programmable devices, becoming integral components of modern industrial automation systems.

One key aspect of the expanding role of PLCs is their versatility and adaptability to diverse applications in industries such as manufacturing, energy, transportation, healthcare, and agriculture. PLCs are used for controlling and monitoring processes, managing equipment, optimizing production, and ensuring safety and reliability in a wide range of industrial settings.

Moreover, PLCs play a crucial role in enabling Industry 4.0 initiatives, which aim to digitize and connect industrial processes for improved efficiency and competitiveness. By incorporating PLCs into smart factories, manufacturers can achieve real-time data collection, analysis, and decision-making, enabling agile and responsive production systems that can adapt to changing market demands and customer preferences.

Additionally, PLCs are driving innovation and technological advancements in global industries by enabling the integration of emerging technologies such as artificial intelligence, Internet of Things, cloud computing, and big data analytics into industrial automation systems. By leveraging these technologies, PLCs can optimize performance, improve reliability, and enhance safety in industrial processes, leading to greater efficiency and competitiveness for businesses.

Furthermore, PLCs are playing a critical role in promoting sustainability and environmental stewardship in global industries by enabling energy-efficient control strategies, predictive maintenance, waste reduction, and resource optimization. By implementing PLC-based solutions for energy management, environmental monitoring, and sustainable practices, industries can reduce their carbon footprint, minimize environmental impact, and contribute to a greener and more sustainable future.

Moreover, PLCs are facilitating global collaboration and knowledge sharing in industrial automation through open standards, interoperability, and connectivity with other devices and systems. By adhering to industry standards such as OPC UA and Profinet, PLCs enable seamless integration with third-party equipment, software, and platforms, fostering innovation and collaboration among industry stakeholders worldwide.

Additionally, PLCs are empowering small and medium-sized enterprises (SMEs) to adopt automation technologies and compete in global markets by offering cost-effective, scalable, and user-friendly solutions for process control and optimization. With PLCs, SMEs can automate manual tasks, improve productivity, and enhance product quality, enabling them to remain competitive and sustainable in today's fast-paced business environment.

Furthermore, PLCs are driving digital transformation initiatives in global industries by enabling the transition from legacy systems to modern, connected automation solutions. By replacing outdated control systems with PLC-based architectures, industries can achieve greater flexibility, scalability, and interoperability, enabling them to adapt to evolving market trends and regulatory requirements more effectively.

Moreover, PLCs are empowering workforce development and skills training initiatives in global industries by providing opportunities for education, training, and certification in PLC programming and automation technologies. By investing in workforce development programs, industries can ensure a skilled and knowledgeable workforce that can effectively leverage PLCs and other automation technologies to drive innovation and growth.

In conclusion, PLCs are playing an increasingly important role in global industries, driving efficiency, innovation, and sustainability across diverse sectors. With their versatility, adaptability, and integration capabilities, PLCs enable businesses to achieve operational excellence, improve competitiveness, and navigate the complexities of the modern industrial landscape.

Preparing for Future Developments in PLC Technology

SECTION 20.5 DISCUSSES strategies for preparing for future developments in PLC technology, considering the rapid pace of technological innovation and the evolving needs of industrial automation.

One crucial aspect of preparing for future developments in PLC technology is staying informed about emerging trends, advancements, and best practices in the field of industrial automation. By attending industry conferences, workshops, and training sessions, professionals can stay updated on the latest developments in PLC hardware, software, programming languages, and application areas, enabling them to anticipate future trends and opportunities.

Moreover, investing in continuous education and professional development is essential for staying ahead in the rapidly evolving field of PLC technology. By pursuing certifications, advanced training programs, and specialized courses in PLC programming, professionals can acquire new skills, deepen their knowledge, and stay relevant in a competitive job market, positioning themselves for career advancement and leadership roles in industrial automation.

Additionally, fostering collaboration and partnerships with technology vendors, system integrators, and industry experts is crucial for leveraging expertise, resources, and innovation in PLC technology. By establishing strategic alliances and networks, organizations can access specialized knowledge, co-develop solutions, and explore new business opportunities in emerging markets and industries, enabling them to expand their footprint and stay competitive in a dynamic business environment.

Furthermore, investing in research and development (R&D) initiatives is essential for driving innovation and breakthroughs in PLC technology. By allocating resources to R&D projects, organizations can explore new technologies, experiment with novel approaches, and develop next-generation solutions that push the boundaries of what is possible in industrial automation, enabling them to differentiate themselves in the market and create value for customers.

Moreover, fostering a culture of innovation and experimentation within organizations is critical for nurturing creativity, agility, and adaptability in responding to future developments in PLC technology. By encouraging employees to explore new ideas, take calculated risks, and challenge conventional thinking, organizations can foster a culture of innovation that drives continuous improvement and drives breakthroughs in PLC technology, enabling them to stay ahead of the curve and maintain a competitive edge in the marketplace.

Additionally, prioritizing cybersecurity and data protection is essential for safeguarding PLC systems and industrial networks against cyber threats and vulnerabilities. By implementing robust security measures such as encryption, authentication, and access controls, organizations can protect sensitive data, prevent unauthorized access, and ensure the integrity and reliability of PLC systems, enabling them to mitigate cybersecurity risks and maintain operational continuity in the face of evolving threats.

Furthermore, embracing open standards and interoperability is essential for enabling seamless integration and scalability of PLC systems in diverse industrial environments. By adopting industry standards such as OPC UA, Profinet, and Modbus, organizations can ensure compatibility, interoperability, and future-proofing of their PLC systems, enabling them to adapt to changing requirements and technologies more effectively.

Moreover, embracing cloud computing and edge computing technologies is essential for unlocking new capabilities and opportunities in PLC technology. By leveraging cloud platforms for data storage, analytics, and remote access, organizations can achieve scalability, flexibility, and cost-efficiency in managing PLC systems and applications, enabling them to harness the power of big data and advanced analytics for optimizing performance and driving innovation in industrial automation.

In conclusion, preparing for future developments in PLC technology requires a proactive approach that involves staying informed, investing in education and professional development, fostering collaboration and partnerships, investing in R&D, fostering a culture of innovation, prioritizing cybersecurity, embracing open standards, and leveraging cloud and edge computing technologies. By adopting these strategies, organizations can position themselves for success in a rapidly evolving landscape of industrial automation, enabling them to adapt to emerging trends, capitalize on new opportunities, and achieve sustainable growth in the digital era.

This is a work of fiction. Similarities to real people, places, or events are entirely coincidental.

AMISH SHELTER

First edition. July 7, 2021.

Copyright © 2021 Stephanie Swift.

ISBN: 979-8223853480

Written by Stephanie Swift.

Amish Shelter

Stephanie Swift

Published by Trellis Publishing, 2021.

"I live three houses down from here. Would you like some coffee?"

She'd never been a big fan of coffee, but for some strange reason, the offer was tempting and made her mouth water. She made a move to get it, but he stopped her and did it himself, and when he brought it over to her, their fingers grazed for just a second, but it was enough to make her knees wobbly.

"Thank you," she said, trying not to stammer.

He sat down across from her, and for a couple of minutes they drank their java in silence, but it was a comfortable quiet that helped settle her frazzled nerves.

"Did you find someone to drive you to Harrisburg? There's a taxi service in Lancaster, if you need one."

Normally, she wouldn't discuss her private life with someone she barely knew, but she felt oddly at ease around Levi and so she decided to trust her instincts and open up to him. Besides, if she didn't tell him what was going on, there was always the chance that Claire, David, or his parents would.

"I used the community phone last night to call the Lancaster police department, and someone is coming first thing tomorrow morning to pick me up."

He squinted as he set his cup down on the table.

"Why do you need an officer to escort you?"

He seemed genuinely concerned, which flattered her but also made her wish she didn't have to tell him the sordid details.

"Lindsey and I were living with my boyfriend, Jeff. We met a year ago, and he was sweet and charming at first, but over time he became very...possessive. I took Lindsey and left yesterday while he was at work so he couldn't follow us, and Claire was the first person I thought of because I knew he'd never think to look here. All we had were the clothes on our backs and my purse, and I used all the money I'd saved up on the taxi ride from Harrisburg to Lancaster. That's why you found us walking here."

She saw the way his jaw clenched and unclenched while she spoke, but she couldn't fathom if his tension was from Jeff's actions or from judging her for being unmarried and "living in sin". That was something she was used to hearing from her extended family members, and it certainly wouldn't surprise her if Levi and everyone else from their community thought the same way.

"I want to go with you," he remarked.

Andrea was taken aback by his response, but even though his chivalry humbled her, there was no way she would ever let him do such a thing, since seeing another man in her presence would no doubt make Jeff livid...and even more dangerous.

"I appreciate that, Levi, but I don't want to drag you or anyone else into this. Claire agreed to watch Lindsey while I'm gone, and it will be safer for everyone if I show up there with the deputy only."

Andrea's heart pounded furiously inside her chest when he reached across the table and held her hand.

"And what about *your* safety?" he asked. "Perhaps you should ask more than one deputy to escort you."

Warmth flooded her entire body, and even though she knew the ladylike thing to do would be to let go, she couldn't bring herself to do it. She couldn't remember the last time a man, other than Lindsey's father, showed her even a small amount of tenderness and compassion, and it was something she truly missed.

"It's sweet of you to worry, but I'll be fine. Jeff should be at work anyway, so if I'm lucky I won't have to confront him at all."

He didn't look convinced, but he didn't try to change her mind again either.

"I can only imagine what you must think of me. I know it was wrong for us to be living together when we weren't married, but I was so lonely after Lindsey's father died, and I guess I let that impair my judgement. I would go back and change it in a heartbeat if I could."

Levi was shaking his head before she finished talking, and when she gave him the chance to speak, she could tell by the tone of his voice that he was serious.

"I'm not here to judge you, Andrea. I've never lost someone I love, so I can't say I understand that kind of pain, and I won't pretend to know what I would do if I were in that kind of situation. I think you're a very brave woman, and I admire what you're doing for you and for Lindsey."

His sincerity brought tears to her eyes, but the moment passed in an instant before she had time to process it.

"I should get back to the barn before my father comes looking for me," he said.

She hated for the conversation to end, but she also didn't want to get him in trouble. They both stood at the same time, and as they made their way to the sink with their cups, the toe of Andrea's left shoe caught on the kitchen rug and nearly toppled her over. Levi grabbed hold of her forearm to keep her steady, and she yelped in pain.

As soon as she let it slip, she wished she could take it back, because Levi zoned in on her reaction quicker than she could bat an eye. He loosened his hold on her arm, but he didn't let her go, not even when Andrea tried in vain to pry herself free. He set his cup down in the sink, and then, ever so carefully, he raised her shirt sleeve, revealing the black and blue bruises that covered her arm from her wrist to her elbow.

For several agonizing seconds he never said a word, but the muscles tightened in his jaw, and when he did speak, she detected an eerie calmness in his voice that made her shiver.

"Are there more?" he asked.

Andrea didn't want to answer him, and even if she did, she doubted she could find it in her heart to tell him the whole truth. She'd managed to hide the marks on her body from everyone else, including Lindsey and Claire, but there was a determination in Levi's demeanor that told her if she wasn't forthcoming about Jeff's abuse he would do whatever it took to find out the truth.

He didn't give her the opportunity to answer his question before he reached for her other arm and pulled up her shirt sleeve, revealing the bruises that were almost identical to the ones on her right arm. Several of them were in the shape of Jeff's fingers, where he'd grabbed her in a fit of rage and squeezed as hard as he could.

"You don't deserve this, Andrea – no woman does. You should be treated with love, kindness, and respect. This...this isn't right."

His face reddened, and she could see the anger burning in his eyes. Before she could address it, however, the back door opened and she heard footsteps in the hallway. Andrea yanked her shirt sleeves down and moved away from Levi seconds before Lindsey came bursting into the kitchen.

"Momma, come see the baby chicks!" she exclaimed, excitedly. "They're so cute!"

Andrea washed and dried her and Levi's cups before joining her. All the while, Levi leaned against the counter and never said another word. As she and Lindsey left the room, she had the uneasy feeling their conversation wasn't over.

* * *

Levi couldn't concentrate.

His working hours had long since come and gone, but he remained in his father's dairy barn, unable to move – unable to breathe normally. He couldn't get the image of Andrea's beautiful porcelain skin littered with black and blue marks off his mind, and it was about to drive him mad. Knowing a deputy was going with her to Jeff's house to gather her things probably should've brought him a sense of comfort, but it didn't.

He wanted to go with her.

Levi twisted and turned on the old wooden stool he was sitting on. He was agitated, on-edge...and a thousand other emotions...and he couldn't get comfortable.

"Levi?"

He turned toward the soft feminine voice and found Andrea standing near the entrance to the barn. He immediately stood when she started walking toward him, and his heart raced a little faster with every step she took.

"Your mother wanted me to let you know she fixed a dinner plate to take home with you," she said. "I wish you had joined us tonight."

He wanted to tell her he couldn't be anywhere near her without having to fight the urge to take her in his arms. He wanted to show her how a woman should be treated, but he also didn't want to overstep his boundaries. There was so much he needed and wanted to tell her, but he had no idea where to start. When she turned to leave, he mentally forced himself to make a move.

"Andrea, wait!"

She stopped, but she didn't turn around, and so Levi went to her. He closed the door entrance to the barn so they could be alone and not risk being overheard, if Lindsey or his parents should happen to leave the house and go looking for them. He noticed right away the frightened look in her eyes, and even though he knew it was probably foolishness on his part, he decided to risk it all anyway. Unfortunately, though, he wasn't good with words. He didn't know the proper romantic sentiments that would get his point across and convey what was on his heart, but he knew he needed to express it somehow.

Levi brushed his fingertips along her jawline as gently as possible, and his heart leapt in his throat as he reveled at the softness of her skin. The heat radiating from her body was a soothing comfort to his soul, and as he let his fingertips drift delicately along the side of her neck, she closed her eyes. Her lips were parted slightly, and even though he didn't want to rush, he was inexplicitly drawn to her mouth and the warmth of her breath on his skin.

Levi cupped her head with his hands and kissed her lips, and much to his relief, she didn't shy away from him or push him away. He was actually surprised when they parted and she grasped the front of his shirt with both hands and stood on her tiptoes for another kiss. This one was deeper and more urgent than the first, and before long they were clinging to each other.

Levi wrapped his arms around Andrea and pulled her as close to his body as possible, but he stopped instantly when she whimpered in response. It wasn't a breathless, passionate whimper that fell from her lips – this one was followed by her whole body tensing up, as if she were in pain.

Levi took a step back. "What did I do? Are you alright?"

She hesitated for a moment, but when she turned around and lifted her shirt halfway up her back, he inhaled sharply when he saw the multitude of bruises covering her bare skin. He clenched his fists by his side, and his breathing became ragged from the rage that boiled up inside him and threatened to spill over. He wished more than anything Jeff was close enough to strike, but he took a couple of deep breaths and controlled his anger. Losing his temper was the last thing he needed to do, and especially not in front of Andrea, who had obviously seen more than her fair share of hatred and wrath.

Levi dropped to his knees and cautiously touched her back before placing his lips against her skin and kissing each bruise. He felt helpless, and it was all he could think of to do to show her the tenderness she so rightly deserved. When she lowered her shirt and turned back around, he put his cheek to her stomach and held her close. Andrea, in return, ran her fingers through his hair, and they remained that way for a long while.

Neither of them said another word, but there was no need. They had each other and he felt peaceful and content – and, for the moment, that was enough.

* * *

Andrea sat in the deputy's car and stared at Jeff's house for several minutes before the two of them left the vehicle and made their way to the front door. She didn't see Jeff's truck in the driveway, which was a relief, but she knew he could return any minute and that terrified her. She retrieved the house key from her purse and unlocked the front door, and the deputy walked in ahead of her and checked each room of the house before he felt comfortable letting her pack her things.

"I'll wait by the front door for you, Miss Watson."

She thanked him and quickly started grabbing her belongings. The less time she spent in the house, the better off she was. Thankfully, there wasn't much to pack other than her and Lindsey's clothes and the few toys Lindsey had in her bedroom. She left behind what wasn't absolutely necessary so they could be on their way.

When she was satisfied she'd gotten everything she needed, Andrea removed the house key from her keychain and left it on the table in the foyer before locking the door behind her and the deputy on their way out. The few minutes they spent loading her belongings into the trunk of the deputy's car, she kept her eyes peeled for any sign of Jeff, and she didn't breathe easier until they were inside the vehicle and headed back to Lancaster.

An hour later, when the deputy turned into the Troyer's driveway, she was happy to discover Levi, his parents, Lindsey, Claire, and David all waiting for her on the front porch. As they helped her unload the few bags from the trunk, she caught Levi staring at her, which made her cheeks redden and gave her goosebumps.

Andrea thanked the deputy for his assistance, and as he pulled out of the driveway, she felt Lindsey tugging on the back of her shirt.

"Is it finally over, momma?" she asked.

Andrea knelt down and gave her a big hug. "Yes, sweetie, it is."

A smile spread across Lindsey's sweet little face, and as she raced off to help Mrs. Troyer in her vegetable garden, Andrea looked beside her at Levi and sighed. "I hope it is."

Levi grabbed her hand and pulled her toward the front door. With Claire and David on their way home, and Lindsey and Levi's parent's preoccupied with their chores, they took the opportunity to steal a few minutes alone inside the house. As soon as Levi shut the front door behind them, he was pulling her into his arms and kissing her with the utmost tenderness.

"I was so worried about you," he whispered. "I almost wore a hole in these floorboards from pacing."

Andrea smiled wearily as she took his hand and led him over to the sofa so they could sit down and talk.

"I have to admit I'm frightened, Levi. I know Lindsey and I can't stay here forever, and I'm sure your neighbors probably don't like having an English woman disrupting their lives."

He shushed her by kissing her, and Andrea sighed contentedly when the warmth of his lips remained on hers long after they parted.

"I think you'd be surprised how accepting we can be," he explained. "I truly believe that *Gott* brought you here for a reason, Andrea. We might not know what that reason is yet, but I want to be there with you as you find your way. This can be a whole new beginning for you and Lindsey, and its past time for you to be treated right – the way you should *always* be treated."

Andrea was still hesitant. "What about Jeff? What if he finds out where we are?"

Levi held her hands and caressed her skin with the pads of his thumbs, and the slow, circular motions eased her troubled mind and calmed her spirit.

"He'd be a fool to step one foot on this property. I'll protect you, Andrea – we all will. You'll see."

His self-assuredness and confidence helped her feel safe and more secure than she had in many long months, and slowly but surely the worry she'd clung to since her arrival began to dissipate. She didn't know what the future held, but as long as God allowed her to put one foot in front of the other, she would follow whatever path He chose for her.

Andrea heard Lindsey searching for her and calling her name, and Levi kissed her one last time before the two of them walked back outside to join her and the others. As soon as they stepped on to the front porch, Lindsey came barreling around the corner of the house.

"Momma!" she exclaimed. "Mrs. Troyer said this one could be mine!"

Andrea gave her a curious look, and when Lindsey jumped the porch steps two at a time, she grinned when she saw the tiny baby chick Lindsey held securely in her hands. She was more excited than she'd seen her in a very long time, and it made her heart swell seeing the huge grin that spread across her dimpled cheeks.

"Can I keep her?" Lindsey asked. "Please, please, please!"

Andrea and Levi both laughed. She traced the soft feathers on top of the chick's head with her fingertip, and she had to admit her heart melted a little bit when it chirped in response.

"Alright," she agreed. "Have you picked out a name yet?"

Andrea nodded, enthusiastically. "I'm going to call her Hope. What do you think?"

Before she could reply, Lindsey took off down the steps and ran back to join Mrs. Troyer as Levi held her close to his side.

"Hope," she said with a smile. "I can't think of a more perfect name."

THE AMISH WAY

JILL BROWN

The Amish Way: A Love Story

Chapter 1

Rachel sat at the table, slowly drumming her long fingers against the hard oak on the table. Yet again, her husband had failed to fulfill his promise to leave work early so that they could share a romantic dinner.

Their marriage had diminished from an inferno down to a slow burn, and Rachel was doing everything she could to restore the passion, but it was virtually impossible to seduce someone who was never around. She'd come to his office a few times bringing him lunch, only to find that he either grabbed her by the elbow and led her away, or simply refused to come out and meet her. He'd hide away in one of the many board rooms.

Tonight, she'd seared an entire chicken and had dressed up in a short black mini-skirt he used to like to see her in. She'd cobbled a meal together consisting of his favorite foods, and had given it her all. Yet, an hour into her wait, she'd guessed that he probably wasn't going to show up.

Just as Rachel had lit a few candles and sat them on the table, the text message came through.

Generally speaking, she was a modern woman who was tolerant and allowed Ted to have his freedom. She knew that it was likely that he saw other women from time to time, which was okay with her, provided she was still the one who held his heart. Yet, as the months droned on and Ted came home less and less it had become apparent to her that she'd been replaced.

This was more than just a little wandering and exploration. It seemed as though he'd entered some kind of serious relationship with someone else. Why else would he become so totally absent at home? Plus, Ted was a very affectionate man in the beginning of their marriage.

Rachel couldn't imagine that he'd simply grown cold. There had to be a reason he'd started to habitually reject her touch. She'd suggested couples' counseling but Ted insisted that he didn't have the time for that. Once, she'd booked them a romantic getaway to Tahiti, and Ted simply canceled on the day they were supposed to leave—claiming that there was some kind of emergency at work.

They'd met in college and had wed shortly thereafter. Their friends and family had been thrilled with the match, Ted—a successful handsome defense lawyer, and Rachel—a school teacher, seemed to have so many things in common. Yet, as time passed, their interests changed.

Rachel became less interested in the constant hustle and bustle of budget cuts and field trips, and she longed to explore her other interests—like attending the ballet and spending hours wandering the halls of art museums. Those things just didn't interest Ted. Ted cared only about two things: money and women.

Rachel sighed to herself as she blew out the candles on the table. For as much as she still loved Ted, it was getting difficult, becoming painful to spend so many nights alone. She'd lay awake in bed and wonder what he was doing, who he was with, and why he'd lost all interest in her. She'd worry about the fact that she'd gained a few pounds, and would consider changing her hair color again. Though, ultimately none of those things ever revived his interest in her.

Tonight, was different though.

Another text message came through to Rachel's phone. *I'm sorry. I love you but I just can't do this anymore. I want a divorce. I think we both know it's the best thing for both of us.*

The message made her furious. What kind of jerk broke up with his wife via text message? He didn't even have the decency to tell her to her face. Plus, how dare he say that divorce was the best thing for both of them. It wasn't as if he had any vested interest at all in taking care of her needs or protecting her well-being.

Rachel turned her phone of, and simply knocked a few of the dishes off the table, onto the floor. It felt good to hear them clatter and break, just like she felt she'd been broken inside.

Then, she simply stood up and went upstairs to go to bed. As she crossed the threshold to their bedroom, she found that she couldn't go and lay in there even one more night alone. There were too many memories of love-making, of sharing their dreams together and their lives together lingering heavily in the air in that room. Plus, the huge wedding portrait, which hung over their bed made her feel sick. When she'd said her vows, she meant it. She'd had every intention of spending the rest of her life with Ted, and now she'd need to come up with some kind of contingency plan. He'd left her high and dry, just like a few of her ex boyfriends. He'd promised her that he'd be different, that he'd take care of her. Yet, somehow, he'd become a person that was willing to break all of those promises. He was going to leave her.

She turned around and went into the guest-room. Rachel brought her knees up to her chest. She had invested so much of herself into her marriage, but now it was all over. She cried silently in the darkness until her body could sob no more and was finally overtaken by sleep.

Chapter 2

Rachel blasted the radio as she pulled out of the quiet suburb of Elenora. Her family had been disappointed to find out about the impending split and had all strongly suggested Rachel come and stay with her sister Grace.

When Rachel found a notice of eviction on the door shortly after her husband had broken the news, she had little choice. Her impending eviction forced the decision. Apparently, Ted had been secretly pocketing money for the divorce for over a month, and hadn't bothered to pay the last few month's fees on their pricey mortgage. He was an attorney, so it wasn't like he didn't know what was going to happen. He was gearing up for trial—already separating their assets in ways Rachel didn't know about. That morning, she'd checked their shared bank account only to find that the balance had dropped to exactly thirteen cents. She'd called her sister in a panic.

"Ted took all our money," Rachel cried into the receiver. "What? Why would he do that?" Grace had answered. "He told me he wanted a divorce and then he cleaned out our bank account." Rachel swallowed. "He took everything, Grace. He took everything I had." She sobbed. Grace transferred a few hundred dollars into Rachel's account immediately—just enough for travel money and gas.

Then, Rachel had hopped into the car and had drive due south, letting the slight hum of the engine sooth her worries.

She scanned through various radio stations as she cried, and even screamed at times. As she passed out of the dense suburbs of Massachusetts and steadily drove into the hilly pastures of Pennsylvania a sort of gentle peace settled upon her. At least she knew she'd given it her all. She'd given that marriage every ounce of love she had inside of herself. If her ex couldn't see or appreciate that, then at least she could leave knowing that she'd done her best. At least she had somewhere she could go. At least she had a loving family, ready to take her in. In that department, she could have done far worse.

When Rachel finally pulled up into Grace's driveway, she was greeted by five screaming children who promptly threw their arms around her and asked for candy. A tiny sticky finger poked at her calf. "You don't even have any toys for us?"

One of the children asked, growing grumpy. Rachel cringed inwardly. She's been so lost in thought that she'd simply forgotten. Then, one of the little boys threw himself on the ground and wrapped his arms around her legs, refusing to let go. When the other children saw this, they giggled and followed suit.

"Oh, come on, you guys!" Rachel said to the kids, as she struggled to walk...dragging them along. She heard chuckling overhead and looked up. There was an Amish man up on the roof, laughing at her plight.

Grace's sister came out on the porch and the children scattered like roaches, for fear that they'd end up grounded for their antics.

As Rachel ascended the stairs to the home she looked over and to the right she noticed the Amish man again. He was perched up there, calmly working, dressed in a white shirt and black pants making repairs. He tipped his hat in her direction and continued to work diligently.

"Sissy!" Grace called, rushing forward. She wrapped Rachel in a tight hug. "I'm so sorry sweetie. I'm so so sorry about Ted. I really thought he was a good guy. Never in a million years did I think he'd do something like this," her sister said softly.

Grace kissed her on the cheek and then peeled out of the hug and looked deeply into Rachel's eyes, searching them. Rachel looked away. "Did you talk to mom yet?" Her sister asked. Rachel sighed. "No, I need to get my head on straight first." Grace nodded, understanding.

Their mom was a wonderful lady, but she'd certainly want to ask a lot of questions. She'd be well-meaning, but eventually she'd ask Rachel if maybe she hadn't made herself available enough, and if she'd ignored Ted's needs.

Rachel wasn't ready for the line of questioning that would surely come from her. Nor did she feel as though she could handle any insinuation that the failure of her marriage had been her fault. She already blamed herself and the last thing she needed was their mother telling her that it was something she'd done which had ultimately driven Ted away.

Rachel followed Grace into the kitchen where her sister poured her a glass of icy lemonade. "I've been going on this thing called Pininterest to find recipes," her sister said as she slowly pushed the glass in Rachel's direction. She pressed her lips up against the cup and sipped. The sweetness of the drink made her smile. It tasted just like their grandmother's recipe.

Rachel placed her purse down on the table. "How are things going with you?" She asked Grace. "Mostly the same," She said. "You know how Bob is. He loves the boys and doesn't believe in birth control. Look at this place. It's a mess!" Rachel looked around. There were toys everywhere, tracked mud all over the carpet, dirty socks, and field hockey equipment. There were video game cartridges on the floor as well as an assortment of G.I Joes.

"So, do you have a plan yet?" Grace asked. "You should take the bastard to court for everything he's worth." Grace said, blank-faced. "He was the first one to file, so I don't think things will work in my favor, but I'll give it a shot. Mainly, I just want my share of the money from our savings account."

Just then, the children erupted in a chorus of petrified screams out on the front lawn. Both Rachel and her sister Grace jumped up in place, and sprinted outside to see what all the excitement was.

Grace's youngest child, Barry was bent over in the yard screaming and gripping at his arm, where a piece of jagged bone jutted out through the flesh. It looked as though Barry had either fallen or jumped out of a nearby tree. "Gary dared Barry to jump out of the tree and he landed on his arm!" One of the boys screamed. Blood was spewing out of the injury and pooling on the ground as the rest of the children continued to howl.

Before Rachel had even taken in the seriousness of the situation in, the Amish man on the roof, sprang into action.

Rachel watched in awe as he slid down his steep ladder, and scooped up the screaming little boy up into his strong arms in less than a minute. Wordlessly, the entire family, including the quiet Amish man, had piled into the family van en route to the emergency room.

As the other children howled and cried in the back, the man ripped off his shirt off and wrapped up boy's arm, creating a tourniquet to slow the bleeding down. Rachel felt guilty for noticing, but was amazed at the man's incredibly chiseled abdominal muscles and biceps. His skin was smooth and tan, and there were many peaks and valleys in his stomach area. All that hard manual labor must have shaped him up into a machine of sorts.

"We're almost arrived to the help, darling," the Amish man said softly to Barry with a slight accent, as Grace sped through various lanes of traffic and honked her horn like a madman at anyone who dared to get in her way.

The man closed his eyes. "Sweet Barry, let's ask Heavenly Father to hold you in his arms right now and to guide your doctor's hands. We'll also ask that he take your pain away." Somehow, through the pain, the boy managed to hear the soft words.

Barry closed his small eyes like tiny crescent moons and listened as the Amish man prayed over him. The man looked up, concerned. "You'll be just fine." He said to the small child, who nodded and blinked at him through his tears.

Chapter 3

When they arrived at the hospital, the emergency room attendants at once placed Barry on a stretcher and tore off with him. Grace trailed along after them in tow. That of course left Rachel with three screaming children, and a shy Amish gentleman.

"I didn't think that Amish people were allowed to ride in cars," Rachel blurted out. Then, she clamped her hand over her mouth, realizing that she's accidentally said something rude. "Our bishop allows an exception for situations that could result in a loss of life," the man returned with a slight smile. "Oh," Rachel said. She was so embarrassed she felt as though her whole face was turning red. A strange feeling danced in her body. He was so handsome that he made her uneasy. In the English world, he could have easily made a living as a model.

One of the children pulled at the Amish man's shirt. "Is Barry going to be okay, Jed?" The boy asked. So, the mysterious man's name was Jed. Rachel took note.

Jed picked him up and the other children trailed along as he led them over to a cluster of empty chairs.

"When I was about Barry's age, my brother dared me to try and jump from one of our trees into another tree. I climbed all the way up and I leapt off one of the branches, but I didn't get a good hold on the other one. So, just like Barry, I fell all the way down onto the ground with a broken leg."

The children ooh and ahhed. "My mother called for our town doctor and he set my leg in a cast for me, and look at it now!" Jed patted his thigh. "It's just as good as new. Your brother will be fine. It will take a few months to heal, but he'll be all better after that. No need to worry. Just be very kind to Barry when he gets home because he'll need your help."

The day droned on into night and finally the children's father, Bob showed up to the hospital, looking frazzled and worried. "I got here as soon as I could. I had to take a plane because I was out of town on business. Where is Grace? Where are they?" Rachel pointed to the double doors and watched quietly as Bob rushed over to the front desk. "We only allow one parent in the back at a time," the secretary said rudely. Bob nodded.

Then the boys trickled over to him. They sleepily started to give him the details of what happened to Barry. Jed tilted his hat to Rachel. "I'll be on my way now. Please give my regards to Barry and please let Grace know that I will be back to work first thing in the morning." He turned to go.

Rachel turned to Bob. "Do you mind if I give Jed a ride home?" She asked Bob. "Go ahead," he said, sitting down surrounded by his many sons. Rachel turned and jogged after the quiet Amish man.

"Wait!" Rachel called. "At least let me give you a ride home." She squeaked out. Jed smiled kindly. "Only in cases where there's a danger of a loss of life are we allowed to ride in a motor vehicle, Miss. I do thank you for the offer, though." He said. "How are you going to get home?" Rachel asked. Jed shrugged. "I'll walk."

Rachel followed him out of the hospital. "Then let me walk with you, at least." She called, running to catch up.

They slowly started down the long gravel road leading away from the hospital. Rachel's cellphone was tucked away in her purse and if her sister needed her, she could call. The hospital couldn't have been more than a mile from their house, so she could easily be back in a flash if she was needed.

"So, what's it like?" Rachel asked. Jed frowned. "I'm sorry Miss, I'm not following." He said. "I mean what is it like being Amish?" Rachel clarified. "It's the only way of life I've ever known," Jed shrugged. They walked a little way more in silence. "What's it like being English? "Jed finally asked, after a long time. "Painful," Rachel finally answered. Jed nodded.

"See that right there?" He pointed. "That's going to turn into a cicada, and that kind only come around once every twenty-three years." He smiled. "You mean like a moth?" Rachel asked. "I suppose they look more like locusts." Jed said softly. "Why do you think they only come around every twenty-three years?" Rachel asked. "Oh, everything has its own life-cycle. All the good Lord's creations operate on patterns and do what they must to fulfill god's will," Jed answered softly.

"Do you really believe that?" Rachel asked again. "I do," Jed said, nodding with his strong jawline. "I don't know what I believe in anymore," Rachel added. "I used to believe in people. That was why I became a school teacher." Jed smiled.

After a while, Rachel's cellphone began to buzz. She accepted the call and placed it up to her ear. It was her boss from the primary school she'd been teaching at for the last ten years. Budget cuts were forcing them to downsize, and Rachel was going to be among five teachers laid off at her school. They asked her not to return after summer. Rachel disconnected the call and sighed deeply.

"I need a minute," she said to Jed as she tried to catch her breath. "Is everything alright Miss?" he asked, as he reached out to steady her. Rachel cried into the palm of her hands. "Everything is just going so wrong, so fast. I don't understand it." She said through a torrent of tears. Much to her surprise, Jed wrapped his arms around her. She could feel the hardness of his muscles keeping her safe. Her body seemed to relax for the first time in a long while. Then, her heart lurched into her throat and she pulled away.

"It seems the English world moves so quickly," Jed said after a long while. "From the outside, it looks like you can do so many things in just a few hours." He said thoughtfully. Rachel had never thought about it that way. "Things are in constant motion for us," She agreed. Her hand accidentally brushed against his and she blushed as a rush of heat flooded through her body. Her heart fluttered at his touch.

"Are you married?" Rachel asked her new friend. Jed sighed, and trained his eyes on the faraway horizon. "I was married a long time ago," he said finally.

"I lost my wife and our infant in child birth four years ago," "I'm so sorry," Rachel responded. Again, she felt like an idiot. "It's okay," Jed said. "I spent a lot of time with her, just sitting beside the hearth, eating dinner after a long day's work. I loved her very much, but when the good Lord sees fit to take someone, we Amish try and accept it." He seemed to have a sense of peace.

They reached a fork in the road and stopped. "This is the road to my house," Jed said, tipping his hat again. Then he pointed to the other road. "It looks as if it might rain soon, so you should take that road home. I can walk you if you'd like." Rachel sighed. He'd already done so much for her family. She didn't want to inconvenience him any further. "No. I'll see you soon though, Jed." Rachel said, timidly shaking his hand. Then, she turned and jogged down the road leading towards her sister's house.

"Wait!" Jed called after her. "Now that your English school has let you go, you'll be needing another job, no?" Jed asked. Rachel nodded, not quite understanding. "My family owns the bakery down that way and we're in need of another hand to help. Would you like to work there? My sister would be glad to have you." Jed asked, seeming a little nervous.

"I'll be there tomorrow," Rachel said. Then, she shook Jed's hand, pecked him on the cheek, and walked away.

Chapter 4

Rachel waited at the house for a long time before her sister's husband Bob returned with the children. Little Barry was in surgery, and if everything went well, he'd be allowed to come home tomorrow. The other tired children filed into the house and went straight into their bedrooms to lay down without even so much as a word. They were a stark contrast to the boisterous children they'd been only a few hours prior.

"I'm sorry about Ted," Bob said as he poured both he and Rachel cups of coffee. Rachel nodded. "For the record," Bob squinted. "I never really thought he was a good guy." Rachel smiled silently as she made her way into the guest room. Bob was being kind and she appreciated it.

Here she was at 35 years old, squatting in her sister's home, with no else to go. Life had taken her back to zero in just a matter of days, and everything she'd worked so hard to build had been destroyed. She climbed into her small bed and pulled the covers up to her neck. Jed was right. Things moved too quickly in the English world. She needed to make some changes.

In the morning, Rachel showered and then walked down to the bakery that Jed's family owned. He hadn't given her a specific time to be at work, but Rachel guessed she should show up around 8am. Yet, when she arrived the Amish were already in full swing.

"You're late," a beautiful woman with brown hair called to her. "I am? I thought I was early," Rachel said. The woman hurried towards her, wiping her hands on her apron. "I'll not tolerate tardiness," She said as she shook Rachel's hand. "My name is Mary," the woman said, leading Rachel into the back room.

"We start at 4:30 every morning. You can start today by kneading that pie crust there. Rachel went over to the table and pushed up her sleeves. "You'll need to wash your hands first," Mary said, tilting her head to the side. Rachel walked over to the basin and lathered her hands up in soap. Then, she returned to the huge pail of dough and began to knead.

"No, no, honey. You're doing it all wrong," Mary chimed in. She rushed over, washed her hands, and then jumped in. "This way," Mary said. Showing Rachel the proper way to make pie crust.

The day droned on and minutes became hours. The work at the shop was hard labor, but Rachel was amazed at all the things she learned in just one day. When all the shop's customers had cleared out, everyone gathered in the store room to pray before heading out. Rachel's heart fluttered and leapt into her chest when she saw Jed walk in and join hands to pray. After they'd given thanks for the day, everyone split up and headed home.

Rachel turned and started to walk the gravel road leading home. "Hey, Miss!" Jed called after her. Rachel's heart fluttered again. "Is this yours?" He asked. Carrying her sweater. "Thank you, Jed" Rachel smiled, gently taking it from him.

"Might I walk you home, Miss?" Jed asked. "Sure," Rachel smiled.

They started down the road. "So, what did you think?" Jed asked. She'd worked harder than ever before, but she also felt an incredible sense of accomplishment. It was also a totally different kind of work than what she was used to, and that felt freeing. There were no lengthy reports to fill out, no parents to call, no screaming children to wrangle—just her, the dough, and her thoughts.

"Thank you so much for this," Rachel answered. Jed patted her gently on the shoulder, and it felt as though electricity was firing throughout her slender body. His touch moved through her in such a way that she found it difficult to breathe. "Goodnight, Miss." Jed said when they reached the tiny fork in the road. He tipped his hat to her. "Goodnight, Jed," Rachel answered softly as she turned to go.

As the weeks droned on, this became their ritual. Rachel gradually learned all the recipes at the bakery and slowly became skilled at making virtually any and everything they sold. There were not only strawberry pies, but rhubarb, coconut, blueberry, marionberry, and so many others. She also learned to make cakes and fresh doughnuts. After she'd mastered those, Jed's family had let her try her hand out in their family restaurant, which was attached to the bakery. Out back, Rachel learned to churn butter, and how to cure ham. All of this gave her a great appreciation for the simplicity of daily life.

Though their relationship had been slow to warm, Mary eventually had become one of her best friends. Thought she used to fuss at her, Mary eventually learned that Rachel could always be counted upon. Bit by bit, the Amish way of life totally eclipsed Rachel's English life. "So, what brought you out here?" Mary asked, after Rachel revealed that she had once lived in Massachusetts.

She'd shared her life story and Mary had comforted her, offering up a little wisdom. "Ted sounds as though he's' not quite a kind person," she said, speaking of her ex-husband Ted. "Though surely painful, it's better that he's gone on. He's given you freedom from his cruelty at least," Mary added. Rachel had never seen things that way, but her friend was right. She could have wasted her entire life on Ted. At least he'd given her that much back. Instead of wasting her life pouring her love into someone who was clearly incapable of loving her in return, he'd at least had the decency to set her free.

One day, the Bishop stopped by the bakery and sat Rachel down for a chat. He commended her on her hard work. "The Lord works in such mysterious ways," He said to her in Pennsylvania Dutch. "You've been a great friend to the Amish," he continued. Rachel sighed. "You have been an incredible friend to me. I felt totally alone when I came here, and yet you've helped me to create meaning in my life again." Rachel smiled.

The Bishop absentmindedly wiped some crumbs out of his beard. "I've been asked by our community to extend a formal welcome to you. If you wish to see more of the way we work, maybe to attend church, and to mingle among us, you are welcome to do so, provided you have a chaperone at all times." The Bishop extended a warm hand to her.

In the months that had already passed, Rachel had picked up smatterings of their language and was able to cobble a few sentences together. "I am so grateful to your community for taking care of me," Rachel responded. The Amish had become her family, and now the Bishop was allowing her to have an even closer relationship with the people she'd come to view as her family.

Then, a strange thought occurred to Rachel. "What would I have to do to become one of you? To become a full member of the Amish community?" Rachel asked. The Bishop seemed a bit taken back by the question. He considered his answer for a moment and then spoke softly, but decisively. "You'd have to leave your old way behind and pledge your life to the church." The Bishop answered. "If one of our men would agree to take you as his wife, we'd formally accept you into our community and you'd live out the rest of your days here. We would be honored to have you, Rachel."

That evening, as Jed walked her home, Rachel turned the thought over in her mind. Less than three hundred English people had ever joined the Amish, yet the Bishop felt as though they would be lucky to have Rachel among them. Was it fate? Was it God's will? Was Rachel really ready for such a huge commitment?

"Do you think I'd make a good Amish woman, Jed?" Rachel asked. He burst out into a fit of laughter. Rachel punched him playfully on the arm. "Why is that so funny?" She said. Jed stiffened. "You're already like us in virtually all ways but your dress," Jed said, looking at her clothing. "Of course, you'd make a wonderful Amish woman. You're already incredible. I see the way you are at the shop. You pay attention to details, you work hard. You're great with the children."

"I think I want to be Amish" Rachel said to him. A serious look scrawled itself across his face. "If you join our people, you'll share our fate, no matter what that is. It can't be like the English way of committing, but then leaving after things get hard." Jed said. Rachel looked injured. "You think I can't hang when things get tough?" Rachel asked. "That wasn't what I meant to imply," Jed said, trailing after her.

She seemed furious now. "You think it's easy out there Jed?" Rachel asked. "It isn't easy. There's no one leading us or guiding us. When things go sour, most of us are on our own. When can't pop over to our mom's house for a slice of freshly baked apple pie!" She screamed. Then, she accidentally stepped right into a pothole and toppled over. "Rachel!" Jed cried as he rushed over and helped her to her feet, pulling her up by her hand. When she was standing upright. He didn't let go. Their fingers remained entwined. "Please accept my apologies" Jed said softly.

They reached the fork in the road, and this time instead of simply saying goodbye, he ran a few fingers through her hair. "I know you're not like the rest of the English," Jed said to her softly. He smoothed down her hair with his strong hands a bit more. "Were you an Amish woman, I'd have surely asked for you hand in marriage, Miss. I'd have not hesitated." He said. Rachel was shocked. Again, her heart leapt up into her throat. "Are you serious when you say you want to be Amish then?" Jed asked.

Rachel turned his words over in her mind again, and then nodded slowly. "I want to be Amish. I want it more than I've ever wanted anything in my entire life." She finally answered. "I'm glad, because I've wanted you more than I've ever wanted anyone in my entire life. Then, Amish you will be."

Jed leaned down and gave her a gentle kiss on the cheek, before turning to go. Then, he paused directly in his tracks and turned back around. "I love you Rachel Elizabeth Forrester. I've loved you since the day I met you. I'll love you until the day I die."

Tears welled up in her eyes. She wanted to say I love you too, but choked on the words. "I have to get home," she said quietly, as she rushed off in the direction of her sister's home.

When Rachel arrived at the store the next morning for work, the Bishop was already waiting for her. He smoothed down the front of his shirt and clasped his hat in his hand. "Let's sit down and talk, Miss Rachel. Jed came to me in a rush last eve," He said. "He wants to take your hand and marry you." The Bishop added. Just hearing the words made Rachel's heart sing. She nodded, smiling. She could feel her face reddening. The thought made her giddy. Would it really be possible for her to marry Jed, to have his children, to grow old by his side? Jed was so different from Ted. Every evening when they walked home, he listened to her. He loved children and he cared deeply about his community.

The Bishop smiled at her and explained the process. She would have to go and live at Mary's house for at least three months. After that, if she was able to acclimate to the Amish way and the community still felt as though she was a good fit, she could wed Jed after formally converting to the Amish in a church service. The bad news though, was that she would have to leave her old way behind. She'd be able to visit with her English relatives three times each year, but that would be it. She wouldn't be able to see the boys grow old, and wouldn't be able to be a part of their daily lives. Again, she'd have to start over at zero.

Later that night, Rachel packed a few items into a suitcase at her sister's house. She'd talked to the family and had been clear about her intentions. They'd cried together, but had given their blessing. They wanted her to be happy. "I can't believe you're really doing this." Grace said. "You're really becoming Amish?" Grace asked in disbelief. Rachel hugged her sister tight. "I love you. I love so so much," she said as she strode out of the house onto the gravel road.

Chapter 5

Three months later, Rachel stood before her new Amish community. She confessed her sins to the parish and asked for their forgiveness. Then, she pledged the rest of her life to them and to God. She promised to protect their community, their ways of life, and to honor her husband—should she ever find one.

Her friend Mary sat in the first pew and cried tears of joy. As the last words of the vow left her lips, the church erupted in shouts of joy.

Later that evening, her new Amish community held a party in a nearby barn in Rachel's honor. There was dancing, delicious foods from the bakery, and lots of music. "May I have this dance, Miss? "Jed asked, as he slowly approached her.

Rachel bushed and nodded yes as she took his hand. He spun and twirled her as she giggled and laughed. She'd never felt so alive or so free. The music shook the barn to the rafters as they dove around each other and soared in time with the music. When the song ended, she stood there smiling at him as her heart thudded in her chest.

Then, Jed stood up on a table and asked for everyone's attention. "The newest member of our community, Rachel, is such an inspiration to me," Jed said. "She's shown me so many examples of the Lord's love and she's made me want to be a better man." Jed jumped down as he approached her.

Then, he dropped to one knee, clutching his hat to his heart. "Rachel, would you do me the honor of being my wife?" He asked.

The Amish erupted into a chorus of shouts and whoops. "Yes!" She cried, as she took his hand. "Hip hip hooray! Hip hip hooray!" The Amish cried in celebration. The perfect night would surely give way to the perfect life, and Rachel knew she was going to savor every minute.

SAVANNAH'S DILEMMA

MARISA MEYER

A Sunrise for Savannah

When Savannah Richmond receives a notice from a lawyer named Alec Murphy about the last will and testament of a certain Mrs Helen Fritz, she was baffled. She had no relatives in Ohio, much less Amish relatives. Convinced that it was a mistake, she declined the invitation but her curiosity got the better of her.

She decides to visit the small Amish town against her better judgement. But little does she know, how things were about to change. Suddenly she finds herself as the sole heir of the Sunrise Farm, and it doesn't take long for her to clash heads with a certain Joseph Yoder.

Right from the start he expresses his dislike of her, but she refuses to be intimidated by him, and the sooner she sells the farm the better. But when she stumbles on a box of letters in the attic, her entire life is turned upside down.

Chapter 1

Savannah Richmond, an attractive and determined young woman in her late twenties had it all. A high profile career in mobile and digital marketing at Harcourt's Digital in Houston, and here she was, conflicted by her own inner demons and the fact she had descended from hero to zero. At home everyone knew her and everyone adored her, well mostly everyone. But here in Millersburg in Holmes County, Ohio, one of the oldest Amish settlements in the state, no-one even bothered sparing her a second glance or giving her recognition. Not that she expected people to fall at her feet, but she definitely did not bend over backwards to climb the corporate ladder for nothing. It was only two weeks ago when she received a call from Alec Murphy, a legal representative of a certain Mrs. Helen Fritz, who enlightened her of this strangers' passing and that her name was included in the woman's last will and testament. Puzzled at first she turned Alec Murphy down almost immediately, but her friend Lucile kept poking her and urging her on to at least see what it was all about. After a good few glasses of wine and contemplation, she finally decided to go. If nothing came of it, at least she would have had a bit of a holiday, a much needed one. The Maldives or even Hawaii would have been first prize though.

Dressed in a stylish tailored outfit, and her red hair pulled back into a stylish bun, she couldn't help but giggle inwardly at the puzzled stares of the plainly dressed Amish couple, who she could only assume to be family members of Mrs Fritz. She could just imagine what was going through their minds. *Who is this Englisch woman? Why is she here? What business does she have with Helen Fritz?* But she knew as little as the next person and had no clue why she was here, and why her name was included in this woman's will. Savannah had been convinced that it had been a monumental administration error and that they had the wrong person.

She glanced around the old room with its dark mahogany furniture that looked like it was crafted by hand rather than in a big factory.

Everything about the place reminded her of her childhood and she felt half nostalgic. She couldn't remember much of her toddler years, but what she knew was that she was adopted shortly after her fourth birthday, by an upstanding family who couldn't have kids of their own. Donna and David Richmond treated her like their own, and she never needed for anything. Brought up in an upstanding neighborhood, she attended a private school, go to university and live a life of luxury. But even that didn't stifle that constant yearning to know more about her birth parents. And for some reason beyond her understanding, this place magnified that yearning.

An elderly man exited a room to her left and came toward them with a warm smile.

"Good afternoon, thank you all for coming, my name is Alec Murphy" he introduced as he sat down in the wingback chair facing them, "I know this is a little out of the ordinary and that you..." he said looking at the Amish couple, "did not expect to have an Englisch visitor, but it was a specific request from Mrs. Fritz to invite her niece."

Savannah's jaw dropped and she looked from the confused couple to Alec Murphy, "I'm sorry, did you say niece?"

He nodded and smiled, "Indeed, according to Mrs. Fritz's will, you Savannah Mary Richmond, is the niece of Mrs. Fritz.

"Surely this is a mistake? Are you sure you have the right Savannah Richmond?"

Alec smiled and flicked through a few pages, "I'm sure. She personally saw to it that we did not have a case of mistaken identity on our hands."

Savannah slumped back against the chair and processed the information. She had an Amish aunt, yet she had never in her life been to an Amish community.

"Alec, if she says she is not Helen's next of kin, then let it be so," the Amish man piped up.

The woman next to him stayed quiet and kept her eyes lowered but Savannah glared at the man, whose name she learned, was Joseph. He was looking more and more familiar to her by the minute, but she was sure she had never seen him before. From under the brim of his hat, his reddish hair and long beard masked his features pretty well, but it was his eyes that drew her attention, they were Hazel, like hers but cold and hard as if he'd had many hardships in life.

"Unfortunately Helen insisted," Alec said and cleared his throat, "On to business. Miss Richmond, are you happy to proceed?"

Savannah nodded, still convinced that she is no relation of Mrs. Fritz, but curiosity had gotten the better of her. Once this was all over and done with she will decide what to do with her inheritance, not that it would be much. Amish people didn't put a value to any earthly belongings.

Alec read the will. She half expected to be last on the list, but she wasn't. Instead everything started with her.

"To Savannah Margaret Richmond, daughter of my beloved sister Anna Fritz, I wish to bequeath Sunrise Farm, to manage in the event of my passing. With the condition that all employees will remain employed by Sunrise, until such time, the farm is sold..."

Savannah's ears rang, she couldn't believe what she was hearing, and by the look on Josephs face and the way the woman's jaw dropped, neither could they. But that wasn't the only thing that had her head in a spin. If Anna Fritz was her mother as Helen Fritz claimed in her last will and testament, that meant that she was born Amish, which confused her completely. How did she end up being adopted if her mother was Amish?

The rest of the reading was a blur, she paid little or no attention as she tried to make sense of it all, and by the time Alec closed the file and Joseph and presumably his wife stormed out of the living room, she was even more at a loss than ever.

"I don't understand," she whispered, "I never knew my birth mother."

Alec was busy shoving the paperwork back into his briefcase, "Well clearly your aunt knew about you all along otherwise she would not have left the farm to you."

Savannah pinched the bridge of her nose before speaking again, "I don't know a thing about farming, what was she thinking?"

He shrugged and extended his hand, "I'll have my secretary contact you to come and sign the legal transfer documents tomorrow Miss Richmond, and of course you could always consider selling, but I don't think that would be advisable not since this Sunrise has provided a very steady income for the community."

She shook his hand and followed him out of the living room and out of the house, "So what, I'm supposed to just give up my entire life and day job to run an Amish farm?" she protested in a high pitched voice.

"Some sacrifices come with a great reward," he said and tipped his hat, "I'll have the paperwork ready for you by Friday, enjoy your stay in your new home."

"Wait, you mean this is it?" she asked surprised.

Alec nodded, "This is the main residence, but as far as you can see to that hill, is your farm land." He pointed to his left, "Over there is the water purification factory where they filter and bottle spring water and next to that is where they craft handmade furniture for local stores in Ohio. It's quite a business Mrs Fritz had started years ago."

"But I don't even know where to..."

"You'll figure it out. Good day Miss Richmond."

Savannah turned around and looked up at the two story farm house with its white walls and grey pitched roof. It was a house that belonged in a story book. The square windows were edged in white and the shutters drawn back from the windows, were painted moss green. This was the last thing she had expected.

Chapter 2

Even the weather had turned against Savannah. After swinging by Alec Murphy's office to get the estate documents and title deeds to the farm it was a deluge. The icy grey sky from earlier had turned into a blackened sky with rain pouring down with a roar. Soaked to the bone she made it to her car and rested her forehead on her steering wheel.

She simply had no choice, she had to get a hold of an estate agent and get the farm advertised somewhere, there was no way she could take on the responsibility of managing a farm, a furniture factory and a water bottling plant. Her passion was in digital media, gadgets and things that evolved technology. She had been lucky that the house had electricity, which was something she didn't expect. She was under the impression that Amish folk lived as minimalists, by growing their own crops, using coal stoves to cook food and candles to shed light. Although this was true for most part, Mrs. Fritz was obviously in her own league of Amish.

She ducked head low and looked up at the sky from under her visor. She realized that the rain was not about to let up any time soon and started her car. The drive back to the farm wasn't as easy as she thought. Although the man road was asphalt the road to the farmhouse was a dirt road, and the rain had carved mini canyons on either side of the road, which she had to avoid at all cost. The last thing she wanted was to get stuck out here with no way to reach anyone. Her thoughts had barely taken flight when she felt her car slide sideways.

"No-no-no!" she cried and tried to steer the car in the opposite direction, but that only made it worse. She turned the wheel to the right, but no matter what the car was heading in one direction, and that was off-road. She slowed down and pulled up her hand break, her car had come to a complete stand still. She waited a few seconds and slowly put it into gear and pressed down on the accelerator, but instead of the car moving forward, it spewed mud and water up against her rear windscreen. The more she attempted to get the car moving, the more she got stuck. It was a futile effort, she was stranded a mile away from the farmhouse in the middle of nowhere.

"Why do you hate me so much!" she shouted and banged the heels of her palms against the steering wheel, "I pay my tithes! I go to church, is that not enough?"

Suddenly the last few days and her conflicting emotions all collided and big mushroomed cloud of anger and animosity shot up in her soul. She may not be a model Christian, but she wasn't a complete wreck either. Once a month she attended church when it was time to pay her tithes, just like her mother and father did so religiously, but that was clearly not enough, she thought angrily. She rested her head back and closed her eyes, if only her mom and dad had been here, they would have known what to do. A surprise tear trickled down her cheek and she swiped it away with the back of her hand.

"Get a grip Savannah, you're not a child anymore," she scolded herself and reached for the keys.

She was about to start he car and try again to get out of this muddy predicament, when a man thrusted his face right up to the window. Her heart stopped in her chest and in a panic she screamed at the top of her lungs. Then she realized it was Joseph. He waved at her with one hand while hugging his coat firmly around his waist with the other hand.

"I'm here to take you back to the house," he called through the distorting rain.

"No I'm fine, I just need a push," she declined.

Joseph shook his head, "No, you're motorcar is stuck, and this rain is getting worse. Greta told me to come and see you home."

Savannah hesitated and then wound down the window, "Is Greta your wife?"

Taken aback by her question he paused and then nodded, "Yah, but right now you I'm getting soaking wet, and it's not a particular favorite thing to do."

She narrowed her eyes and looked at him, "You expect me to walk all the way in the rain?"

He nodded, "I'm afraid so, unless you want to wait here until your motorcar is swept away."

That sent her heart racing in a panic, she glanced back over her shoulder, she could hardly see a few feet into the torrential rain, then gathered her bag and shoved the title deeds under her shirt and opened the car door. It was like the ice bucket challenge all over again. The moment she set foot out of her car, she was soaked to the bone. Much to her surprise, Joseph was there with a horse drawn buggy, and although didn't offer complete shelter from the rain, it offered some.

A few minutes later, Savannah broke the silence, "You don't like me, do you?"

Joseph kept his eyes on the road, "Why would you think that?"

"Because I'm not Amish, and I'm a stranger."

He glanced sideways at her, "It's not you, and it's the general Englisch arrogance.

She raised her brows, "I'm not arrogant at all!"

Joseph laughed and shook his head, "You come here, convinced that you are no relation to Helen, to do what? Claim a farm that's not really yours to claim. My wife and I have been working on the farm for several years, we've invested all our time into it and you have no idea how to run it."

"So it's all about land for you, I thought Amish didn't place any value in belongings," she retorted.

"A farm is not a belonging, it's a life. A life we value."

Savannah shivered as the cold air sliced through her clothes and hugged her arms around her, "You don't know a thing about me, yet you judge me."

"I see what I see, and what I see is an Englisch woman who relies on modern technology and who is a slave to her own pride."

Joseph's words were like a slap in her face. He made her sound like a boastful peacock. She didn't like him one bit; if anyone around here was arrogant it was him.

When they finally arrived back at the farmhouse, she got out of the buggy and without a word she stalked away from him. He was not worth her time, and unless he paid her some respect she had absolutely nothing to say to him. He can be grateful that she wasn't planning on staying here and running a farm, because he would have been the first on her retrenchment list.

Chapter 3

It's been almost two weeks since Savannah Richmond's arrival and Joseph had to do everything in his power to keep his anger at bay. All she did was sit behind that computer of hers, or have that cellular phone stuck against her ear. What annoyed him even more was that Bishop Stoltzfus had nothing to say and that he had no idea what her plans were with the farm.

"Joseph, you need to give her some time, she only just found out that Helen was her aunt," his wife Greta said softly.

"She does not need time, she needs to go back home to where she came from," he muttered under his breath as he broke a piece of bread, "She will run the farm to the ground."

"You don't know this, the Lord works in mysterious ways."

Joseph looked lovingly at his wife and his heart softened, she was a loving woman who always tries to see the good in people, but his gut told him that Savannah Richmond did not have the interest of the farm at heart.

"You're right, I don't know, but just yesterday there was a man at the farm looking around and making notes. I think she's considering selling it."

Greta's hand went to her chest and she inhaled deeply, "Why would she even consider that? Sunrise has been a part of our community for years."

"She doesn't care," he simply said and slumped back against his chair.

"You must go talk to her Joseph, there are jobs at stake, you must make her understand."

Joseph stood up and paced up and down with his thumbs hooked under his suspenders, "She's too stubborn and arrogant to listen."

Greta shook her head and worried her lip, "Maybe I will talk to her, and she might feel better talking to another woman."

He shrugged and said, "You can try, but don't get your hopes up."

Greta sighed; she knew how passionate Joseph was about Sunrise, and how much time he had put into the place to make it what it was today. When Helen first came up with the idea of purified bottled water and selling it to the community and surrounding towns, he was all ears, and within a year they had built the plant. It had nothing to do with making money, but all about bringing a community together and creating employment for the growing Amish people of Ohio.

She waited until Joseph went to check on the horses before she went to her room. She kneeled next to her bed and prayed for God to intervene and bless the newcomer. Somehow she couldn't help but feel sorry for her. She had no idea what she had gotten into, and finding out that Helen was her aunt must have been enough of a shock for her to deal with.

Chapter 4

It was still dark outside when Savannah got up one early morning, she had spent the night tossing and turning, not sure what to do about her predicament. Her holiday was quickly coming to an end, if that's what you could call it. And she knew that she had tons of work to catch up on once she gets back to the office. With only a few more days left, she had to seriously consider her options. So far none of the potential buyers got back to her with an offer. What was even more puzzling was that every time her phone rang, she hoped that it wasn't a buyer. She was getting used to this way of life, not the Amish way per say, but the peace and tranquility that she would never have in the city. For the first time since she climbed that never-ending corporate ladder, she wasn't running from one meeting to another, or wheeling and dealing her way into a sale. She was actually relaxed and the stress she had now was not even close to the stress she had under normal circumstances. Every day since her altercation with Joseph, she had attempted to get a little more involved with life on the farm. It was the only way she could so Joseph that she wasn't just a short sighted city girl with no farm savvy.

With her cup of tea and one of the bran muffins Greta had brought her the day before, she went outside and sat down on the wooden bench on the porch. The sun peeked through the hazy morning fog that blanketed the entire landscape before her while the sky was painted with elaborate and vibrant oranges, reds and yellows. The sight was simply breathtaking.

"Good morning Savannah," Greta greeted as she entered through the small gate.

"Morning Greta, you're early today."

Greta smiled and Savannah noticed the bunch of flowers she held in her hands.

"Today is Helen's birthday," she said endearingly, I was wondering if you would like to come with me to pay our respects.

Savannah blushed and hid her face behind the brim of her cup. She realized that she hadn't once made any effort to find out who Helen really was. She only assumed that she was adored by everyone who worked on the farm, and that she was her aunt. She felt a twinge of guilt knot her insides and she cleared her throat.

"Let me put this inside," she said and excused herself.

Minutes later she joined Greta and the two of them took a leisurely stroll to the cemetery.

"Tell me about Helen," she asked.

"What would you like to know?"

She shrugged, "Anything, I mean, I never even knew of her existence. What was she like?"

Greta smiled softly, "She was a caring and compassionate soul who gave selflessly of herself."

That was exactly how she imagined her, and how the employees on the farm portrayed her. They weren't shy to tell her how much they loved Helen.

"I tried to look for some photos of her in the house, but I couldn't find any, do you have any I can look at?"

Greta laughed, "Photos are not permitted here, but she was a lovely woman."

Well that was a bit useless, Savannah thought, but left it at that. She would simply have to use her imagination and imagine Helen as an older version of Mary Poppins who loved children and spread joy wherever she went.

"She loved this place, and the people," Greta whispered and she could hear the tremble in her voice.

"Joseph told me, how is he related to Helen?"

Greta went quiet and they walked a little while before she spoke up.

"They aren't related, Joseph was Kemp's best friend, they were like brothers. Kemp was Helen's son. After he died, Joseph took it upon himself to be there for Helen through thick and thin. She took it very hard in the beginning, but eventually she invested all her time and effort into running Sunrise."

"Helen had a son?" Savannah asked curiously.

Greta nodded, "It was a barn accident, almost ten years ago. Kemp had insisted to help in the barn rising, but that day the weather was awful. The elders wanted to stop and carry on the next day, but most of them insisted to push on and get it done. Kemp was just in the right place at the wrong time, he was only fifteen years old when he died."

"I'm so sorry, I didn't know," she whispered and clasped her hands before her.

"It as a long time ago, at lease she had Joseph in the end."

"What about Joseph's parents?"

Greta knelt down and placed the flowers on Helen's grave and said a silent prayer before speaking again.

"Joseph was an orphan, the Bishop and his wife took care of him as a child, but after Kemp died, Helen became his caretaker."

No wonder he's so passionate about the farm, she thought. It was much more than just a novelty pass time or job security, Sunrise meant something to him, and it was something she could never relate to. But maybe, just maybe, if she allowed herself to open up and actually get to know these people, she might change her mind. What she didn't understand was why Helen didn't just leave the farm to Joseph, it simply made no sense.

Chapter 5

Over the next few days, Savannah had come to learn and understand why Joseph was so angry with her. And if she had to be honest with herself, she could quite easily have been in his shoes, and she would have reacted the same way he did. With this little bit of insight she did her utmost to try and be nice, which failed most of the time, but she wasn't ready to give up. Sooner or later he would have to accept the fact that she was the owner of Sunrise, for now anyway. The farm was still up for sale, but she was in no hurry to sell anymore. Maybe they could come to some agreement to have Joseph and Greta run the farm while she continues with her life in the city. And every now and again she could come here and spend a week or two just to catch up and get away from city life. In concept it sounded like a good plan, but whether or not it would work, was another story all together.

Instead of spending her time behind her laptop and making business calls, she decided it was time to get more involved in the farm and really get to know the people who worked here. Greta had involved her into their weekly quilting sessions on a Wednesdays and bread baking on Thursdays. The rest of the week, Savannah got to know the people who worked on the farm and they were slowly starting to grow on her. Although they worked really hard, they loved what they did and never complained. They were a grateful people with big hearts. The modern world and sceptics out there really did a number on the Amish people by making them out to be some sort of a cult. But in essence they were just normal people with a different set of rules and high moral values.

Time had gone by so fast and by the time the weekend arrived, Savannah was even more confused than ever. Laying in her bed and staring up at the ceiling she tried to figure out what to do next. By Monday she would have to go back to work, and after three weeks at Sunrise, the corporate ladder seemed more like a prison to her. From the carousel of thoughts that spun through her mind, clarity formed.

She had been in this house all this time and the only spaces she knew were in the bottom half of the house, the kitchen the living room, the bathroom and the bedroom she slept in. She hadn't bothered to dig around and get to know the old women who stayed in this house. She shot up and slipped her feet into her slip-ons then reached for her gown and put it on. It was time she got to know Helen Fritz. She walked to the stairwell and made her way up the stairs, the walls were decorated with a few landscape paintings and ornaments that hardly matched. There were only two rooms upstairs, one looked like a small office and the other was a bedroom, that was small and stuffy. It looked like a kids room and Savannah realized that this must have been Kemp's room. She entered the room and glanced around, a single bed stood in the corner with a nightstand to its left. On it was a bible and a small wooden horse. To the left of the room was a free standing closet painted green with floral borders on the door. Again no pictures of family or friends, and no magazine posters, other than the cuckoo clock against the wall, it was bare.

She exited the room and closed the door behind her; at the end of the short hallway was a narrow staircase. That had to be the attic; she thought and ventured up the stairs. The attic with its low beams was small, and the amount of stuff stored made it even smaller. Dust had settled on everything over the years, and cobwebs ran along the borders of the ceiling. A shiver ran down her spine, she hated spiders more than any other creepy bug. Everything in this attic had been out of sight out of mind, long forgotten like old memories buried in the confines of a lost mind. With the only light coming from the small round window at the end of the attic it was hard to make out much, so she made her way through the junk to where the most light was. She had no idea where to start and turned around to assess her surroundings. A shoe box caught her eye, it was tied with string and on it in big letters were written *Private.* Curiosity got the better of her and she reached for the box, found a spot to sit down and untied the string. It was filled with papers and letters, she took out the envelopes who were bunched together and set them aside. At the bottom of the shoe box she found a small doll made of material but it had no face. And next to it a small babies rattle, but what she didn't expect was to find a photograph. It had already deteriorated with age. It was a photo of a woman holding two babies in either arm. As far as she knew Helen only had one son, so this could not have been her. Turning it over she tried to read the faded inscription, raising it to the light to see better it said *Mary and Joseph, born 24 June 1991*. She realized then that this must have been a part of Josephs past. Helen had told her Joseph was raised by the Bishop, so this must have been his birth mother. The woman in the picture was beautiful, even in her Amish clothes, but she looked sad.

Savannah put the picture back in the box and then started at the top of the pile of letters. As she read through the letters one by one she started to get the bigger picture. The woman in the picture must have been Annabelle, and Joseph had been one of a twin. None of the initial letters had mentioned anything about his twin sister Mary though. Intrigued by what was unfolding before her she kept reading. Letter after letter telling the tale of heartache, love and infidelity, something that was highly frowned up on by the Amish.

Towards the bottom of the pile of letters, there was one envelope that stood out, it was a white envelope with doves printed on the flap, and the return address was a small suburb in Houston. With trembling fingers and a feeling of premonition Savannah opened the letter and started to read it, word for word, line after line, until the letters distorted and looked like running ink before her eyes.

The letter had been addressed to Helen and was from Anabelle and in it she confessed to having had an affair with Helen's husband Caleb and how she had fallen pregnant. She described in detail how terrible it was to live with that secret for so long, and how she tried to tell the truth, but couldn't bring herself to do so. But it was the last paragraph that broke the bow.

...I couldn't take them both, so I had to leave Joseph behind, but I know that he would grow into a strong man, just like his father. As for Mary, I had finally decided it was time to do the right thing. I had given her up for adoption; it was an open adoption but I have decided to let her grow up without knowing me, it is for the best. The couple who adopted her is a lovely couple and they will take great care of her. Their names are Donna and David Richmond; according to the social worker they have christened her Savannah Mary Richmond. One day, when I'm no longer around, I hope you will find it in your heart to reach out to her and introduce her to her brother...

The room spun and the letter floated to the floor like a feather. She slid off the box she sat on and fell to her knees as tears streaked down her face. She was shaken to the core. All this time, she had a twin brother, right here in Ohio and she never knew! She went through the motions of shock, sorrow and anger. How could a woman give up her children, even worse, separate twins? What a terrible thing to do!

She sat up in the attic for hours as she tried to come to terms with everything, and when she finally calmed down she gathered the letters and stuffed them back into the shoebox. She felt lost and confused, but happy at the same time. Her emotions were like a ball of tangled wool, a complete mess, but one thing was certain. Joseph deserved to know the truth.

With determination she made her way over to Greta and Joseph's house, not quite knowing what to say to them, but for a start she will hand him the letter.

She knocked persistently on the door, "Greta, Joseph!" she called.

The door opened up and Greta's smile faded instantly, "Savannah? You've been crying is everything all right?"

"Can I come in?" she whispered.

"Sure." Greta stood aside and let her in, "What's wrong?"

"Is Joseph here?" she asked.

"No, he's at the barn, is there anything I can help with?"

Savannah worried her lip with the shoebox clutched under her arm. She had no idea how to start or what to tell Greta, but perhaps it was a good place to start.

"Maybe you can help," she whispered and walked through to the kitchen, "I found this in Helen's attic."

"You found a shoebox?"

"Well, yes, but oh... I don't know Greta, I honestly don't know."

Greta reached for the shoebox and opened it up, "I'm not quite sure I follow, you found a bunch of letters."

Savannah reached for the letter on top and handed it to Greta, "If only these were just letters."

Greta sat down and opened the letter and started to read while Savannah watched her nervously and with anticipation. Greta too went through the motions of utter shock, her jaw dropping and tears threatening to spill before she gently folded the letter closed. One could cut through the tension like a hot knife through butter and neither woman knew what to say as they both contemplated the weight of the situation.

"We need to tell the Bishop," Greta said first.

"Why the Bishop, what good will that do? We need to tell Joseph," Savannah objected.

"You're right, we need to tell Joseph, and then tell the Bishop."

It was obvious that Greta was overwhelmed by this news as she grabbed a cloth and started to wipe the already spotless table.

"Tell me what?" Joseph asked as he suddenly appeared in the doorway.

Greta gasped and the salt and pepper shakers she held in one hand went crashing to the table and cheeks turned red. Savannah felt the blood drain from her face as she whipped around to look at him.

For the first time since her arrival at Sunrise, and after spending most of her time with Joseph and Greta did the strong resemblance between her and Joseph make sense. He had the same color hair as her, those hazel eyes were almost an exact match to hers. Even the shape of their noses matched. It was as if a veil had been lifted.

"Are you both just going to stand there and stare at each other?" he asked petulantly as he looked from his wife to Savannah.

Greta stepped forward, "Joseph I think you need to sit down."

Joseph studied the two women and frowned, he knew exactly what this was all about. Savannah had found a buyer and she was here to gloat. Instead of sitting down he crossed his arms and pushed out his chest.

"If this is about you selling Sunrise, then you're in for..." he started.

"Savannah is your twin sister." Greta said at the same time.

"...a fight Miss Richmond..." Joseph paused, "She's my what?"

Greta reached for the letter and held it towards Joseph, "Savannah is your twin sister, Helen's sister Annabelle was your birth mother she..."

"Joseph, I didn't know," Savannah interrupted, ringing her hands nervously together.

Joseph looked at the two women, as if they had gone completely mad and then at the letter he had in his hand.

"Here sit down," Greta said and led him to the chair, "You need to read the letter, then you'll understand."

Joseph moved slow, almost too slow as if time had momentarily slowed down enough for him to try and process what just happened. And as he read the contents of the letter, realization swept over him and things finally started to fall into place.

The day he saw Savannah, he was surprised at how much she reminded him of himself, the red hair and her stubbornness. It was all so surreal. He too went through the motions until anger sprung up from the fountain of his soul.

He stood up and tossed the letter aside, "I don't care what you are, but I won't let you sell Sunrise for any amount."

She may be his sister in blood, but she was Englisch and her plans were to sell off Sunrise and move on with to her Englisch life.

Savannah stepped closer and reached to touch his arm. "I'm not selling Sunrise; I've decided to stay here. This is where I belong."

Joseph shook his head and took of his hat, dragging his hand through his hair, "You can't just wake up one day and decide to be Amish, you've been in the city your entire life."

Greta stepped closer and rested her hand on his chest, "Joseph, she is your twin sister."

He knew in his gut that it was true, even though his brain was fighting the logic, he knew. He closed his eyes and held his breath. He had so many questions now that the truth was out there, but he also knew that he would probably never find the answers.

Savannah's heart pounded in her chest as she looked at her twin brother. Things may be daunting at first, but if she could prove to Joseph that she was as much a part of Sunrise as he was, he might one day accept her as his sister. After all, it was never her choice to go; she was as innocent in this as he was. Impulsively she flung her arms around Joseph's waist and hugged him, and a sob tore through her chest. She always wanted a brother since she can remember, and now her dreams had finally come true.

"Oh praise the Lord!" Greta exclaimed and wrapped her arms around both of them. "God does work in mysterious ways."

They all cried and laughed, and the rest of the day they spent reading the rest of the letters and spending time together. Savannah told Joseph about her adopted parents and her life as a child, and Joseph shared parts of his life.

Sunrise was no longer just a farm; it was a symbol of reunion and a new day.

***

Psalm 30:5[1]

---

1. *https://bible.knowing-jesus.com/Psalm/30/5*

For His anger is but for a moment, His favor is for a lifetime; Weeping may last for the night, But a shout of joy comes in the morning.

NAOMI'S PROMISE

ELAINE LANE

61

Lancaster City, Pennsylvania, 2017

Rock music blasted off a boombox speaker. A mechanic in blue overalls crouched beside a dismantled motorcycle, the deep thump of the bass rattling the tools littered around him.

"—Yoder! Hey, Yoder!" The shout cut through the music and jolted Jacob from his focus. He stretched out an arm and dialled the volume on the boombox down.

"Did you hear what I said?" The assistant manager of Jim's Auto Repair, Pete, stuck his head into Jacob's work space.

"No, sorry," said Jacob, taking off his cap to run a hand through his unwashed hair. He stopped mid-motion and blinked down at the engine grease coating his fingers. "Say it again?"

"Don't take this the wrong way, okay?" said Pete coming forward to stand in the middle of the little garage space, "I wouldn't ask you if it wasn't relevant."

"What is it?" Jacob sat up straight. "You're making me nervous talking like that."

"You're Amish, right?" said Pete.

"I was," said Jacob, rubbing the tattoo at the back of his neck and looking away. "But what does that have to do with anything?"

"There's some Amish people out there. I think they might be looking for you."

Jacob stared at Pete, thinking maybe he'd heard wrong. They were looking for him? It had been almost twenty years since he'd had any contact with that world. Time and new technology had changed many things here on the outside—the internet, smartphones, Google, Facebook, Youtube, Amazon, Netflix. . . But Jacob didn't doubt that the Amish lived exactly the same way now as they did two decades ago. He wasn't sure if he wanted to see the proof of that with his own eyes though. It was a past he'd left behind long ago.

"Oh, and uh," Pete said, "there's a pair of police officers with them."

When Jacob went to meet the strange group standing outside in the hot, dusty yard of Jim's Auto, the police officers immediately came up to him. "Are you Jacob Yoder," said the taller, older-looking officer, "grandson of Benjamin Yoder?"

"Yes, that's me." said Jacob, looking between the officers and the Amish group standing a few feet away. They avoided his gaze the moment he turned their way. Oh, that's right, thought Jacob, I'm still under the Bann. He had forgotten what being shunned felt like.

"We are very sorry to tell you that your grandfather has passed away," one of the officers said. "He was trying to repair the roof and. . ."

##

Bird-in-hand, Pennsylvania, 2017

Jacob left his motorbike and helmet next to an oak tree at the end of the dirt road and made his way down the hill on foot.

The house Jacob grew up in was just a tiny, one bedroom log cabin with a loft. Grandpa slept in the bedroom and Jacob slept in the loft. But more often than not, Jacob slept wherever he felt like, especially in the summer, when he'd fall asleep outside, under a tree by the stream, or on the hill overlooking Naomi's house.

It was just his secret, but he used to spend long hours sprawled in the dark, on that hill, staring at the distant light of the gas lamps twinkling from her bedroom window. In the weeks before he'd left, he'd sat at that hill and pondered, over and over again, whether he could ask her to run away with him. He'd gnawed over the idea with hope and fear and a dizzying kaleidoscope of things in his heart, until he was left with no choice but to just pull her aside one night so he could finally tell her. Run away with me, Naomi.

But he never told her. He couldn't. Not after what she'd said.

Caught by an impulse, Jacob turned away from his grandfather's log cabin and headed instead towards the old footpath leading up to the hill where he'd once watched the glow of Naomi's bedroom light from afar. A mild wind rustled the trees as he climbed the hill.

Standing in the open space of the hilltop, Jacob looked out over the countryside he spent the first sixteen years of his life in. When his gaze landed on Naomi's family home, he froze. The Stoltzfus' house was gone. In its place was a small cluster of buildings that could not have been anyone's home. What the hell?

Jacob knew that time changed things. It had been twenty years after all. But the Amish didn't sell away family land so easily. What would they do without land? Live in apartments like the English in the city?

He turned and ran back down the slope, past old streets and familiar landmarks—that bridge over there, that windmill, that signboard that's still there after twenty years—until he stood in front of one of the buildings he'd seen from the hilltop. Up close, it looked like a schoolhouse.

The sound of children shouting at each other drifted to him from an open window nearby. Jacob walked closer and peered in. So it really is a schoolhouse, he thought. I wonder what the other buildings are for. He scanned the room: rows of chairs, children shouting at each other, another one crying on the ground, and a teacher at the blackboard writing equations calmly. Something's wrong with this picture.

At the back of the classroom, the two kids lunged at each other, hands grabbing at shirt fronts and suspender straps. From experience, Jacob knew that fists would fly in about a minute or less.

"Hey," Jacob called out to the teacher. "Your students are fighting, why aren't you doing anything?"

The teacher kept writing equations on the board, as if she hadn't heard anything. What's wrong with her? Something about her made him stare. . . But all Jacob could see was that she wore the same plain dress and white kapp as every other unmarried Amish woman in town. Then she turned to face the room and Jacob caught the sudden dismay bloom on her face at the sight of the chaos behind her.

That face. That silver-blond hair peeking from under her kapp. Those wide, grey eyes. It was Naomi Stoltzfus.

Jacob stared at her through the open window as she mediated between the quarreling students, her small hands gesturing in the air. Something about the way she talked to the children, something about her delayed reaction struck him as strange. He couldn't put his finger on it.

She suddenly glanced his way and Jacob's pulse jumped as he ducked out of sight. He crept away from the window, careful not to be seen. His heart raced in his chest. Jacob didn't think he was ready to face Naomi again. Not after the way he'd left all those years ago.

Without a single word of goodbye.

##

Bird-in-hand, Pennsylvania, 1997

Sixteen-year-old Jacob Yoder carefully eased the borrowed motorcycle behind a dense shrub of holly. The rolling tires crunched loudly over twigs and leaves on the ground. He hung the bike's keys on a chain around his neck, just to be sure he wouldn't misplace them.

Sunday school activities had finished more than a few hours ago and the school grounds were mostly deserted but Jacob looked around to check again. If he got caught lurking where he wasn't supposed to be, and with forbidden technology too, his Bann might just be extended for life. But. . .

He thought of Naomi's small, delicate hands flipping a book, the soft, silver blonde strands of hair escaping her kapp, the hidden smile in her grey eyes whenever her called her name and she'd look up from her reading to meet his gaze. But, it's worth it.

Tonight, he would tell her, once and for all.

Jacob took a hair tie out of his pocket and pulled his brown hair back into a little topknot, wincing at the twinge of pain from the back of his neck. He rubbed a hand over the inflamed skin and the new tattoo there. I wonder what she'll make of this, he thought. Better not let anyone else see it though. Jacob wasn't sure if getting a tattoo was a huge violation of the Ordnung or not. It wasn't like any of the adults talked about tattoos or explicitly warned them against it. Getting tattoos just wasn't something the townsfolk of Bird-in-hand had ever thought about.

But Jacob had never been like most of the people here. He probably never would be. Would Naomi—the schoolmaster's golden daughter, the paragon of filial obedience and Amish piety—accept him as he was? Was it selfish of him to want to draw her out of this insular, old-fashioned world they lived in and make her share the other half of Jacob's world? The half that he stepped into whenever he showed up for part-time work at the auto-repair shop, and whenever he hung out with the non-Amish friends he made there. . . Was it wrong of him to want to share with her all those things that made Jacob who he was?

Distant laughter and shouts of encouragement drifted over to him from the parking lot on the other side of the schoolhouse.

Naomi Stoltzfus felt the sweat rolling down her back, beads of it dripping into her eyes. Her kapp was damp too. She longed to take it off and feel the cool wind ruffling through her hair, but there were boys here; it would be improper. On the other side of the net, the opposing team was deciding on whose turn it was to serve.

In the distance, the last of the sun disappeared behind the tops of the trees.

They had set up a volleyball net on the empty, gravel-lined buggy stand and parking lot of the town's only school and had been playing since early afternoon. It was almost too dark to see the ball now. From the nearby stand of oak trees, crickets had begun to chirp in a rhythmic chorus. They would have to break to prepare for the evening sing soon.

The Chickadees' would be hosted by the Beilers this week and Naomi could easily imagine the little Beiler kids sneaking bites of the snacks meant for the guests. The Chickadees currently consisted of twenty boys and thirteen girls. They considered themselves a middling low, middling conservative youth group, traditionally known for and united by one thing: their love for sports.

Before Naomi had joined, the popular sport in the group had been baseball. But by the time Naomi was of age, it had shifted to volleyball. Naomi privately thanked God for that every Sunday because it was the only sport she knew. If Jacob hadn't dragged her into playing volleyball with him all those years ago, she'd have turned into a pale, indoor-bound girl who only read books and did domestic chores. She was the schoolmaster's daughter after all. Her father gave her books to read, her mother gave her house chores to do. And Naomi liked making her parents proud that she could follow the fine examples they set for her.

At the rear of their makeshift volleyball court, Naomi bent her knees, arms at the ready as she tried to make out the other team's server. Blond, blue-eyed and easygoing Sam Schrock waved at her from the serving zone.

Next to her on the back row defense, Mary-Anne giggled and inched towards Naomi. "He really likes you, doesn't he?" she said. "Has he asked you to ride in his buggy yet?"

"I hope he doesn't," said Naomi.

"Why not?" said Mary-Anne. "He's nice."

Sam Schrock might be nice, but he wasn't Jacob. Regardless of what the rest of the community of Bird-in-hand thought of Naomi's oldest childhood friend—a social deviant, a rebel, a bad influence, a rotten apple from a rotten tree—to Naomi, Jacob Yoder was. . . How could she describe what Jacob was? Under those slightly drooping lids that made him look sleepy or indifferent to others, Naomi knew that he had the clearest hazel eyes, and sometimes when he smiled a certain way, a little dimple appeared on his left cheek. When he laughed—

"Naomi, watch out!" one of the girls shouted.

Naomi blinked into focus just long enough to see the ball rocket towards her face. It was too late to dodge, nevermind receive. It smacked her in the nose and bounced off, rolling to a stop at one of the middle blocker's feet. Naomi clapped a hand over her nose as she felt a thin trickle of blood drip down over her upper lip.

"Naomi!" Mary-Anne rushed to her side. "Are you alright?"

Naomi nodded, letting go of her nose to look at the tiny smear of blood on her hand. "I'm fine." She swiped at her nose again to confirm. "It's not bleeding anymore."

Reuben, the oldest in the group, clapped his hands to call everyone's attention. "Right, then! I think that's enough playing for tonight. Go home, wash up, and let's meet again at the Beiler's by eight."

The Chickadees dispersed with calls of 'good game!' and 'see ya soon!'

"Are you sure you're alright?" said Mary-Anne, her green eyes full of genuine concern. Behind her, David Hershberger had brought his buggy around from the other parking lot and now stood next to the horse's head, looking in their direction. He lifted his hand in greeting when he caught Naomi's gaze.

"I am," Naomi said. "You go on ahead. Your boyfriend's waiting."

"Don't call him that yet!" Mary-Anne said, flushing. "He's just giving me a ride home."

"Of course he is," said Naomi with a wink.

"But what about you?" said Mary-Anne.

"I'll wash up at the sinks and walk home," said Naomi, rubbing at the dried blood on her upper lip. "Then I think my dad will probably drive me to the Beilers. Or I'll just walk again."

"Okay," said Mary-Anne. She waved at Naomi as David Hershberger snapped the reins and the horse trotted off.

Naomi watched the two of them ride away, sitting side by side on the buggy, happily chatting. David seemed like a good match for Mary-Anne. Both of them were kind, patient and hardworking. Both of them were model youth who followed the Ordnung and were well liked by everyone. Naomi could easily see these two getting married by the end of their rumspringa.

At the sinks next to the outhouse, Naomi splashed water onto her face and rubbed away the dried blood under her nose. The gaslamp she had set on the floor cast a weak, flickering light, barely enough to see by. For some reason, she couldn't get her mind away from the perfect picture Mary-Anne and David had made as they drove away. Was she envious of them?

A sudden shadow detached itself from the treeline. It was the only warning she got before something grasped at her wrist and pulled her into the bushes, a hand over her mouth muffling her shriek. And then she was in complete darkness. . .

Thump, thump. What was that sound? Thump, thump. A heartbeat? Her own heartbeat galloped away in her chest, but this one was slow and steady. Naomi became aware of the warm hand on her wrist, the other over her mouth, the heat of the body pressed close to her own, and the strong, steady heartbeat next to her ear.

There was a man behind her. She was being held by a strange man in the dark. She stiffened in fear and drove an elbow into her assailant's gut.

He grunted and whispered, "Stop it. It's me!"

Naomi sucked in a startled breath and froze. That voice. And that familiar scent: engine grease, metal, sweat, wet grass, and cigarette smoke. Jacob? What was he doing here? He was under the Bann, he can't be here. And why did he snatch her into the bushes?

Jacob drew his hand away from her mouth. "Look over there," he whispered, pointing at where Naomi had been washing her face less than a minute ago. Tall, blond. . . It was Sam Schrock. He stood by the sinks, looking around for Naomi. He picked up her abandoned gaslamp with a puzzled frown.

"I swear she was here just a second ago," Sam muttered.

"I don't like him," Jacob murmured, his warm breath ghosting over her ear. She suppressed a shiver and jostled him away slightly.

"You can't be here!" she whispered. "What if someone saw you?"

Sam raised the lamp, peering in their direction. "Is that you, Naomi?"

I am an idiot, thought Naomi. Did he hear me?

Jacob gripped her wrist tighter as Sam walked forward to peer into the darkness. A rustle among the bushes to their left had all three of them looking in that direction. A fox kit leaped out of the foliage, waving its little, white-tipped tail. A larger fox, the mother no doubt, chased the kit into the open. It froze in place at the sight of Sam and the gaslamp he held aloft.

"Now!" said Jacob, sliding his grip down her wrist to grab her hand tightly. He pulled her further off the cleared paths of the school grounds and into the dark forest. They made a racket disturbing tree branches, bushes, and twigs as they passed, but whatever reaction Sam had to the sudden noise, Naomi didn't have time to find out. Jacob was running too fast.

"Hey!" Naomi shouted with a wheeze. "Slow down! Why are we running?" She placed a hand over her chest where her heart pounded so fast it scared her just a little bit. Her heart never beat like this during volleyball. She really wasn't meant for running around in the woods.

Jacob stopped and looked back. His eyes were bright, his breathing a little faster than usual, but he wasn't as winded as Naomi. "I don't know," he said, rubbing the nape of his neck. "I guess, I felt like it." Naomi caught something like a smudge of ink trailing over the skin of his neck, but he shifted and it disappeared out of sight. Was it just a shadow?

"You felt like it?" she said, incredulously.

"I've got something I want you to see," he said, grabbing her wrist again and pulling her along, at a walk this time.

"Stop dragging me everywhere," she said.

"If I didn't drag you everywhere, you'd spend your life behind a desk, studying."

"I read, not just study," she said. It was an old argument they had never resolved. Bickering over it had become a habit at this point. "There's a difference."

"Yeah, yeah," said Jacob. "Oh, here it is!" He parted a dense clump of holly bushes to reveal something that gleamed silver, black, and red in the filtered moonlight.

"What is it?" Naomi looked between the bushes and Jacob's grinning face. He glowed with so much excitement, Naomi almost lifted up her hand to shade her eyes.

Jacob pulled it out slowly into the open. Black grips, the gleaming curve of silver handlebars and side-view mirrors, a round headlight, a wheel, an engine, a red-painted body, another wheel, and a license plate.

"Jacob, what. . ." said Naomi, in shock.

"It's a 1980 Yamaha XS650," said Jacob, waving his hand at it like a farmer announcing his best wares at the market.

"I have no idea what that means," she said. "But how did you get a motorcycle?"

"I'll tell you later," said Jacob. The whites of his eyes and teeth stood out in the darkness. He gripped her fingers and squeezed. "Will you come with me tonight?" he said, solemnly.

"They'll be expecting me at the Beilers," she said.

"Just for tonight," said Jacob. He rummaged in the bushes, drew out a helmet, and fitted it on her head, strapping it securely. Then he clapped his hands over her helmeted head and lifted her face up. He looked her in the eye, leaning in so close that she couldn't help but notice how his eyelashes fanned out and curled darkly against his skin, how his pupils dilated wide in the moonlit darkness. "Let's go for a ride, just for tonight," he said.

"I'll get in trouble," she said, without much conviction.

He let her go, stepping back to strap on his own helmet and loop his leg over the motorcycle. "Tell them I stole you away against your will."

"Stealing away maidens like this," said Naomi, as she tentatively got on behind him and wrapped an arm around his waist. "You are an evil villain, mister."

"You love me," he said, laughing. He kicked the engine to life and didn't hear the response she whispered into his back. For decades afterwards, Naomi would wish that she'd shouted it in his ear instead. I do love you. . . Jacob Yoder.

##

Bird-in-hand, Pennsylvania, 1997

The cold wind whipped past them, buffeting their clothes and the exposed skin of their wrists and neck. Jacob loved the roar of the motorcycle's engine, the way it hummed as it sped down the highway like a living animal, faster and wilder than a real horse. The first time he took this bike to the highway and rode it at the maximum speed limit, he whooped inside his helmet until his ears rang with echoes.

But this time, with Naomi riding behind him, it was all he could do to keep his focus on the road. He was almost afraid to breathe, all too aware of the way Naomi's delicate arms fit around his waist, the soft, subtle press of her chest on his back. . . Whoa, don't go there, Jacob, he thought to himself, cutting that train of thought before he could dwell too long on it.

They rode westward along the PA-340 highway, straight along the US-30 towards downtown Lancaster. Sixteen minutes later, Jacob entered the campus grounds of Franklin & Marshall College, coasting slowly to a stop in front of a well-maintained two-story building. To Jacob, it had always looked like it could be a courthouse or a government building. Tall, white columns supported a grand porch, and broad stone steps lead up to the glass double doors. Black painted park benches, electric street lamps, and trimmed hedges decorated the front lawn.

All was quiet except for the rhythmic chirp-chirp of the crickets in the nearby stand of oak trees. Jacob watched Naomi take off her helmet and arrange her hair back into her kapp. She stared around at the deserted campus and Jacob stared at her face as he hung his helmet on one of the bike's handlebars.

"Shadek Fackenthal Library," said Naomi, looking up at the large gold letters inscribed into the white painted gable of the library's facade. Her wide grey eyes, taking in everything in front of her, looked otherworldly in the light of the electric lamps. She turned those eyes to Jacob and he swallowed, his mouth suddenly feeling a little too dry. "Hey," she said, so softly he wouldn't have heard her if it hadn't been so quiet, "why are we here?"

Jacob shrugged as casually as he could. "I thought you'd like it, that's all." He waved an arm at the building. "There's books," he said, lamely. "And it's really pretty inside."

Naomi looked at the library. "It's closed," she said.

"What?" Jacob ran up to the double doors and grabbed one of the handles. His pulling only rattled the door. "But the lights are all on! See?" He waved an arm at the windows. "It's bright as daylight in there."

"I think the English just do that," said Naomi. "It's all electric anyway."

Jacob slumped his shoulders and rubbed at his neck. "I'm sorry. I brought you all the way here for nothing."

"Jacob," said Naomi, "what's that on your nape?"

"Oh, this?" Jacob clapped a hand over the back of his neck, flushing. "It's a tattoo."

"A tattoo?" Naomi said. "You got a tattoo? When? Let me see." She reached for his collar.

"Wait, wait!" Jacob flung her grasping hands away and turned so she couldn't see it. "Before that, I have something to say first."

Naomi's eyebrows shot up. "You're planning to run off and join a circus? Is this tattoo an initiation mark from the circus then?" She chuckled.

"I'm serious, Naomi." Jacob looked down at his feet, his mind awhirl with all the things he wanted to tell her. He had rehearsed this in his head so many times, but now he had no idea where to begin or how to say it.

His plan had been to show her how amazing the library and the college was. And then he'd casually bring up the idea that she could study here, be a college student. She was smart and she loved to study. And then he'd mention that he had a job offer at an auto shop and parts dealer. She could get scholarships and loans and he'd work to support them both. They could. . .

They could live together. Here in the city.

But before all that, there was one thing Jacob needed to say first. He opened his mouth. . .

Naomi stared up at him, her grey eyes luminous under the glow of the street lamp. She looked like a spirit. "Yes?" she said.

But Jacob couldn't speak at all. Now he understood that phrase in the Psalms: my tongue cleaves to the roof of my mouth. Naomi was still looking at him, waiting. Her lips parted to say something and—

Jacob ducked down and caught her mouth in his. He had no idea what he was doing, but her lips were soft and. . . And this was what he wanted to say. He kissed her slowly, tentatively, trying to pour everything that she meant to him into the way his mouth moved against hers. Naomi reached up to wrap her arms around his shoulders and they kissed until they were both breathless.

When they broke apart, Naomi's small hand was on the nape of his neck. Jacob ducked his head down, resting his forehead lightly on her shoulder so she could see the black lines scrawled on his skin. She traced the still-healing tattoo with a finger.

"So," she said, "what does this script mean?"

"It's Hebrew," Jacob murmured. He straightened up and met her gaze. "It means Na'omi."

They stared at each other, the chirp of the crickets in the trees filling the silence between them, the sound swelling and ebbing like an irregular tide. Jacob wondered if Naomi understood what he wanted to say. He couldn't read the look on her face now. He loved this part of her too, the way she was always so careful, so self-contained, so completely unlike him. But he wished he knew what she was thinking now.

Naomi pulled his head down and kissed him again. It lasted for only a few seconds, but for her to suddenly initiate a kiss like that. . . He stared down at her in wide-eyed shock. "Promise me something," she said, threading cool, smooth hands into his hair and pressing their foreheads together. He felt her breath against his cheek, warm and soft.

"Anything," said Jacob.

"Come back to the Church," said Naomi. "Tell the Bishop you repent." She gave him a smile like the dawn, her eyes bright with a painful hope. "Receive baptism with me. I want to live an Amish life with you."

Jacob looked into her eyes. Run away with me, he wanted to tell her, but Naomi's words echoed in his head. What other answer could Jacob give her except. . . "Okay." He placed his hands over hers. "I promise." How could I live my life without you?

##

The ride back home was like a dream. Naomi sat behind Jacob on the motorcycle and imagined their future together. She pressed close to his back, locking her hands around his middle. With the warmth of his body so close and the solid feel of him in her arms, she imagined what it would be like to have something like this everyday, to have him all to herself like this every morning, and to fall asleep next to him every night.

A five minute walk away from the outermost homestead in Bird-in-hand, Jacob pulled the bike to a halt and let her off. Any closer to town and the rumble of the engine would give them away. Naomi gave him back his extra helmet and he took it without a word. Then they stared at each other in awkward silence.

Things had changed between them. Before this night, or if they hadn't kissed and said everything they said back at the Shadek Fackenthal library, both of them would have simply waved goodbye and parted ways. But now neither of them made a move to leave. I should give him a goodnight kiss, thought Naomi. I should say something more than just 'goodbye' or 'goodnight'. But she didn't move.

Perhaps it had to do with being in a new place, or something about the atmosphere of the Fackenthal library lawn that made it easier for Naomi to say and do all those things. She had kissed him there, she had opened her heart and said things she'd have never imagined she'd be able to say out loud. But now, back in familiar territory, in the place where they grew up together, it wasn't so easy.

Jacob took her hand and dropped something in her palm, closing her fingers over it. "It's the keys to this bike," he said. "You can hold it hostage until I deliver on my promise."

Naomi looked at the set of keys strung on a long silver chain. "A hostage?" she said.

Jacob looked down at his gloved hands. "I don't trust myself to. . . well, if you have the keys, I won't be able to ride away on this thing," he patted the bike's handle. "Call it a token of my promise or a reminder or whatever."

Naomi stared at Jacob's bowed head. She thought of kissing him again or running into his arms and never leaving. Instead, she hung the chain around her neck, tucking the keys into the bodice of her plain dress. "I'll keep them until you need to return the bike to your friend," she said.

Jason smiled down at her. For a split second, Naomi thought there was something a little sad in his smile, but then he leaned in and kissed her and she forgot all about it.

"Are you keeping this bike in that old barn?" she said, when they broke apart. "Wouldn't you need the keys to move it there?"

"Yeah, I'll be walking this bike to the 'secret lair,'" he said, the corner of his mouth quirking up at the emphasis. "I don't need the keys for that."

As she set out for home, Naomi looked back at Jacob one last time.

He stood there on the side of the road, supporting the bike with one hand. With the other he waved and blew her a kiss, his gestures large and dramatic. *I love you too, Jacob Yoder,* she thought quietly. Someday, she'd say it out loud.

If only Naomi had known that she'd wake up tomorrow morning to a town without Jacob Yoder in it. If only she'd known that she'd spend years and years—decades—wishing that she'd done something more to make him stay. No matter what anyone said.

Bird-in-hand, Pennsylvania, 2017

Naomi's hand shook as she wrote the last equation on the chalkboard. At the grocery store, early yesterday evening, she'd seen two older women talking by the fruit stand. She'd caught the shape of the words coming out of their mouths.

Old Yoder's grandson is back in town, did you hear?

I saw him. Completely fallen to the material world, that boy! He was flaunting his motorbike and his clothes. And his ears were decked out in jewelry!

Jacob was back. Naomi gripped the piece of chalk tighter and forced herself to keep writing until the last number. Her peripheral nerves had improved a lot in the last few years. She could do daily tasks and even teach without much impediment now. Except...

Naomi turned to face the class and found chaos. One of the younger students was crying near the back of the class while two older students squared off in a heated argument over the crying girl. Naomi's eyes told her they were having something close to a shouting match. But her ears heard only the usual silence. Only complete, maddening silence.

Naomi smacked her hand on the board. Thud, thud, thud. She felt the sound of it on her palm. A small part of her treasured those last tidbits she had left of the audible world. But the rest of her was devoted to being a useful member of her community.

Despite her hearing loss, she wanted to be a good schoolteacher. But she couldn't even realize that her students were causing trouble right behind her back, while she was in the room with them. She walked up to the quarreling pair.

What's going on?, she felt herself say.

Jamie made my little cousin cry!

It's not my fault. She's just a crybaby.

Naomi sighed and glanced out the window for a second. Her heart jolted in her chest at the sight of a dark face peering in on the class from outside, backlit by the afternoon sun. But in the next moment, it was gone.

##

Bird-in-hand, Pennsylvania, 2017

When Jacob returned from the schoolhouse, still in a state of mild shock at seeing Naomi again, he found a visitor waiting for him at his grandfather's log cabin. She sat on the porch steps, her belly round with child. For a moment, Jacob couldn't place who she was.

"I'm Mary-Anne Hershberger," she said, with a smile. "Naomi's best friend."

"Oh," said Jacob, blinking awkwardly.

"I'm sure you'll meet Naomi while you're in town," Mary-Anne said, standing up and walking slowly down the steps towards him. She held out her hand and dangled something silver in the air. A set of keys on a chain—the keys to Jacob's old Yamaha XS. He'd left it behind, like he'd left everything else behind.

"I want you to know," said Mary-Anne, "I need you to understand what happened after you disappeared twenty years ago."

They sat together on the porch, Mary-Anne on Old Man Yoder's rocking chair, and Jacob on the porch steps. Jacob looked out at the weed-grown yard. The wooden floorboards creaked under her chair as she rocked it slowly.

"We didn't find out until much later," she said, "but sometime after the Bishop banished you, Naomi used her savings to buy the motorbike from your friend. And she started learning to ride it in secret."

"Naomi did? Why?" Jacob twisted to glance up at Mary-Anne. "She's never been interested in—"

"Why do you think?" said Mary-Anne with a hard look in her eyes. "She tried searching for you in the city. We even asked your friends at the auto shop. But it was like you'd just disappeared. You were as good as gone forever, so why do you think?"

"Why are you telling me this?" said Jacob, staring down at a clump of weeds growing through the gaps of the porch steps. "So she's still riding that bike?" he said. "And what? She never got married because of that? Because she was doing things against the Ordnung? So it's my fault?" But even as he said it, Jacob thought of the way Naomi kept writing equations on the board, back there at the schoolhouse, oblivious to her students shouting at each other, to Jacob calling out to her from the window. It was like she couldn't hear anything.

Jacob grabbed at the clump of weeds and tore them out. The leaf blades came away in his hand, ripped in half, but the roots remained stubbornly in the ground, under the porch steps.

"Yes," said Mary-Anne. "It's your fault, Jacob Yoder." She stood up, one hand over her round belly, and threw the Yamaha's keys at him. "It's in that barn, your old 'secret lair'. You'll know what I mean once you see it." She descended the steps and walked off without another word.

Jacob thought he had an idea of what he'd find in the barn. But when he unlocked the bolt and threw open the door, nothing could prepare him for the sight of the crushed motorcycle, lying on its side in the middle of a pile of his old childhood collection of forbidden technology. It was just another useless scrap of metal and parts now, the same as that dismantled radio next to it, and the discarded microwave Jacob had found and taken apart out of curiosity when he'd been fourteen. He swept the other stuff away and pulled out the warped and dented Yamaha XS.

Jacob ran his fingers over the chassis. The red paint was scuffed, like it had been scraped off by rough pavement as it skidded on its side, violently propelled across the road by inertia, and maybe impact with another moving vehicle. Road rash on a bike, he thought. He tried not to imagine the same thing happening to Naomi, but horrible things were circling around in his head.

Why did they keep this? To show him what he'd done to Naomi if he ever came back?

During one of his darkest hours, about three years after he'd begun living on his own in the outside world, a Jehovah's witness missionary had approached Jacob with a Bible in hand. Jacob had tuned the man out and turned around in his cot to face the wall, hoping the man would just leave him alone.

But at some point, the missionary had begun reciting the Psalms. *By the rivers of Babylon, there we sat down and wept. . . How can we sing the Lord's song in a foreign land? If I forget you, O Jerusalem, may my right hand forget her skill. . .* Then a familiar phrase had caught Jacob with an intense, almost crippling pang of longing.

As he stood there, in the middle of the old barn, with the smell of rotting hay all around him, and the metallic tang of rust from the scrap parts his teenage self had hoarded, Jacob recalled that phrase and the first time he'd ever thought it—twenty years ago, on the steps of the Fackenthal library, with Naomi looking up at him, waiting for him to speak, her grey eyes luminous under the glow of an electric street lamp.

May my tongue cleave to the roof of my mouth, if I forget you.

Standing in the middle of the barn, Jacob put his face in his hands and wept.

##

Lancaster City, Pennsylvania, 2017

The employee's bathroom at Jim's Auto had only one stall and two urinals, but there were three faucets and the tiled sinks were wide and deep enough to be troughs. Jacob turned the water off as he scrubbed at his grease-darkened hands, rubbing the special mechanic's soap all the way up to his forearms.

Someone knocked.

Jacob stopped and stared at the door. *Don't they know this is a communal washroom? Is it a newbie?* "It's not locked!" he called out. "C'mon in."

The knock came again, a bit more insistently. Thud, thud, thud.

"I said, it's open!" he shouted, rinsing his hands quickly under the tap. But the knocking didn't stop even as he turned the water off. Thud, thud—

Jacob threw the door open. "Didn't you hear me—" The words died in his throat.

Naomi stood in the doorway, dressed in Amish plain dress. She looked completely out of place in the back room of Jim's Auto shop. Behind her, the rest of Jacob's co-workers stared. But Naomi simply stood there, in front of the employee's washroom, looking up at Jacob like he was the only one in the room.

"Naomi," Jacob said. "I am so sorr—"

Naomi pulled his head down and kissed him. She kissed him like she would never let go. Distantly, Jacob heard hoots and catcalls, but Naomi was kissing him and all else was secondary. But then, like a flash of pain, he remembered the warped metal of the Yamaha XS, the scratched paint on the chassis, the way it lay there in the barn, a broken thing in a pile of broken things. He put a hand between them and pushed her away.

"Naomi," he said. "What happened to you, what I did, leaving just like that. . ."

The same night they came back from their nighttime road trip to Franklin & Marshall college, after he had parted ways with Naomi at the edge of town, Jacob came home to find the Bishop, the ministers, and the deacons waiting for him. He remembered walking up the yard and wondering why all the gas lamps in the house were lit, as if there were important guests.

Sixteen-year old Jacob had peered into the main living room to find the entire council of ministers waiting there, sitting with his grandfather in somber silence. He remembered the grief in his grandfather's eyes when he looked up to find Jacob in the doorway. Jacob had known then, with that one look, that he had been banished, that he had committed the last straw in the eyes of the community. To rebel on your own is one thing, the Bishop had said, but to corrupt your peers too. . .

"So I left," Jacob told Naomi. "I couldn't—"

Naomi pressed a hand to his mouth and shushed him. "I love you, Jacob Yoder," she said.

Jacob coughed. "What did you just say?"

Behind Naomi, Jacob's co-workers clapped and cheered. Naomi followed Jacob's gaze and turned around to blink at their audience in surprise. Then she grabbed his wrist and pulled him towards the front of the shop. "Do you understand me when I talk?" she said. "I can't really hear myself. Did I slur?"

"No," said Jacob, but then he realised that she couldn't hear him and he wasn't in her line of sight. But before he could make his response clear to her, she pulled them to a stop at the front desk where the receptionist immediately handed Naomi a placard and a fat, black marker with a conspiratorial wink.

"What. . ." said Jacob.

Naomi threw Jacob a smile as she uncapped the marker and wrote something on the placard. "Just to be clear," she said. "In case I slur or talk too softly. I want you to know this." She turned to face Jacob and held up the placard high over her head, as if she were in a rally. It said: I love you Jacob Yoder. Marry me.

Jacob barely heard the cheers, the whistling, and the shouts of encouragement echoing around the room. All he had eyes for was the woman in the plain dress and kapp, standing there with a placard in her hands and love in her gaze. Naomi's mouth quirked up with a little bit of mischief as she raised her arm and wrote on the inside of it with permanent marker the Hebrew name: Ya'aqov.

Jacob laughed and rubbed the back of his neck where Naomi's own name was tattooed. He felt his eyes grow hot with tears and he swiped at his face. Even as he cried, he couldn't stop smiling as he walked towards Naomi and took the marker from her. He set it slowly down on the receptionist's desk.

Then he took Naomi's hand, wove his fingers through hers, and pulled her out the door. I'm stealing you away, he thought as he looked back at her. But he didn't need to say it, because by the look on her face, she was planning to steal him away too.

ANNIE'S CHOICE
NIKKI SALEM

Chapter One

The sun was beating down hard on Anna as she walked through the market. Her heart was light with the feeling of summer finally setting in. She made her way through the busy crowds, avoiding eye contact with any English who were touristing in her community, and found her way to the baker's stall. The air around it was filled with the sweet smell of baking bread and sugar. She wanted to get something special for after dinner, a treat that she didn't ordinarily indulge in. The line was long, she didn't mind.

"So is it good here then?" a voice behind her asked. Anna turned slightly, half expecting it to be a tourist who was going to drill her questions about her community, it wasn't. He was a handsome young man, maybe a year older than her, his eyes were greener than anything she'd ever seen. He was definitely not English, he was dressed modestly and looked like he'd walked out into the market instead of riding in a car. She relaxed a little, glad to not be interviewed on her lifestyle or religion.

"It is," she nodded, turning back forward.

"I'm Zachary, new to town, just transferred in as the teacher," he offered.

"Oh! Welcome then, we've been in need for a new teacher for a couple weeks now," she agreed politely. The line moved forward and she followed it.

"Are you from here originally?"

"I have lived here my whole life," Anna said. The man smiled and his cheeks dimpled at the pull.

"So what would you say is the best thing to get here then?" he asked, conspiratorially. Anna was still a little cautious even though he was obviously a simple person like herself, she always felt tense with strangers- it was the aftermath of her upbringing.

"They have a sweet bread with apple folded in, if it's not all gone you should try some," she explained. It was her turn, and she quickly ordered. The man didn't talk to her again until she started to leave.

"I hope to see you again," he said, smiling again, he stepped forward to make his order.

The sun was hot on Anna's face as she walked away quickly in embarrassment. He was entirely too bold, too friendly, for a stranger. She was a married woman, it should have been obvious with the color of her clothing and bonnet, and yet he'd been almost indecent in flirting with her. She had been so caught off guard, though, that she hadn't reacted in any way to show she wasn't interested or amused by his advance.

Anna loved her husband and it ashamed her to think of how he would feel seeing her reaction.

She'd known him for four years, he knew every reaction she had. If he saw anything new he was sure to mention it, to marvel at it like a gift he had forgotten to open. She loved him, loved that he loved to keep getting to know her even though it had been two years.

The morning they got married it was raining.

It was during a Sunday service, as all marriages in her community are, and the rain was tapping against the windows and roof as though it were dying to sneak in and get a peek at the ceremony. Anna sat down next to James, her new husband, her dress was hand sewn by her mother, to listen to the rest of the day's church service, and she felt whole for the first time in her life. He wasn't looking for a placeholder, for someone to fill a gap in his life, he only wanted Anna. James was kind and sweet, even to the animals of his farm. He raised them with care and when she watched him she couldn't help but wonder what he'd be like as a father.

The father of her children.

Her family cooked a huge meal after the services, inviting the whole church.

Everyone had approved, blessed them, wished them well.

It was the best day of her life.

So to think that some stranger would go to her and try to encroach on any of that, try to take away from the relationship that defined her life, disturbed her. Anna was no flirt, no easy catch, and she didn't take kindly to anything that could allude to that.

The trip was hot, the sun heavy on her, and by the time Anna finally arrived home, she was exhausted and ready to change into clothing that wasn't so heavy. The house was nice and cool, insulated from the hot sun. She wiped sweat from her brow, and peered out to the back yard from the kitchen.

She almost dropped the baked goods immediately.

Something was wrong.

Their barn was open, and one of the steer was eating the grass beneath the kitchen window.

It was far too hot for the animals to be out. Usually James kept the animals in the barn where it was shaded, cooler, and there was plenty of water, until the sun started to set and the air cooled. He cared about them, not just for their ability to be good meat, but to ensure they were living good lives.

Nothing was protecting them from the heat.

He wasn't anywhere in sight, and Anna's heart started speeding immediately.

Something was wrong, she could feel it in her bones, she needed to go to her husband, she needed to find him. The animals had gotten out before, either by an unsecured door, or by accident, and she'd never felt this way when seeing it.

Something in her heart, in her body, knew that this time was different.

Quickly stopping what she was doing, Anna fled from the kitchen, back out into the hot summer's sun. Cold sweat covered her neck and back, terrified even though she wasn't entirely sure why. She couldn't see him in their field, but his buggy was still on the property. She hadn't seen his shoes next to the door when she came in, which meant he was still out there somewhere.

Where *was* he?

Anna forced her thoughts into a standstill, made herself try to calm down and focus.

She needed to check inside the barn. He could have just found a problem with it, and put the animals out while he repaired it. He may have been exhausted from the sun and took a break without closing up. She may find him sleeping, propped up against the inside of the barn. There was also the possibility he was just cleaning out the shelter.

Dread filled her, telling her none of this was true, but she clung to the ideas even as she entered the barn.

Her eyes took a moment to adjust to the dark shadow of the inside of the building as she stepped out of the sunlight. Something dark on the ground caught her attention, and she stared for a moment until she could see clearly.

The second she realized what it was, breath left her body in a quick gush, and Anna rushed forward. Her husband, the kind farmer who'd sat beside her on that rainy Sunday, was out flat on the floor of the barn.

"James," she gasped, running to his side.

James was on his stomach, out cold, but he was still breathing.

She knew she needed to get help quickly.

Anna never touched horses growing up, her father had built furniture and she never drove the buggy. The only times she'd even touched them in her whole life was while she'd lived with James. She'd fed them a couple times, he showed her how to shoe them even though he didn't expect her to ever do it.

Now, without pause or thought, she mounted a horse and frightened it into a gallop as she clung to it. It bounced away beneath her, but she didn't let it shake her loose. It terrified her, but she'd do anything for her James.

She needed to get into town.

It didn't matter how scared she was, how quickly the horse was running, or how hot the air was, she needed to get help for her husband.

The trip, although a quarter of the time it would have taken her to walk, felt like it took years, each second a wasted one. When she finally made it to the town's doctor, she was pouring tears. Her words came out in gasping blurts, struggling to make a sentence. James was her entire world.

He was everything she knew, everything she loved.

She needed to get him help.

Chapter Two

The English hospital was too crisp.

Every edge, every light, every sound, felt sharp and artificial. Like looking at a sickly animal and knowing that something just wasn't right about it. She sat still, keeping her hands in her lap, and watched over James.

It had only been half a day since she found him, but it felt like ten lifetimes had passed. Her husband, large and strong, was still unconscious. He was in a garb the hospital had dressed him in, under sheets so white they seemed impossible. He looked almost English, and the idea would have been funny if it weren't for the situation. Three different machines were reading different parts of his existence that she couldn't even fathom.

There was one beeping that told her his heart was still beating, though, and she cherished that one.

The Doctors had only done a couple scans, they said there would be more. The nurses who followed told Anna that he'd been kicked in the back by a horse or cow, that it fractured parts of his spine.

They said he may never wake up again.

If he did wake up, he'd never walk.

Anna's heart ached watching him, knowing what a sad existence would lay ahead of him if he woke up. She began to hope she'd wake up as well, that this was just a dream brought on by the heat of summer, and she'd be able to move past it.

She'd only ever known him as strong, as active. He'd carried her more times than she could count, either in teasing or in love, and she couldn't imagine him not even being able to carry himself.

She didn't wasn't sure if she was strong enough to help him carry that weight.

And what if he didn't wake up?

What if he stayed sleeping for the rest of his life. She wouldn't be able to drag his life further in any artificial means. Stuck in this too-sanitary world that forgot that god made them of the Earth and that people shouldn't stray too far from it. Anna's heart caught in her throat at the thought, and she leaned forward, wrapping her hands around his.

His fingers squeezed hers back.

Fresh tears, fat and thick, burst from her eyes immediately, plopping heavily from her cheeks onto the ground between them.

Anna closed the distance, her empty hand touching his face.

"James," she whispered, sucking in a sob.

"I want to go home," he murmured out, sounding still asleep.

Anna gasped, sobbing, and couldn't help but let a smile slip onto her lips.

***

They sent him home in a wheelchair.

The chair the hospital sent was metal, still stuck with the cloying scent of bleach and metal. It looked uncomfortable, too shiny, too fake. When they made it back to the town, and he was helped out of the van a driver from town took them in, he was helped into a woven wood chair instead. It had a quilted back and seat that was hand-made by women of the village years ago.

Made with love instead of metal.

James didn't speak much, not that he ever had. The community was eager to help, they had set up a ramp for him in the weeks that Anna had been by his side in the hospital. They'd filled her kitchen with food, filled their home with quilts and gifts to aid his recovery. The church even left a letter saying his medical expenses would be covered until she thought she could take over.

It was overwhelming, touching. Anna felt loved by her church, by the families around them that saw their hardship. She cried happy tears, touched by these movements. She spent most of their first day back thanking people, letting visitors come in to wish James better health.

He wasn't so hospitable.

By the time Anna noticed this it was passing dinner, they'd had people over feeding them. He was having trouble holding his fork, and Anna had to help lift his hand to let him feed himself.

This only soured his mood more.

When they slept that night, him in a special slinging system they'd given him to support his back, he turned his face away from her.

All their time at the hospital, his hand in hers, it had felt more at-home than that night in their own bed.

The next morning she got up early.

Many people had given them baked goods, offered to stop by and cook for them, but Anna wanted to do it herself now.

She wanted to show him she still loved him. James was her life, sworn to him at their church, and she'd do anything to ensure he was happy and knew he was loved. She baked bread, made soft boiled eggs, sliced fruit, and even made fresh juice from apples off their own farm. Anna gathered it all on a tray, and brought it to their room.

She'd only done this for him once before, when he'd been so sick with a fever he couldn't stand.

The memory made her smile, remembering how needing he'd been then. How rewarding it felt to be able to serve him as she felt she should.

She wanted to treat him like he deserved.

He was still asleep when she made it to their room, the sun far past risen. She set his food down on a small table beside the bed, and sat beside him. His face was smooth with dreams, and Anna slid her fingers over his cheek and jaw. His beard was groomed, but it was still a wonder to think that it marked how long they'd been married. Two years. Every hair that grew there was able to exist because of their marriage. Images of him with a graying beard, wired and bushy, came into her mind and Anna caught a smile slipping onto her face.

"Husband," she said softly.

James stirred slightly before opening his eyes to her. His eyes were soft at first, fogged by sleep and tiredness.

"I made you breakfast," she said, standing. Getting the tray, she brought it over to the bed.

His mood soured almost immediately.

"I'm not in the hospital anymore, I don't need to be served in bed," he said angrily. His face was slowly turning red, and Anna's heart started to speed in worry.

"I know that, I just thought it might be nice if-"

"Did you ask me if I wanted this?"

"No, I just wanted to be kind," she tried to say.

"I'm not here for pity, I am still in head of this household, and I expect my meals at the table," he almost shouted. His voice was rising, and although the house was empty she felt humiliated.

She wasn't trying to embarrass him.

She was trying to show her love.

"I'll put it at the table, then," she said simply, her face coloring red in discomfort.

"I'll be out there when I can get myself into the chair," he said bluntly as she left.

Anna ended up having to go back and help him into the wheelchair, his legs unable to swing over the side of their bed on his command. As she pushed him into the kitchen, still able to see how angry he was, she only had one thought on her mind.

This wasn't the man she married.

Chapter Three

Time passes slowly when the one you love has turned on you.

He was becoming cruel, and she felt guilty for thinking it.

James would adamantly say that he wanted to do things for himself, and then when he proved time and time again that he couldn't, he was spiteful and frustrated when Anna eventually had to help.

She was always tired.

If it wasn't from the work of her heart getting used to this, it was from having to do all of the farm work herself. Many people had offered the first week, a few the second week as well, but after that people stopped offering.

She was sure if she asked, many people would have offered.

Nobody would have willingly left her to do it on her own.

Her husbands pride is the only thing that kept her from mentioning it to the church. She was happy to carry the burden if it meant that he wouldn't be ashamed of his situation. After the fourth week back home, he stopped attending church with her. The church leaders visited, without question, but after they left he was in an even worse mood.

Anna was finding herself seeking any excuse to get out of the house.

She volunteered at the church, she would go to town to sell eggs more often than she did before, she visited family more often.

It felt like a betrayal to be wanting to be out of her husband's surroundings, but he made her feel even more alone than she did without him. There was a sign up on the church, on their fifth week back, that the school was going to need assistance the following Tuesday. Anna agreed to do it without a second thought.

Maybe in giving back to the church, to her community, she could absolve herself of the guilt of slowly despising her husband.

That morning before she left, she helped James into his chair, and had food prepared for him for the first half of the day. He didn't leave the house most days, instead he sat in the kitchen and stared out at the barn, as though he could undo the tragedy by glaring at it hard enough. A cane that she'd bought him, in the hopes that he'd eventually find the energy or strength to try it, still sat unused by the kitchen window.

He had Anna sell the horse that did it the first week they were back.

"I'll be back after noon, is there anything you want from town?" she asked him as she donned her bonnet.

He didn't reply, instead James kept staring out at the barn. His beard wasn't well kept anymore, his hair was getting long as well. She decided, while looking at him, she'd clean him up that night if he'd let her.

"Good bye, my husband," she said gently as she left, the summer sun a cool balm from his hot spite.

Anna had forgotten about the new teacher until she arrived at the school that Tuesday morning.

He was just as handsome, just as striking, as when she first saw him. She arrived before any of the students, wanting to be prepared and able to find out what her duties were before things got too hectic. It felt almost too intimate, being alone with him, after how he'd treated her just a couple months before.

"Good morning," she greeted him, anyways, as she stepped into the new school.

He was marking papers on his desk, and looked up at her with surprise.

"You're the volunteer today?" he asked, as though he was expecting someone else entirely.

"I am," she agreed. "What will I be doing?"

"I'm having to take the students to a couple farms to show how math is going to help them with their daily lives," he explained. "Some have been questioning it," he shrugged, a smile on his face as though he found it endearing that the children questioned him.

"That sounds fine," she agreed. "I'm just a chaperon, then?" she clarified.

"That's right," he said, setting down his pen. "Do you have children yourself?" he asked. She was taken aback by the personal question, but didn't let it play on her face.

"I don't," she said plainly. It was better that she didn't have children, considering her husband's situation. The second that thought passed her mind, her stomach knotted in guilt again, and she tried to fight away the sensation that was growing to be familiar. Children were something she'd wanted her whole life, something that was expected of her. She didn't need to betray herself or her community like this just because she was mildly unhappy.

"I have the same sadness," he nodded. "My pupils are good, though, and they shouldn't give you trouble," he offered her a smile.

"That's good to hear," she admitted. She was the youngest child, and so had little experience with children that were younger than she was growing up.

"I'm sorry about your husband, by the way," he said gently. "If there is anything that you or he need help with, please don't hesitate to let me know," he said.

It was the first time any man had offered to help her in weeks.

The first time she'd heard such a soft voice from a man since her husband's accident.

"Thank you," she said earnestly.

The first children came, and she and he immediately stopped talking: almost as if they'd agreed to. She spent the day corralling the children around, helping explain and answer questions when Zachary was busy.

He was good with the children. Kind, patient. Even when a couple children got into mischief and started bothering the chickens at one of the farms they visited, he explained to them patiently why they needed to respect all of the animals. Anna watched him with a curious eye, seeing bits of who James used to be in him. She could imagine Zachary as a good father, raising a family with a calm and patient mind.

He'd never yell or fuss.

He seemed genuinely kind.

She tried to remember when she saw her husband as that, before his accident. When she'd been so eager to get home to him, so willing to get him treats and do anything she could to show how thankful she was to him.

How much she loved him.

It was getting harder and harder to do that, but as the school let out that afternoon, she caught herself wanting to capture the magic again. She stopped at the bakery on the way home, and picked up a couple of his favorite sweets.

He wasn't himself, he was hurt.

It was her job as his wife to make him feel whole again, to let him know he was loved.

When she arrived back home it was with a fresh heart and mind, starving for his affection and love.

"Husband, I'm home," she called as she came in and took off her shoes. She headed to the kitchen with her basket, and he was still in front of the window, his lunch untouched. "The children were very energetic, I haven't moved around that much since we were moving into the home," Anna joked, setting the sweets on the kitchen table. "I got a special treat for you," she continued. He didn't respond, and Anna felt a familiar worry clutch her heart. Leaving the table, she went to her husband's side. His eyes were open and moving as he gazed over the same view he'd been staring at for a month and a half.

"Anna," he said softly. His voice sounded broken. Biting her lip in worry, she lay her hand on his shoulder.

"What is it?" she asked, trying not to pressure him too much.

He turned to her, his eyes were tired and when they rested on her face, she was sure he wasn't seeing her.

"What kind of a god would take a farmer's ability to work the land?" he asked, his shoulders slackened.

Anna felt like a widow.

Chapter Four

The church continued paying his medical expenses.

Every visit from the doctor was still nerve wracking, though, and she was always eager to see him leave. She wasn't sure what she expected, or what she really wanted. This man wasn't her husband anymore, wasn't who she'd built a home with. He wasn't the same man she'd fallen in love with while watching him tend to his livestock.

He was a shell.

Without purpose, without god.

She wasn't going to argue with him. She didn't want to push him away even further by trying to press him back into god's arms. His relationship with religion wasn't her business, wasn't in her control. You can't help somebody go to the church, they have to want to be there themselves.

Their bed was always cold in the center.

He never rolled over to her, even after his spine had healed enough that he wasn't in the sling anymore.

He never reached out to her.

Anna had begun to accept the fact that she'd never have children.

Many times the idea of volunteering at the school again had tempted her. She'd get to be around children, even if she could never have any she'd get to help shape the next generation.

She had to stop herself, though.

Nothing had happened between her and Nicholas.

They'd never touched, never said anything affectionate between one another, but when she'd see him in town their eyes would meet and guilt would flood her. She didn't see him as just a family member of the church. She didn't see him as just a neighbor. As a friend, even. The last sparks of who her husband used to be were in the teacher, and it drew her to him.

She longed for Nicholas to complement her, to look at her.

She wanted his attention.

So, she was guilty. She may have never touched another man besides her husband, and not even her husband as of late, but even the thought of wanting another man's attention felt treacherous.

James had done everything he could for her when they were happy together.

He'd treated her like a partner in life, more than just a marriage in the church, but also in their hearts. He'd shown her love and kindness she'd never expected, even her parents had married because of their families wanting the properties joined.

Anna had been given an opportunity with James to have so much more, to be so much more. They were going to have children that would know only good memories, who would want to stay with the church because it created such happiness as their parent's love.

It wasn't working out that way.

Instead they slept two feet apart.

He'd only eat after she left the room, now that he could hold a fork.

He didn't talk to her unless he needed something.

Anna was thinking of other men when she couldn't sleep.

Of Nicholas.

She wasn't who James married anymore, either.

One night, when summer began to draw to a close, she wheeled James out into the backyard, and cut open a watermelon in front of him. He watched her with disinterest, even though it had once been his favorite food. It was ripe, shiny in the setting summer sun, and as she handed him a slice, he didn't look her in the face.

Still, she sat close to him and watched the fireflies start to light up the grass.

"Do you still love me?" he asked, lifting the fruit to his face.

"I do," Anna said. She could never lie about that, her love had changed but it was still there.

"Do you still like me?" he looked over at her, his eyes sad. He looked like he'd aged years, not months, since the accident.

"I don't know," she admitted.

She couldn't lie about that, either.

He dropped his watermelon slice to the ground, and set his hands in his lap.

"I want to go to bed," he said quietly. His voice was flat, emotionless.

She wasn't sure if she hurt him or not, if he was going to yell at her again, or if he was just going to leave her alone.

She did as he said, though, and wheeled him in. Anna didn't say another word to him as she washed the watermelon juice from his hands and helped him change into sleepwear.

She'd failed as a wife.

She was supposed to support him, be at his side and be his strength, regardless of what they went through together. She was supposed to be there for him and be loyal in not only body- but heart.

She didn't feel loyal anymore.

Anna cleaned up the house, alone, and dreaded going to bed.

She didn't want to lay next to him.

Didn't want to feel this guilt.

The sun had long set, though, and she was wasting oil by staying awake.

She closed the house, changed into bed clothing, and climbed into the bed where her husband lay.

He seemed to be asleep, and she longed to lean over to him. She wanted to reach out, touch him, be sure that he was still the warm man she'd married. She could seek out scars she knew only he had. She could look for moles that she'd discovered only after they married.

Anything to prove he was some impostor.

Anything to prove that her James hadn't changed so much.

She ached for this, but she knew it wasn't possible.

She'd have to sleep alone in a shared bed, feeling more wanted by a teacher who was a stranger than her own husband.

What was keeping her from divorcing him? What was keeping her from leaving him and seeking Nicholas? Nicholas who smiled so warmly at her, Nicholas who had been kind and offered her help. Nicholas who wasn't her husband.

The guilt mingled with grief for her marriage, and Anna felt a sob break out of her throat. Her husband didn't move, she assumed he was completely asleep and oblivious to her pain, and so Anna let herself cry.

She cried for her marriage, that had so much promise in the beginning.

She cried for the children she'd never get to have.

She cried for herself, for losing faith in her husband.

She cried for her husband who lost faith in god.

The pillow beneath her quickly became drenched, but she kept crying, unable to stop the flood now that she let it start. She hadn't let herself cry since the night after they came back to their home. She told herself there was no need to cry anymore, that she had her husband alive, and that was more than enough.

It didn't feel like enough anymore.

She would have given anything to feel his arms wrapped around her.

Would have traded the world for it.

She eventually slipped into a fitful sleep, unable to find peace in her pain.

Chapter Five

Anna woke a little later than usual the next morning.

Her head pounded from the tears shed, her heart and mind felt numb. She didn't want to think about any of it, didn't want to consider what to do with how she felt.

As the food baked, a bread pudding similar to the one she had made the morning after they were married, she set on making herself a bath. She could still smell the salt of the tears on her skin, could feel how tightly it had drawn her, and wanted to wash it away. As she slipped into the bath, she thought she heard something in the kitchen, but attributed it to the hot oven stone, or logs, shifting.

The water was cool on her skin, and she would have usually feared getting sick, but she was too tired to worry herself. She already had the rest of her morning planned.

She'd bathe, then take the food out, set it out on the table, and then have to wake her husband. She'd wheeled him out to the kitchen every morning since the accident. She'd cut his food for him if he couldn't, some days his arms wouldn't even let him feed himself. She'd clean him up, dress, him, take him to town if he wanted (which was rare), and do whatever she could to make him happy.

He was an entire day's work all on his own.

She reminded herself of her wedding vows, though, and it caused her to push through.

Another sound thudded in the kitchen, pulling her out of her thoughts, and she worried that the breakfast had overturned and fell in the oven. Standing quickly out of the tub, she roughly towel dried her body and shoved on her undergarments before sliding into a dressing gown and rushing out to the kitchen.

Her heart stopped at the doorway.

There was a man standing in the kitchen.

Her James.

He was standing at the oven, watching over the baking breakfast, leaning almost all of his weight on the cane that had been abandoned by the window until then.

"James," she gasped out, staring at him as he turned to her. She couldn't help but double check his face to make sure it was him, to be sure this wasn't some stranger that had broken into her house.

"Annabelle," he said gently, lovingly, in that voice that he'd used to say his vows.

"You're standing," she said softly, unsure what else to say. Her hair dripped onto her robe and the kitchen floor, the only sound between them.

It felt obvious, but she had to say it. Had to confirm it was happening.

He turned further, to be independent of the wall he'd leaned against, but he started to wobble, and Anna rushed to his side.

He didn't gripe as she helped him.

He didn't glare.

James looked sad, apologetic, and Anna was sure she was dreaming.

Had her husband come back to her?

After two months?

"Breakfast smells incredible," he said as he let her help him walk to the table.

She never thought he'd walk again, never thought she'd hear his footsteps on their floor. Here he was, letting her help him. He hadn't willingly let her do anything for him without making sure she knew how miserable he was to accept her help.

"I'm a while away from carrying you in from the barn, like when we first married, but I want to work to get there again, for you," he said softly, taking her hand as she sat beside him. Anna could feel tears welling in her eyes, and turned her face to hide them. "Come here," he said gently, opening his arms to her. Anna's voice broke out into a sob now, and she quickly stood and leaned into his arms, holding him tightly. "If you want me to court you again before we get to that point," he started to say.

"I'm so sorry about what I said last night," she shook her head, leaning back to look into his eyes. James raised his shake hands and wiped the tears from her face.

"I've been terrible to you," he admitted, the words were a bigger admission than she'd expected. "You've been incredible to me, and in questioning myself in god's world, I made you question your place in mine," he brushed a few wet strands of her hair away from her face. "I love you, Annabelle, and I will work my whole life to prove that to you," he continued.

"I love you too," she nodded, before wrapping her arms around his shoulders again.

It felt so good to hold him, to be held by him.

She'd missed him, even though he'd only ever been a few feet away.

She never wanted to be that far away from him again.

He was her husband, he always would be, and she'd do anything to ensure that she never forgot that again. Nicholas couldn't compare, he was a vague copy, a poor knock-off. James was the only man who'd ever made her feel complete, made her feel like there was more in the world for her.

That there was actually love for her.

She planned on spending the rest of her life thanking him for coming back to her.

ANGELA'S ANSWER

MEGHAN MASON

Angela wiped the tears from her eyes as she arose from her bed. It was only five in the morning, but now that her husband was dead, she was a young widow with too much on her plate to handle. There was her young, seven-year-old daughter, Becca, and her mamm, Alma, to look after. It was hard to believe that just one short year ago, her Amos had passed away from a freak farming accident. Amos had been out choring, and the sun had been very hot that day. Amos must have become dehydrated and collapsed, because that was the only reasonable answer that anyone could come up with as to how he had lost control of their buggy, causing the horse to veer off the road into a ditch. The buggy had fallen on top of Amos, killing him instantly. The horse was alright, but the buggy and her husband were certainly not. Everyone in the modest sized Amish community gathered their resources to fill in for the poor man, so that Angela and Becca could finish out the harvest season. The men took care of the field work, and the women folk took care of the household choring so that Angela could take her time to grieve for all she had lost. She and Amos had been engaged to be married since the spring dance when they both turned sixteen. By seventeen they had married, and by eighteen, boppli Becca had come along. Angela was happy with her life on the farm, and everything had come to a sudden and tragic halt with the death of her beloved Amos. Even now, a year after his death, Angela still felt the pangs of grief wash over her, as she had every morning since his passing. Today was no different, as she began her morning routine of cooking the breakfast, caring for her ailing mamm, and preparing young Becca for school,

"Guder mariye schlofkopp," Angela said in her native Pennsylvania Dutch.

"Good morning, mamm," came a muffled reply from a sleepy Becca.

"Time to rise and shine, and get yourself ready for the day," said Angela.

"Alright, but I am so tired," complained Becca, "there are too many chores to do before school."

"I won't have you complaining, Becca. When your daed left us, we had no idea we would inherit his daed's buggy making business. Now we have the farm to care for, plus my mamm, plus the running of the business," explained Angela, for what felt like the hundredth time. She had known little about Amos's family, who had lived in an Amish settlement many miles from their own. It had come as quite a shock that the buggy making business had then fallen to the widow and her child upon the death of Amos' daed. Too many deaths, too many responsibilities, and too little time, thought Angela, as she laid out Becca's school dress and apron,

"Don't forget your bonnet, maedel," reminded her mamm. With that final reminder, Angela returned to the kitchen to finish breakfast preparations and wash her mother, Alma. Alma had married late in life, and had given birth to only one child. Naturally, the responsibility for her care fell to Angela. Even though she tried her best to keep everything running as smoothly as possible, Angela was beginning to feel the major strain of just getting through each day.

After seeing her daughter off to school, Angela began the litany of duties that was now her life. When she had discovered the buggy making business that she had unwittingly inherited, she arranged for the small business to relocate to her town of Springbrook, Pennsylvania. That way, everything she needed to care for was near to her. Angela traveled to her buggy business by foot every morning, leaving her mother, Alma, in the care of another Amish woman who had grown children. It meant that Angela could be free to run the business, but return home at noon to resume care of Alma. Alma was bedridden with a myriad of health problems, and there was much care to be given. She loved her mother, and was not about to pawn off any more of her care onto anyone else than was necessary. Despite it all, Angela bore her cross as best she could. This allowed her absolutely no time for friends or social occasions. Whenever a time arose that involved getting together with her fellow Amish community members, she found it too difficult and heartbreaking to leave her mamm alone, even for an abbreviated time. Becca was still too young to be given care duties for Alma, and she had wanted her daughter to be free from as many responsibilities that Angela had come to acquire.

Angela's overburdened life continued month after uneventful month, until December rolled around. Word spread that a Winter Dance was to be held at Bruder Helms farm across the village. Angela dismissed the event from her mind, as she always did, but once Alma got wind of it through her caretaker, she spoke to her daughter about it,

"Angela, Mrs. Hamlin told me about a Winter Dance that Bruder Helms is holding down yonder at his barn. I want you to go. Ya do enough to care for me and Becca, plus that ol' buggy shop. Give it a rest, and join people your own age. You deserve a life better than this one ya got. Gott himself would agree!" Angela was surprised by her mamm's words. After all, Alma barely spoke outside of using Pennsylvania Dutch, and when she did use the more modern Englisch, it was to convey something very serious or important to her daughter, granddaughter or caretaker. Alma slipped back into her old language, and expressed that despite Amos' untimely death, that he had lived a full life,

"Er hot en iwwerflissich lewe gfaahre," Alma mumbled to her daughter. Alma had loved her husband so much, that she felt as though she would betray his memory if she was to attend any function outside the home. Amos had been her only true love, and her only experience with a man. Alma looked at her daughter sternly,

"Get Becca to stay a few hours with me, and the both of us'll be alright, while ya go and try to have a bit of fun in yer life!"

"Mamm, what if something goes wrong, and you or Becca need me? What then?"

"Then Becca will run over and git ya," was all Alma was willing to say at this point. She was determined, even in her weakened state, that Angela should have more in her life than only work and worries. Angela resolved to think it over, and decide either way over the next few days.

Meanwhile, across the village on Newborn Farm, there lived a young widower named Gabriel. Gabriel had married Samantha, the girl he thought could do no wrong, but that was not to be as true as he had envisioned. They had married and despite a somewhat troubled union, Samantha had given birth to a daughter, Emilia. Shortly thereafter, Samantha had vanished in the night. The townsfolk had hunted high and low for her to no avail, when two days later, they discovered Samantha had drowned in one of the larger lakes nearby. It was rumored that maybe Samantha had tried to run off, fallen in the water, and succumbed to drowning. Other rumors involved a secret lover from Englisch Town, or some other tantalizing story, but Gabriel knew she was unhappy with him and Emilia. Samantha was not a young woman to settle down, as her Amish tradition dictated. No matter how hard Gabriel tried to make life enjoyable for Samantha, there was to be no pleasing her. She was unhappy to her core, and the boppli had not brought her any happiness at all. In fact, Samantha was very distant from the boppli, and a nurse maid had had to be brought in from the start to care for the poor girl. Luckily, Emilia was far too young to understand the complications with her mamm, and had no memory of Samantha's death. All Emilia had ever known was her father's love and attention, and that of the nurse maid that looked after her when Gabriel had to go out to the fields. It was a guilt that plagued Gabriel every day. He questioned whether there was more he could have done to prevent Samantha's departure, but life was what it was, and Gabriel slowly came to terms that he would raise his girl alone. He was loath to become involved in any future entanglements with womenfolk, as Samantha had brought him only heartache and pain. He tended to his animals on the farm, and harvested the wheat fields every season like clockwork, and before he knew it, three years had passed by since the death of his wife. There was no doubt he was reclusive, and stayed at home with Emilia, except for church services. Gabriel was an exceptional handyman, and did take on the occasional extra project for a neighbor or family member, but that was it. His only friend and confidante was his bruder, Laz, and it was rare that they had time to sit and speak together. Laz had a growing family of his own, and that left little time to socialize. It just so happened that on this day, the very same day as Angela was debating attending the Winter Dance, Laz had made the time to pay a visit to his bruder,

"Hello, Gabe! How have you been managing? Well, I hope?"

"Well enough," was all that Gabriel said.

"The family is headin' down to that Winter Dance, you know?" explained Laz, "You should go too. Give you a chance to experience a somewhat normal life, Gabe. It does the maedel no good to be isolated on this farm with no womanly influence. How do you expect her to learn her traditions and duties, for heaven's sake?"

"Emilia is doing just fine, and don't be telling me otherwise. The family wants to meddle in my affairs, but I am not traveling down that road again. Samantha took my heart and destroyed it. The only blessing that came of it is Emilia. I'm not going anywhere, especially some barn dance," Gabriel replied.

"Well, bruder of mine, it seems you have little choice in the matter, as mamm has the final say in such things, as ya well know it," chided Laz. Their mamm was infamous for putting her foot down as to the well-being of her two sons. She had sent Laz on this mission to see her eldest son, and force him to attend that dance. She knew Emilia was growing fast, and that a mother was what she needed, not an embittered father with limited time. She had made it quite clear that Laz was not to return home without securing his bruder's attendance at that Winter Dance! Laz was not thrilled at being the one selected for this daunting task, but knew his mamm meant business, and dutifully went to prod Gabe until his stubbornness gave in. After about two hours of pleading with his bruder, Gabe agreed to make a brief appearance to satisfy his family, but he was not going to make more of an effort than that. Laz left satisfied that at least he had gotten a small commitment from Gabe to attend, and that their mamm would be placated for the time being.

After a few days to think things through, Angela finally consented to attend the Winter Dance. It was now only a mere two weeks away, and she had lots to do to prepare Becca to care for her grandmother. She wrote a list of instructions a mile long, which was not necessary, as Becca had watched her mamm enough times to care for her grandmother alone for some time now. It was only that her mamm prevented Becca from taking on too many responsibilities, in the hopes of sparing her daughter the hard life she had become accustomed to. Becca reassured her mother that she would alert her should anything go awry, and that she had better focus on what dress to wear to the dance. After all, Angela did not go anywhere, and had nothing very pretty to choose from. It was all work dresses or somber looking church dresses that she stared at, as she began to reconsider her opinion about going to the dance at all. She chose a rather less depressing looking gown of lighter blue, and decided it did not matter what she wore anyway, because she had no intention of conversing very much, let alone dancing!

The evening of the Winter Dance arrived, and the village was a bustle of activity, busy with preparations for the occasion. Gabriel donned his church clothes, put on his hat, and climbed into the buggy. He had his misgivings, but if it would appease his mamm, then a short appearance at this dance would certainly be worth the trouble. He bade Emilia goodnight, leaving her in the care of her nurse maid for the hour he planned to be away. He told his horse to giddy up, and he arrived shortly at Bruder Helm's farm. It was lit up amongst the trees with home-made twinkling lights, and he could hear music coming from inside. There were many buggies parked alongside the road, but what surprised him was when he saw a young woman dressed in blue, walking solitary up the long road from across the village. Gabe wondered to himself what on earth a single woman would be doing walking out alone to a community function. It was rather an improper sight, but Angela was far too independent at this juncture in her life to be bothered with the conventions of her somewhat conservative Amish village. She trudged along the road leading up to Helm's Farm, only to be met by an austere looking young man who appeared to be staring at her. Gabriel got down from his buggy, and couldn't help but stare into the unwaveringly cold face of Angela. There was something about this woman that garnered his attentions, though he fought it tooth and nail. What was it about this odd woman that he found so entrancing? Angela fought off his gaze, and entered the barn. Gabe looked down at the ground, surprised at himself for even looking at a woman. He had sworn them off a long time ago. He tethered his horse to a post, and decided to drop in quickly, but he had to fight off the urge to discover who the woman in blue was. There was something very different about the way this woman carried herself, and it had certainly caught his attention, however unwilling he was to accept it.

Angela stood off to one side of the barn, watching the others dance or make merry with conversation. She had no one really to talk with, since she never ventured out of the house or her business. Instead, she decided to stand off apart from the other guests. She felt awkward and alone, and regretted her decision to attend. She had seen the strange man in the buggy once before, she thought, at the buggy shop. She remembered that he had come in for some minor repair while she had sat in the office area. She had thought little about the man, other than that she had seen him in passing. She spied him once again, standing alone in the doorway of the barn. He appeared very handsome in his somewhat worn out suit. Despite the years and isolation, Gabriel had retained his youthful and rugged good looks. He still managed to cut a fine figure of a man without even trying. Gabriel felt intensely out of place, as he found his way to the cider table. He decided he'd look a bit less conspicuous if he had a cup in his hand, so promptly took one, and then saw her across the room. She was standing there all alone. She talked to no one, and no one seemed interested in engaging her in any sort of conversation. He thought this a little pathetic, and watched her in silence. Against his better judgement, he decided the best thing to do, was to grab another cupful of cider, and make his way over to this solitary woman in the corner. Angela did not notice his approach, and just stood there glancing around at others enjoying themselves. She jumped as Gabriel tapped her upon her shoulder, and proceeded to introduce himself. He had no idea what or why he was doing this, besides the fact that his heart seemed to be doing the acting rather than his brain.

Gabriel stared into Angela's face as he offered her a cup of cider,

"I could not help but notice you from across the barn. You are alone, I take it?" inquired Gabe.

"Yes, as is per my usual circumstances," she stiffly replied. She then looked at him directly, prepared with all her might to throw off his attentions, but as their eyes locked, something strange stirred deep within her. It was as if his eyes were a sea of blue, and she felt completely entranced by his piercing eyes. He too, felt some foreign spark, as he could not stop admiring her understated beauty. She was soft in her face, even though he could tell that she tried to put up a cold front of indifference to those around her. Her cheeks were slightly rosy, as she took the cup offered to her,

"Thank you," was all she could muster, as she felt flustered and numb, not knowing what to do with her hands besides grasp the cup tightly.

"You are most welcome," replied Gabe, "I hope I am not unwelcome. I saw you and thought you to be the only woman in the barn worthy of my attentions." The words seemed to tumble from his mouth before he realized what he had said. The weird part was that he had ceased to care what his logical mind was telling him, and that was to walk away. His eyes were locked upon her, and they obviously had a connection of some sort that was unrivaled by anything he or she, for that matter, had ever experienced. It was as if two magnets were being drawn to one another, despite each one's negative past relations and experiences. Here were two lonely souls that had sworn themselves to a life of solitary existence, who now had eyes only for each other with no apparent reason. It was as if the stars had perfectly aligned this night, and the two were inexplicably drawn together by fate.

Angela allowed herself a sip of cider, as Gabriel gave in to starting a meaningless conversation with her about the prettiness of the lights outdoors. It was as if each of them were being guided towards one another, and instantly fell into easy conversation. Angela felt nervous no longer, as Gabriel's confident demeanor took over, and she felt instantly smitten with the stranger who had simply offered her a cup of cider. They continued standing there, talking about this and that, when he found himself saying,

"Angela, would you like to walk a bit outside amongst the light and trees? The fresh air would be nice," offered Gabriel.

"Of course. That sounds lovely," she replied automatically, as if she had no further will of her own.

Gabe and Angela took their leave of the barn dancers, and slowly began to walk under the stars. Gabriel grasped her hand as he took her beyond the buggy area towards the horses and cows that were still out at pasture. It was late for them to be out, but the barn had been needed for guests, and it was warm with a gentle breeze. He guided her along as any gentleman would, and she suddenly felt a warm glow spread across her face,

"I have not held the hand of any man since the hand of my late husband," she whispered almost to no one in particular. Gabe held her soft hand in his, and replied with much the same sentiment,

"Nor have I, I must confess. My wife passed on a while ago, and it is just me and my little young daughter."

"Oh! I hadn't realized you were a widower," said Angela, quite surprised to have found a kindred spirit in another who had lost a spouse not too long ago, "I, too, have an only daughter. I tend to the buggy shop in the village, and then return home to care for her and my mamm."

"Is that not too much work for one woman to handle? Not that you are incapable, I am certain. It would seem more proper for you to have a husband to share the load, would it not?" Gabriel replied.

"Perhaps, my mamm says so anyway," she said rather sadly, but still had her hand in his as they walked along in the moonlight.

"I find you to be a rare woman of independence and dedication. Not many women would have the strength to handle all of what you seem to handle every single day."

"Perhaps not, but I am devoted to providing my Becca with a better life than the one I've been thrown. That is not to say I am not thankful for my blessings. I am healthy, I have a child to love, and a mamm who loves me enough to send me here to this dance, even though I had no intention of going," Angela explained, not wanting Gabe to think her ungrateful to Gott.

"Well, I am certainly glad your mamm made you come this evening. I have also come at the request of my own mamm," he chuckled. "It appears as though we both have concerned family looking after our well-being."

"Yes, apparently so," whispered a suddenly shy Angela. What could make her feel so much so suddenly? She could scarcely breath as he guided her over to a fence covered in vines from the garden. He grasped her hand ever tighter, but with a fervency that conveyed only the most sensitive of feelings, as he placed one hand simply upon her cheek. They looked at one another, somehow knowing there was no going back to a life of solitude.

"Forgive me, but I am entirely taken with you," announced Gabe, as he brought her hand to his lips in a most gentlemanly manner. He would not dare attempt anything further, as it would be considered entirely inappropriate, but then again, they were adults, not two silly young teens going courting. Gabe fought every instinct to embrace her. Angela fought every instinct to give in, but her sense of unwavering propriety won out, and she suddenly let go,

"Oh, I am quite taken with you also, but I think it best we meet again sometime very soon. I must be returning home, as I was only to be gone an hour. Becca is at home with mamm alone, after all," she stammered.

Though sorry she had released his hand, Gabe knew and respected their Amish ways, and had no intention of disparaging her character or his own,

"Allow me, please, to drive you home in the buggy. It is quite late, and I would not want to think of a woman walking alone in the dark at this hour," he pleaded.

"Alright...I would be pleased if you could escort me back home." And off they traveled down the road back to Angela's home.

After Gabriel had seen Angela home safely, he stopped his buggy some miles from his own farm, and looked up at the night sky. It was unbelievable the turn of events the evening had taken. He had reluctantly come to the dance wanting nothing more than to leave, but instead had found this enchantingly wonderful woman. She was totally unlike the other women in the village. Her independence was admirable, but he was touched by her circumstances and hardship that forced her to avoid the rest of the community. He understood her feelings all too well, and recognized his own loneliness in her face that night. Above all else, he thanked Gott for leading him to this person, who might just be the only woman who could break his solitary existence. He could sense what a loving heart she possessed, as she cared so deeply for her daughter and mother. She was everything he thought a perfect woman to be; strong, hard-working, devoted to her obligations, and she was beautiful in a soft and quiet sort of manner. It seemed as if she carried the weight of the world in her eyes. He wanted nothing more than to ease her life's responsibilities. He wondered whether this was Gott's will for him to remarry. This would mean a mother and a sister for his dear Emilia. He fought off the temptation of the dream, as he was unsure how Angela would return his feelings, but she had reacted so naturally when he had expressed his interest in her. A soft rain began to fall, beckoning him back to reality, and he continued back towards his farm. Once home, he dismissed Emilia's nurse, and tried his best to get some sleep. He resolved to call on Angela the next day at her home, and his stomach was fluttering with unexpected nerves.

Once Angela got through her front door, both Becca and Alma were peppering her with questions as to how the night had gone. For she had been gone for double the time she had originally intended, and Alma knew, as a mamm always knew, that something had taken place at the dance. What it was exactly she knew not, but she was determined to pick her daughter's brain till she found out the answer,

"Out with it, then. Your face has not seen such a wide smile in a very long time. You can avoid it all you want, but I know when my daughter is happy and when she is not. You have spent these past years unhappy, and now you suddenly smile as if the angels themselves have sung to ya this night!"

"You are not wrong, mamm, but do not get ahead of yourself. I did make the acquaintance of Gabriel from across the village. He is a widower, not unlike myself in many regards, and he was definitely a breath of fresh air, that I hadn't intended to breathe ever again after Amos..." spilled Angela, as a few tears of happiness fell from her eyes.

It was not at all what she expected the night to bring, and she was overwhelmed with a sudden fit of exhaustion,

"Good night, mamm. I will speak more about it tomorrow," and she went to her room, and fell into an unusually peaceful sleep. She began to fall into a strange dream where Amos appeared to her, and said how much their love had meant to him. He took her hand in his, and told her to welcome the coming of Gabriel. She awoke with a start, and a light sweat upon her brow. She had not dreamt of Amos in months, and the nature of the message was totally unexpected! It was as if his spirit had descended from Heaven to release her of her burdens. Angela sat up in bed, and began an earnest prayer to Gott, requesting His guidance in all things, but especially regarding her situation with Gabriel.

The following morning Angela arose from bed at her regular five o'clock time, and resumed her normal life of daily choring. Little did she know that Gabriel was already up and about, preparing himself to visit her that very day.

Around noon time, Angela glanced out the kitchen window as she washed up from cleaning around the house, only to see Gabe's buggy ambling up the road towards her home. She had avoided her mamm's nosy questions thus far, but she sensed that she already knew what was afoot. Alma heard the clip clop of horse hooves, and sat up,

"Why, who could be callin' on us today, I wonder?" announced her mamm. Becca had been out in the chicken coops gathering eggs, and had already seen the man in the buggy approaching. She wondered if this had something to do with her mother's good spirits the previous night, and she dropped her egg basket to greet the visitor,

"Hello, sir. What brings you here today? Do you need a repair on your buggy or something," Becca inquired with a slight smile.

"Why, no, not exactly, little miss. Last evening, I had the pleasure of meeting who I can only assume to be your mamm by the look of you," replied Gabe, "Is she at home?"

"Yes, she sure is. Why don't you come in, and you can talk to her," A precocious little Becca offered. She decided he was a nice man by the looks of him, and much to her delight noticed the small figure of a girl riding next to him! She was no higher than his knee, and Becca felt delighted that another child had appeared for once,

"Oh! What is your name? Mine is Becca. Would you like to play dolls?"

"Can I," asked little Emilia, as he helped his daughter down from the buggy.

"Yes, I think that is a grand idea. You girls get to know one another, while I converse with your mamm," suggested Gabriel. He immediately took a liking to the friendly and outgoing Becca, who so willingly took Emilia under her wing to play. He allowed the girls to run off towards the house, and out came a surprised looking Angela. Today he noticed that her hair was in a looser bun than the night of the dance, and she looked even prettier for it.

"Hello, Gabriel," she said, as she tried wiping her damp hands upon her apron. He had caught her doing chores, and she felt a bit untidy, but was thrilled to see him nonetheless,

"Please, come in, and I'll make you up some tea," and she began to turn towards the house. Gabe took hold of her arm to pull her back towards him, as he needed to get the words off his chest that had been forming all through the night,

"Angela, please, give me but a moment of your undivided attention before we go inside? I have thought of nothing but you since meeting you at the dance. I even prayed about it, and I have felt that you are a blessing sent to me from Gott himself. We are both alone. We belong together, and I feel I can provide you with an easier life. Moreover, I can offer you my love and my farm. I offer all that is mine to you and your daughter and mother. I think we are an excellent match, and I find that I have fallen in love with you from the moment I laid eyes on you. I know how sudden this is, but we are not youngsters just starting out.

The community will accept our union as we are both widowed. Please say yes," and Gabriel stood there in a mess of nerves, as he hoped she would agree to marry him in the Spring.

Angela was taken aback by the sudden display of affection, but truthfully, she had felt the exact same way. After the dream, she had come to terms with her feelings of loss, and allowed herself to feel love again for the first time since Amos. She could not help but weep at his offer of love and total acceptance of a woman he had just met. She was glad that he had brought Emilia, so that the girls could meet and test the waters,

"Come in why don't you. I cannot do anything until you meet my mamm," she smiled, and he took this as a positive sign.

The two of them entered the house, and Alma was already sitting up in her bed. Her bed was in the large open sitting room for ease of care, so she had had a peak through the window at the two lovebirds,

"Good afternoon to ya', young man," she said quite formally, "Come in then, because I know what you're on about, and I can recognize love when I see it. I may be an old woman, but there are some things a woman can sense, especially in her daughter," as she glanced towards Angela, "My question to you, young man, is this: Kannst Du Deitsch Schwetza?" This translated into *Can you speak Dutch,* which Angela knew was the ultimate test of his worthiness. To her mamm, the only man good enough for her daughter after all she'd been through was a true and upright Amish man, who was able to conform to the old ways and blend them with the new.

Gabriel cleared his throat, hesitated for a moment, as if to search for the right words, and finally spoke back to her mamm. What he said was the following, much to the utter surprise of all in the household within earshot,

"Mir gleiche die Amische brieder bsuche *(We enjoy visiting our Amish people).* Amos, Er hot en iwwerflissich lewe gfaahre *(Amos, he lived the abundant life.)* Nau is awwer bsll Zert *(Now it's about time!)*

I love your daughter, and am ready to fulfill my duties as her faithful husband under Gott. I apologize, but my Dutch is a bit rusty, but I do know one thing, and that is this," as Gabe sat down to become eye to eye with Alma, and addressed Angela,

"Sie hot die hose aa *(She wears the pants in the family)*," as he gestured towards her mother, clearly knowing the traditions of the older generation,

"and I seek to garner your permission to enter into marriage with your daughter."

From the look of shock on her mamm's face, neither one of them had suspected that Gabriel was so familiar with the old language such as he was. Little did the ladies know that his own mamm had taught him well, and had brought him up to respect his elders. She had made sure he knew Pennsylvania Dutch enough to speak properly to relatives and older members of the community. This was a blessing in disguise, as Angela's mamm was not easily impressed, as Angela noted that Alma was beaming from ear to ear!

"Young man! You impress me. Of course, I give my permission. Now, go get yer little boppli and Becca, and let us celebrate as a family!" she cried out. Alma was elated that her daughter had finally found a man to care for her and Becca. She cared little for her own care, as she knew that the young man would see to the best care possible by the women of the village. Any young person who had been brought up in the old ways, was an exceptional choice for her daughter, and secretly she could not wait to make the acquaintance of the woman who had raised such a gallant young man! She would keep that to herself, for now was the time to make certain that the girls got along well enough to be sisters. At that thought, the two girls came bouncing out of Becca's room, each with a dolly in her hand, and jumped up at the table as Angela set down a cake she had luckily baked just yesterday afternoon. The tea things were arranged around the cake, and everyone sat down together, as Gabriel recited,

"Ich saaag dank am disch (*I offer thanks at the table*), and may Gott grant us the strength to become one family," and Gabe got up from the table, ran to Angela, and took her in his arms. He swung her around for all to see their happiness, as two separate and formerly lonely souls had found their way to one another against all odds. This day they would all remember with fond joy for the rest of their lives, as the moment that a new union was formed under the guiding hands of Gott himself.

A FAMILY FOR RACHEL

STEPHANIE COLLIER

Rachel Conrad pushed her feet against the wooden planks on the back porch as she rocked the sleeping baby in her arms and watched his father plow the pasture behind the house. Under different circumstances, the scene probably could have passed as a picture-perfect family moment, but the sad truth was…it wasn't her family.

She sighed as she looked down at one-year-old Mark Bowman, who was resting peacefully with his chubby little face pressed against her shoulder. It was late Friday afternoon, so it wouldn't be long before she would have to say goodbye and return to her home and face the long weekend, and the thought made her heart ache. When she agreed to help Mark's father, Isaac, care for the infant after his wife passed away six months prior, she never expected to become so attached to him – and Isaac too.

Rachel's gaze drifted once more to the large open field. There were storm clouds lingering on the horizon, but with any luck the rain would hold off until Isaac could finish plowing the last two rows. He pulled up on the reins to stop his horse and plow, and as he removed his hat and splayed a hand through his thick brown hair, Rachel took a couple of deep, even breaths to quell her pounding heart. He retrieved a handkerchief from the pocket of his trousers and quickly wiped his brow before putting his hat back on and signaling the horse to start moving forward again. She knew it probably wasn't ladylike to stare at the handsome widower, but she just couldn't make herself look away.

Much to her dismay, Isaac was the subject of many conversations within the small circle of single women in their Amish community. She had to remind herself repeatedly that she was nothing more than the nanny hired to care for his son, but there were so many nights when she dreamed of becoming more. Perhaps it was foolish, but she believed in her heart that God brought them together for a reason. Maybe someday Isaac would feel the same way.

A rumble of thunder echoed in the distance, causing Mark to stir and open his eyes. Rachel began humming his favorite lullaby to try and lull him back to sleep, and it wasn't long before the soft tune and the momentum from the rocker made his eyelids grow heavy. It also didn't take long before Rachel heard the pitter-patter of raindrops on the tin roof covering the back porch.

She stole another tentative glance at Isaac and was relieved to discover he'd finished plowing just in time before the rain fell. As he steered the horse and plow toward the barn, Rachel stood with Mark and entered the small wood-frame house through the back door. She tiptoed down the hallway to the nursery and carefully laid him in his crib before making her way to the kitchen at the other end of the house.

A few minutes passed before she heard the back door open and close, followed by Isaac's heavy footsteps in the hallway. When he walked into the kitchen, she held a finger to her lips to signal to him that Mark was sleeping, and he gave her an understanding nod.

His hair and clothes were slightly damp from the rain, and she resisted the overwhelming urge to brush away a couple of loose tendrils that were stuck to his forehead. She moved closer so she could whisper without waking Mark, but being near him proved more difficult than she expected it would, and for a moment she couldn't find her voice.

"There's some beef stew simmering on the stove, and there are biscuits in the oven. I'll see you Monday morning."

As she turned to leave, he wrapped a hand around her arm to stop her, nearly stopping her heart altogether. His grip was firm, but not at all rough, and the heat from his touch seared through the thin fabric of her dress and warmed her entire body.

"A storm is moving in, and it's too dangerous for you to drive," he whispered. "Stay and have dinner with me."

His invitation caught her off guard, but she didn't object. Honestly, the thought of sharing a meal with him excited her more than she cared to admit, but she tried to remind herself that from his standpoint it was more than likely an innocent request and nothing more. When she agreed to stay, Isaac went to one of the overhead cabinets and removed two plates and two glasses. She walked over to a drawer in the counter, where the cutlery was located, and took out two forks and two knives and placed them on the dining room table along with a couple of napkins.

He motioned for her to have a seat at the table, and as she sat there watching him move around the kitchen, she couldn't help but notice how happy he appeared to be. Not that he wasn't usually a happy man, but this was different. During the first few months after his wife's passing, she rarely saw him smile, which was, of course, understandable, but it did her heart good to witness him slowly emerging from his shell as he went through the healing process.

Isaac filled their plates with stew and biscuits, and their glasses with lemonade, before sitting across from her. It was the first time she'd dined with him, and she felt somewhat uncomfortable and unsure of what to say or do. After he said grace over the meal, Rachel laid the napkin in her lap and tried to keep her hands from shaking.

"I appreciate you cooking, Rachel. This looks delicious."

She gave him a shy smile. It wasn't in her job description to cook his meals, but she did so out of the kindness of her heart, because she knew he already had so much to tend to with raising Mark alone and trying to work.

"You're welcome. I enjoy doing it."

Her voice cracked, and Rachel cleared her throat and silently reprimanded herself for being so timid. It wasn't as if this was the first time she'd ever eaten a meal with a man, but it was the first time she'd ever felt awkward doing so. If Isaac noticed her apprehension, he didn't mention it. They ate in silence for a long while, but it was a comfortable silence, marred only by the rain pelting the tin roof and intermittent thunder.

"I hope this rain moves out before the festival tomorrow," he remarked.

Rachel furrowed a brow. It was the first time in several days she'd given any thought to the festival, which had been orchestrated by some of the women in the community to help raise money for the King's, a family from their church who'd fallen on hard times. Because of her full-time job caring for Mark, she'd had little time to help with the festivities, but she did donate a couple of her handmade quilts to be auctioned off.

"I hope it does too," she replied. "Were you planning on going?"

She tried to sound nonchalant about it, but the thought of being near him somewhere that didn't involve work made her feel hopeful they could eventually move beyond their employer/employee relationship. Festivals didn't occur very often in their community, and the only other place they both frequented was church, but that wasn't exactly the time or place to socialize on a personal level.

Rachel kept her eyes on her plate, but she held her breath, waiting for his reply.

"*Yah*, I told Bishop Jacob I would help him set up the podium and stage for the auction, so I'll be there most of the day."

Her heart soared, but she contained her excitement and continued taking small bites of her meal, stopping every so often to sip her lemonade. Although her hands trembled like a bashful schoolgirl's, she managed to hold on to her knife and fork.

"I can watch Mark for you while you help the Bishop, if you need me to."

He smiled at her, but he didn't accept her offer right away, which bothered her more than it probably should have.

"My parents are supposed to be there, and they volunteered to watch him for me. You already do so much for us, Rachel. I don't want to impose on you, especially on your day off, but thank you for offering."

She hoped her face didn't portray the disappointment she felt. It was ridiculous, really. After all, this was Isaac's family they were talking about, and she wasn't his keeper or Mark's mother, so she had no right to feel possessive of them.

The heavy rain slowed to a steady rhythm and the thunder dissipated as Rachel focused on finishing her meal. There were so many times when she couldn't wait to see Isaac, but there were also moments that hurt being near him, when the somber reality of their situation gripped her hard and refused to let go. This was quickly turning into one of those moments, and she knew she should distance herself...fast. The last thing she wanted was for Isaac to see her cry.

Rachel wiped her mouth with her napkin and carried her dinnerware to the kitchen sink. Isaac remained at the table and continued eating, which Rachel hoped would give her the chance to slip away easily, but before she could rinse her dishes and make a quick getaway, she heard him push his chair away from the table.

"Rachel, do you mind if I ask you a personal question?"

When he walked over to the sink and stood beside her, she kept her focus on washing the dishes to keep from looking at him. They'd never had a serious conversation about anything other than Mark and his late wife, Julia, so she couldn't imagine what he wanted to ask, but her heart raced while she waited.

"*Neh*, I don't mind. Go ahead."

He pulled up his shirt sleeves and helped her with the dishes, and Rachel made every effort not to touch him in the process. It wasn't that she didn't want to, but she knew even the slightest skin-to-skin contact with him would just weaken her resolve and leave her feeling even more depressed.

"Do you think it's possible for a man's heart to heal after he's lost his wife – to the point where he's able to love another woman?"

Rachel's hands began to tremble again. Part of her wanted to believe that he might be talking about her, but he'd given absolutely no inclination that he felt anything for her other than friendship, and she knew that could only mean one thing – he'd fallen in love with someone else. The realization was like a dagger to her heart.

"I believe God allows our hearts to heal and then expand to include someone else," she answered, softly. "He designed us to love others, and I don't think He meant for that to end, under any circumstance."

Hot tears sprang to her eyes, and she almost choked on her own words, but somehow, she managed to speak without crying. She waited for Isaac to reply, but he never did, and when they finished washing the dishes, Rachel hurriedly dried her hands with a dishcloth and smoothed her apron with the palms of her hands.

"It sounds like the rain has stopped, so I best go before it gets dark. Perhaps I'll see you tomorrow."

She turned away from him and went to the hallway to collect her cape, but unfortunately, he was much quicker. There was an expression on his face she'd never seen before, but she couldn't discern what was going on behind his beautiful hazel eyes, and maybe that was for the best. He held her cape open for her, but he didn't let go right away once he wrapped it around her shoulders. For a moment, she stood with her back to him, enjoying the feeling of his warm breath against her neck. When he released her, she stepped away from him, breaking the connection that was only tightening the vise around her heart.

"Good night, Isaac."

Before he had the opportunity to reply, Rachel opened the front door and walked away.

* * * *

Isaac scanned his surroundings for the hundredth time, but there was still no sign of Rachel. There were people milling about everywhere, and it seemed as if every man, woman, and child from the community was attending the festival...except the one person he truly cared to see. He caught sight of his parents sitting at one of the picnic tables under a grove of oak trees, with Mark in his stroller beside them. He waved when they looked his way, and he attempted a smile, but his heart was heavy.

Where could Rachel be?

"Isaac? Are you ready?"

The sound of Bishop Jacob's deep, booming voice interrupted his thoughts and brought him back to reality. The minister stood nearby, with both hands gripping one side of the makeshift podium they'd constructed for the auction taking place that afternoon. Isaac hurried to join him, and together they lifted the heavy podium and set it in place. With any luck, it would be the last thing the elder needed his help with, because he desperately wanted to take a walk and look for Rachel.

"Are you alright, Isaac?"

He focused his attention on Bishop Jacob, who was now staring at him intently, and he gave him a tentative smile. He really didn't want to get caught in a lengthy conversation over something he was still trying to work out on his own. He trusted the Bishop completely, and there were many times, especially during the last six months, when he'd darkened his doorstep, in search of council or a kind word, but this time was different.

"*Yah*, I'm fine," he replied. "Is there anything else I can help you with?"

Bishop Jacob looked at the completed stage and podium and smiled as he shook his head. "*Neh*, this is perfect. You should get some lunch and spend time with your family. *Denki*."

They shook hands and Isaac left his side and began wandering through the huge crowd of people. All the women had on the same attire, with their long dresses, aprons, and bonnets, so picking Rachel out was no easy task. He felt like kicking himself for letting her leave his house the night before without finishing their conversation. It had been a very long night, with little sleep, and not because Mark kept him up. He'd suffered through many sleepless nights over the past couple of months simply because he couldn't stop thinking about Rachel.

Something changed between them last night that he couldn't quite put his finger on. He hoped she understood he was referring to her when he asked her opinion about loving another woman, but it was hard to read her reaction. When she left suddenly, he felt almost certain she was upset because she didn't feel the same way and she didn't want to hurt his feelings. He needed to talk to her so he could find out once and for all where they stood and if he had a chance. The realization that she might be avoiding him made his heart hurt, and it also hastened his search.

Several people stopped him to talk, but he managed to get away from them quickly. When he reached the last booth, and found Rachel sorting through some jars of honey and homemade jellies for sale, his heart started pounding fiercely, partly from relief but mostly from the mere sight of her.

Her long, wavy brown hair was gathered behind her neck and tied with a satin blue ribbon. She grinned as she talked to the owner of the booth, and her beautiful smile lit up everything around her. It was impossible not to be captivated by her beauty, but there was so much more to her than that. Her compassionate heart, loving spirit, and generous soul were just as beautiful.

Isaac walked up beside her and lightly touched her back, which caused her to jump and almost drop the basket she had looped around her arm. He caught it and held it upright to keep the contents in it from crashing to the ground.

"I'm sorry. I didn't mean to startle you."

Rachel laughed softly. "It's alright." She picked up a jar of strawberry jam and paid the owner for it before placing it inside her basket. "Are you through helping Bishop Jacob?"

He nodded, and they stood in awkward silence for what felt like an eternity before he motioned toward an empty table nearby. "Can I talk to you for a minute...alone?"

She started for the table, and Isaac caught a faint scent of lavender when she walked past him. The aroma wafted through his senses and made him light-headed as he tried to fall in step beside her without stumbling over his own feet and making a fool of himself.

"I owe you an explanation about last night," he said. "I feel like we ended things on the wrong foot."

Rachel held up a hand to stop him from saying anything further. "It's alright, Isaac. You don't owe me anything. I understood what you meant."

It wasn't the reply he hoped for. If she did understand him then he didn't misread her reaction at all, and his worst fear was true – she didn't feel the same way about him. He stuffed his hands inside his pants pockets and shuffled his feet on the ground. It felt as if someone reached inside his chest and placed a chokehold around his heart.

"Rachel..."

She leaned into him, but they were interrupted before he could finish his sentence.

"Isaac! There you are! We've been looking all over for you!"

He turned in the direction of his mother's voice, and it didn't take long before she was closing in on them, pushing Mark in his stroller with one arm and her other arm draped through a woman's he didn't recognize. He felt Rachel move away from him, and just like that, there was a distance between them that felt more like an ocean than just a couple of feet.

When the women reached his side, his mother placed a hand against the stranger's back and nudged her toward him, nearly causing them to collide with each other. Isaac took a tentative step backward and gave his mother a weary look. He knew what she was up to before she said a word, and he felt his temper bristle in response.

"Isaac, this is Ruth Kurtz. She just moved here a couple of weeks ago from one of the communities in northern Lancaster."

He tipped his hat to her, and he tried to smile, but it was a half-hearted attempt, at best. He couldn't be rude because he knew his mother's behavior wasn't Ruth's fault. His parents made comments on several occasions that it was time he moved on, and so far, they'd done everything possible to try and make that happen.

"Oh, I'm sorry," his mother continued. "How rude of me. Ruth, this is Rachel Conrad. She's Isaac's maid and Mark's nanny."

Isaac's blood turned cold as he shot her a resentful glare. She was never one to mince words, but calling Rachel his maid was taking it too far.

"Mother, Rachel *isn't* my maid..."

He wanted to reprimand her, but Rachel kept him from doing so by stepping between the two of them and holding out her hand to Ruth.

"It's nice meeting you," she said. "I hate to rush off, but I really should be going."

They shook hands briefly before Rachel turned to leave, but not before bending over Mark's stroller and kissing his cheek.

"Rachel...please wait," he urged.

She didn't look at him, and when she walked away from them, Isaac felt a piece of his heart go with her.

* * * *

Rachel tickled Mark's stomach as she sat beside him on his blanket the following Monday morning. He loved laying on it and playing with his toys, and in no time, he was cooing and smiling up at her. His laughter was exactly what she needed. The house had been empty and quiet most of the day, which wasn't helping her somber mood in the least bit.

When she arrived that morning, Henry, one of Isaac's farmhands, was there waiting for him so they could make the drive into Lancaster for supplies. Because of this, she and Isaac didn't have time to speak to each other, except for a brief "hello". When the men returned three hours later, they immediately started working on one of the plows, stopping only to eat lunch.

It was probably for the best he remained busy and away from the house – and from her – because she didn't know what to say to him anymore. She felt consumed by a losing battle – not only with his mother's obvious low opinion of her, but from trying to vie for Isaac's attention among the other eligible women in the community.

Within a matter of minutes, Mark fell asleep on his blanket, and Rachel decided to clean up the kitchen while he napped. There wasn't much to tend to since Isaac and Henry washed and put away their dishes when they finished their lunch. Rachel nibbled on her bottom lip as she looked around for something to do. Being idle gave her far too much time to dwell on circumstances she couldn't change, so she tried to stay busy as much as possible.

She wet a dishcloth in the kitchen sink and started wiping down the countertops and dining room table, but not long into her task she heard Isaac and Henry's talking outside. She peered out the window above the sink just as Henry hopped on his wagon and steered his horse toward the main dirt road that would lead him home. Soon thereafter, she heard the back door open and close.

Rachel returned to her cleaning, but with just a few heavy footsteps, Isaac was standing in the kitchen doorway. He remained there while she worked, holding his hat and twirling it around and around in his hands, until he finally stepped inside the kitchen and laid it on the dining room table.

He approached her then, and Rachel sucked in a breath when he stood before her, leaving her no choice but to back up against the counter for support. He was so close she could see the tiny specks of dirt and oil on his cheeks and neck from working with Henry. His sleeves were rolled up to his elbows and the top two buttons of his shirt were undone. He looked rugged, masculine...and determined.

Isaac took the cloth from her and threw it in the sink before grabbing her hands and holding them securely. Her heart raced inside her chest, and her knees shook so badly she worried they might buckle and send her crashing to the floor.

"Is Mark asleep?" he asked.

She cleared her throat and nodded, not trusting herself to form coherent words. He looked down at their joined hands and when he returned his gaze to her again, she noticed he had the same expression on his face that he had Friday afternoon before she left. When he raised her hands, and brought them to his lips, she thought for certain her heart had stopped beating.

"I apologize for being so forward, but now that we're finally alone, there are some things I need to say. I don't want to waste another minute, so please just listen and let me get this off my chest."

She felt a lump form in her throat, and she was thankful he wanted her to remain quiet and let him speak because she wasn't sure she could say anything that might be audible over the drumming of her heart.

"When Julia died, I thought my life would never be the same. It felt like she took a huge part of me with her. Something was missing that I feared could never be replaced. I was angry at God for taking her from me and leaving Mark without his mother. I was angry that He took her instead of me. As terrible as it sounds, I didn't want to live anymore."

Rachel felt her eyes swell with tears, but she kept them at bay, not wanting to upset Isaac any more than he already was. He looked over her left shoulder and out the kitchen window, and his gaze was forlorn and distant.

"When I hired you to care for Mark, I never dreamed it would have such an enormous impact on my life, but little by little I started feeling better, like the broken pieces of my life were coming together to make me whole again. I have you to thank for that."

He looked at her and smiled and she tightened her grip on his hands, not wanting him to let go...ever.

"I think you may have misunderstood me when I asked if you thought it was possible for me to fall in love again. I wasn't talking about another woman. I was talking about *you*, Rachel. But then again, maybe you did understand, and perhaps you don't feel the same way as I do. Either way, I can't let another day – another second – pass by without letting you know how I feel."

He leaned forward and kissed her forehead, and she shivered as the softness of his lips and the heat from his breath lingered on her skin.

"Please don't take to heart anything my mother says. I have no interest in dating Ruth Kurtz or anyone else she tries to set me up with. I know her heart might be in the right place, and perhaps it's my fault because I haven't told her or my father yet how I feel about you. I *will* do that though...and soon."

He bent to kiss her again, but his lips bypassed her forehead and rested instead on her cheeks. She closed her eyes and enjoyed the feeling of his lips brushing against her nose and caressing her face. She expected him to kiss her lips, but he never did, and when he stopped and leaned back to look at her, she became suddenly aware of her ragged breathing.

"If you don't feel the same way about me, Rachel, I will try to understand, and I'll never speak of this again. I promise. I don't want to jeopardize our friendship in any way, but I do need to know if I stand a chance. You mean so much to me...and Mark too. I hope you know that."

He touched her chin before sliding his fingertips over her jaw and down the side of her neck. By this time her chest was rising and falling in rapid succession and she gripped the countertop behind her to keep from swooning.

"I do know that, Isaac. I feel the same way about you. I'm so sorry I overreacted the other day. I thought you were talking about falling in love with another woman, and it broke my heart. I didn't know what to say or do. I just knew I had to leave before I started crying, because I couldn't let you see me that way."

He held her head in his hands and this time when he leaned in to her, he pressed his lips against her own. His mouth was hot and demanding, and Rachel let go of the countertop and clung to him instead. The power he yielded was unlike anything she'd ever experienced before, and when they finally separated, she was so overcome with emotion she had to remind herself to breathe.

"Will you stay and have dinner with me tonight? I want to cook something for you. One of my specialties."

Rachel nodded. "I would love to, but you don't have to do that, Isaac. I can prepare something. You've been working so hard, and…"

He silenced her by kissing her again, but this kiss was gentler than the one before it. His lips barely brushed her own, but it had the same impact.

"I want to do this for you," he continued. "I still have some work to finish in the barn, but I'll be back as soon as I can get away."

She couldn't speak, so she simply nodded, and after one last kiss, he was picking up his hat from the dining room table and heading for the back door. Rachel remained in place, leaning against the kitchen counter for the longest while, not trusting her shaky legs to carry her very far. She could still feel his kiss, and as she traced her fingertips across her lips, she closed her eyes and smiled. Her dream was coming true, and she couldn't remember a time when she'd ever felt happier.

The sound of Mark whimpering prompted her to move, and she went to him and picked him up from his blanket. She kissed his little face and twirled him around a couple of times, which made him laugh. It was such a beautiful sound, and one she would never tire of. Her heart soared when she imagined the three of them becoming a family and never having to face another long weekend in her empty home. It was enough to bring tears to her eyes.

Rachel carried Mark to his nursery so she could change his diaper. She looked forward to sharing dinner with Isaac again, especially since she'd never had a man cook for her before. There were so many new experiences taking place – each one more exciting than the one before it. She felt light on her feet and she couldn't stop smiling. It was a wonderful feeling.

As soon as she changed Mark's diaper, she heard the creaking of the back-door hinges as someone opened it, and she slipped on Mark's shirt and pants before picking him up.

"Let's go see daddy. He must have forgotten something."

With a spring in her step, she left the nursery and bounded down the hallway, but it wasn't Isaac who greeted her when she turned the corner. Much to her surprise – and dismay – it was his mother.

* * * *

Isaac put his sandpaper down and stepped back to examine his work. It took longer than he expected to repair the broken plow handle, but it was coming together at last. The sound of a horse whinnying caught his attention, and he furrowed a brow as he looked toward his two horses in their stalls at the opposite end of the barn, where they were busy eating their grain.

Isaac put the sandpaper down on his work bench and went to one of the windows facing the house, and his heart fell to his feet when he recognized his parents horse and carriage in his driveway. Rachel's horse and wagon, on the other hand, were gone. He muttered a few choice words under his breath as he raced toward the house and burst through the back door.

He heard his mother's voice as soon as he entered the house, and he found her sitting at the kitchen table, bouncing a giggling Mark up and down on her knee. He searched the rest of the small house, but Rachel was nowhere to be found.

"Where is Rachel?" he asked.

His mother stopped playing with Mark and finally acknowledged his presence.

"I sent her home."

Isaac felt his temper rise, and he took a couple of steady breaths to try and remain calm. "You did *what*?"

She stood and walked with Mark to the living room, leaving Isaac no choice but to follow her.

"I told her she could go and that I would take care of Mark. It was almost time for her to leave anyway, wasn't it? Really, Isaac, I don't know why you keep her around. There are so many women in our community who would love to marry you, and you need a partner – not a nanny. I mentioned to her that she might want to start looking for another job soon. I can watch Mark for you."

Isaac closed his eyes and shook his head.

"Mother, I love you, but you don't have the right to choose who I should and shouldn't marry. I have no interest in Ruth Kurtz or any of the other women you've introduced me to."

She rolled her eyes heavenward before sitting on the sofa.

"Oh, stop being ridiculous, Isaac. I'm only trying to help you."

Isaac walked over and stood in front of her. "If you want to help me, then you need to accept the fact that I love Rachel, and I plan on asking *her* to be my wife."

Her jaw slacked open and her eyes became wide and expressive. "Rachel? Well, why didn't you tell me? I thought she was nothing more to you than your employee."

Isaac shook his head again. He loved his mother dearly, but there were times when she could be too crass for her own good.

"I've never thought of her that way. She isn't a *servant*, Mother. I love her and Mark loves her, and that's all that matters." He sighed. "I need to find her. Please stay here and watch Mark until I get back."

Before she could object, he was out the door and taking the reins in her carriage. He steered the horse onto the main dirt road and veered to the right, in the direction of Rachel's house. Thankfully, he didn't have to go far before he came upon her in her wagon. He yelled her name, but the sound of pounding hooves on the gravel drowned out his voice. Isaac ushered the horse to go faster, and within seconds he was pulling up alongside of her. As soon as she saw him, she jerked up on the reins to bring her horse and wagon to a stop and Isaac followed suit.

He noticed right away that her cheeks were wet with tears, which made him even angrier at his mother for intervening. He jumped down from the carriage and climbed aboard her wagon so he could sit beside her.

"I'm so sorry, Rachel."

He wiped the tears from her cheeks before pulling her into his embrace.

"I don't think your mother will ever approve of me."

He frowned. She sounded so tired and defeated, and it broke his heart.

"My mother has never been one for gentle words. I don't understand why, but please don't take it to heart. She's always been that way – with everyone."

She let go of him and leaned back in the seat, but he held on to her hands and rubbed them gently to try and keep more tears from falling.

"She didn't know how I feel about you, but she does now, and I apologize for not telling her sooner. Please don't give up on us. I won't let this happen again. You have my word."

He kissed her lips, and the brief contact was enough to send a jolt of heat rushing through his veins.

"I would never do that, Isaac. I can put up with anything or anyone for you – even your mother," she replied.

Her comment made him laugh out loud, and when she grinned at him, he felt his spirits lift.

"Then come back to the house and let me fix that dinner I promised you. With any luck, my mother won't be staying long, but if she does, we'll get through it together."

She nodded in agreement, and he kissed her one more time before returning to his horse and carriage. As they both turned around and headed in the opposite direction, he looked up at the sky and mouthed a short prayer of gratitude to God for bringing Rachel into his life when he needed her the most. He knew without a doubt in his mind that Julia would be happy for him and Mark too, and that filled him with a profound sense of peace he hadn't felt in a very long time.

He'd stumbled across the answer he longed for, and it was Rachel. Because of her, he'd discovered it *was* possible for his heart to expand and find love again…and he couldn't wait to spend the rest of their days making memories that would last a lifetime.

A PROPER AMISH MAN

CHELSEA MCCANN

Abigail knew the path to the Church by heart. She could walk it blindfolded if she had to. Once, her brother Eli had dared her to. She made it halfway before she tripped on a rock and sprained her wrist. Everyone laughed, but she argued it could have happened to anyone.

She remembered her mother, red faced, her thick, black hair slipping from her bonnet when she discovered what her middle daughter had done. *"Dat is niet wat de dames doen!"* That is not what ladies do.

She continued to walk the path every day, sometimes twice a day. That was what ladies did in Amish country; they went to church. Usually Abigail was accompanied by one of the little ones. She was one of eleven: Mary was the eldest, then Ruth, Miriam, Eli, Aaron, herself, Samuel, Isaac, Hannah, Sarah and then finally Baby Jilly who had accompanied her that day.

Jilly held Abigail's hand as she skipped down the path. Her black hair was in two braids on either side of her head, and her boots were worn from the six little girls that had worn them before her. Abigail figured she should have scolded Jilly for skipping, *dat is niet wat de dames doen,* but as she wasn't her mother she figured she would let her get away with it.

"What are we gonna sing today?" Jilly asked her big sister. She was five. Abigail was sixteen.

"I'm not sure," she said. "Whatever Pastor John has planned for us, I guess."

"Ik hoop dat het iets leuk om te zingen," Jilly said, accidentally slipping into the Dutch their parents spoke at home, and whenever they were talking with other elders in the town. *I hope it's something fun to sing,* Jilly had said.

Deep in her gut, Abigail had the impulse to correct her; tell her that speaking Dutch would only drag her further into the community, and that she would never be able to escape. However, she could not poison her baby sister's mind.

Her poison was off in the distance. A few months before, her community had opened their gates to tourists coming to examine Amish life. It was a controversial topic among members of the community, and a good chunk of the men had voted against it, but the majority won. There was a school group there, of boys and girls about Abigail's age. As her and Jilly walked closer, she was able to examine them more. She was envious of the girls with short hair, cut to their chins, and the paint on their face that she would never be allowed to wear. The boys had shaggy hair, and were cute; unlike men in the town. Except perhaps Lucas . . .

"OMG she's so cute!" one of the girls pointed to Jilly as they walked by. "Look at her little dress!"

Jilly, like a good little Amish girl, ignored them. They were sinners after all. And following in her sister's example, Abigail did the same.

****

The church was a one room building in the center of town. The old white stone was drafty, as many of the buildings that Abigail visited, without a fire burning except in the coldest of winters. Her and Jilly bowed their heads as the entered, and then walked over to the piano where Pastor John sat.

"Good morrow, girls," he said. Pastor John was old, about fifty or so, with whiting hair and lines around his mouth. He was easily the kindest man in the whole community. He had come to them as a teen from the outside world. His parents had died in a fire, and his brother and him ran away from their foster parents. They found solace in the community, and after a few years were baptised. Pastor John became a pastor. His elder brother became Abigail and Jilly's father.

"Hello, Uncle John!" Jilly beamed.

Pastor John laughed. "How about some hymns?"

They warmed up first. Jilly still had a baby voice, but as the youngest walking member of the community she warmed the hearts of the elders whenever she sang in church. Abigail, however, had a gorgeous voice. As they sang their praises to God and Jesus, there was a creak of the door opening, and the steps of people walking inside.

The first thought Abigail had was that the school group was not allowed to be inside of the church; they were sinners, and they would taint the building. Pastor John did not seem to mind, however, and Abigail just continued singing, trying to tune out Jilly's baby squeaks and the sounds of the teenagers whispering. She accidentally glanced over at them once, and saw a blonde haired girl there front and center smiling. Uncomfortable, Abigail looked away, back at Pastor John.

The teenagers left eventually, to most likely go play with the baby sheep that had just been born, and their lesson ended as well. The girls thanked their uncle the pastor, and began their walk home.

****

Lucas was the shepherd's son. He lived next door to Abigail's family farm, which was about a half a mile away. He was the eldest, the only boy with seven sisters. He had a steady future, with no threats to his family's welfare. He was good looking, strong, and a man of God.

As Abigail was exactly the same age as Lucas, it was no secret that they would be pushed together at some point. She fought it forever, making it a point to torture Lucas when they were children. She had pushed him into the river once, ruining his clothes and nearly breaking his arm. She remembered her mother that day vividly: *dat is niet wat de dames doen!*

However, the more she tried to fight it, the more her feelings for Lucas grew more and more, until eventually she felt as though she was going to burst. Of course, being a lady, she was not allowed to tell him.

About a week before that mentioned singing lesson with Jilly, a letter that had been addressed to her was tucked into the chicken coop. She had discovered it when she went to fetch the family's eggs that morning.

She couldn't read it in front of Hannah, Sarah or Jilly as she knew they would tell her parents. She tucked it into her apron, and impatiently waited until she had a moment alone.

That moment came when she went to go check on their cow, Miss Lavinia, who was due to give birth at any day. She hid inside the barn, completely alone, and practically tore open the letter Lucas had written her:

My dearest Abigail,

As a proper Amish man, I should be writing this letter in Dutch, however I just cannot bring myself to do that. This town has us restricted in so many ways, but fortunately it seems that it is completely alright with the two of us being together. I did not want to alarm you, but I wanted to tell you that this evening I will be meeting with your father and I will be asking to court you. I hope this is okay, yet in my heart I know that it will be. I know you love me as I love you, and I am looking forward to this journey together. Now as a proper Amish man, I must say this: Ik hou van jou. I love you!

Lucas

Abigail had nearly cried when she had read the letter. Her darling Lucas . . . he was actually hers!

That night, just as he had promised, he came by right after they finished their dinner. He asked to speak with Abigail's father, Pastor John's brother, who was named Ethan. Ethan was a large man; bred in the outside world but easily adapted to life within the community. Had Abigail not been told of her father's past she never would have guessed it. The three littles ones (Sarah, Hannah and Jilly) were unaware.

Lucas was tall as well, with broad shoulders that were good for carrying injured sheep. He had sandy colored hair and bright blue eyes that lit up his entire face. Abigail tried not to melt when she walked into their home.

"Lucas!" Jilly and Sarah, who was a year older than her, ran over to him and gave him a hug. Abigail expected a scolding from their mother, but then quickly remembered she was rather soft on the two little ones.

"Hello to the two most beautiful little ladies," Lucas said, returning the hug. He then extended his hand to Ethan and shook it.

The two had excused themselves. Abigail, pretending she did not know what was going on, helped her mother with the dishes, all the meanwhile trying to hide the fact that her knees were clacking together with nerves. After what felt like hours, her father poked his head into the doorway.

"Abigail," he said. "A moment, please."

"You're in trouble!" Sarah taunted.

"Mind your manners," their mother said.

Abigail thought that if her father was asking her to go outside that was a good sign. Wasn't it? She wiped her wet hands on her apron and excused herself. It was beginning to be cool.

"Lucas." She nodded her head.

"Miss Abigail." He smiled.

Ethan shut the door. "Abigail, Lucas here has asked for my permission to court you. I have said yes, but as I am not a man of stone I wanted to know if that would be alright with you."

Abigail pretended to think for a second, but she was so happy she could not stand it. A smile burst out of her. "Yes!" she squealed.

Ethan laughed, and then patted Lucas on the shoulder. "Make sure to take care of her now," he said. "She may not be my eldest daughter, nor my youngest, but she still means the world to me."

Abigail and Lucas nodded their heads to each other, as that was what a courtship entailed, but Abigail had a feeling that wasn't going to last.

****

After dinner that night and after everyone went to bed, Abigail slipped out the bedroom window to the barn. If she was caught, she would tell her parents she was checking on Miss Lavinia, when in fact she was going to meet Lucas.

He was petting Miss Lavinia, who still had yet to give birth. "She might be having twins," he said, as Abigail entered the barn.

"You're never supposed to insult a woman's weight," Abigail mused.

"In a good way," Lucas said, smiling. "Twins means more money. More dairy. More beef."

Abigail shuttered. "They're not even born yet and you want to send them off to slaughter?"

"In the outside world, they have people who don't eat meat," Lucas said. "Because they can afford to do stuff like that."

Abigail pet Miss Lavinia's snout, and the cow, uncomfortable, closed her eyes and allowed herself to be soothed. "Ever think about leaving the community?" she asked.

"And being shunned?" Lucas scoffed, but his face read that he wasn't completely opposed to the idea. "Where would we go?"

Abigail shrugged. "Somewhere big," she said. "Like . . . Philedelphia. Or New York City. Or Hong Kong!"

Lucas laughed. "Hong Kong is in a different country."

"But we could never go there if we didn't leave," Abigail said. Miss Lavinia opened her eyes and gave her a sorrowful look. "We would be trapped here forever, narrowing our world, not seeing everything. Don't you want to see everything?"

"Do you never want your parents to speak to you again?" Lucas asked.

"I wouldn't mind," Abigail said, which was the half truth.

"What about Jilly?"

To that, Abigail had to be more creative. "We would take us with her!"

"Your parents wouldn't be okay with that and you know it."

Abigail felt defeated. Miss Lavinia mooed, and it sounded painful. She was sure to be in labor soon, if not beginning to already. Before Abigail could tell Lucas this discovery, his arms were wrapped around her waist.

She turned around into his kiss. It wasn't the first time he had kissed her. Though pre marital *anything* was against the rules, the two of them were relaxed when it came to kissing. There was no way that everyone who kissed someone else ended up in hell, and the two of them agreed not to progress it any further. But sometimes, like moments like that, when he literally knocked the breath right out of her, Abigail found it hard to resist.

"I wish we could leave," he whispered, when he paused.

"Neither of us are baptised," she replied. "We could and if we didn't like it -"

"I'm the only son."

Abigail didn't say anything. She knew how much of a struggle that would be for him. It would be a struggle for her too, even though she had plenty of brothers and was not the sole heir to her family's farm. She looked at Miss Lavinia. She would miss her, and her siblings, especially little Jilly, but she did not know if she could miss the community life. The problem was it was not a revolving door; the only ticket out was a strict one-way.

"Well," she said. "We will figure something out."

Lucas didn't reply. He just held her tight.

****

About a week later, Miss Lavinia had given birth to a new calf. It was a boy. Jilly named him Jedidiah, because she felt like that was a good name for a cow. A day after she gave birth, Abigail found herself headed down the familiar path to the church with Jilly, to their weekly lesson.

When they got there, however, they did not find a lonely Pastor John; they discovered he was with someone else. He was tall, taller than

Lucas and Ethan, with bright blonde hair to his shoulders. What struck Abigail the most was that he was wearing outside world clothing.

"Hello, Abigail. Jilly," Pastor John said. "This is Mac McMullan."

Mac. That wasn't a name, was it? Abigail nodded politely and said, "How do you do?" Jilly didn't say anything. She didn't understand the difference between who she was allowed and who she was not allowed to talk to, so she reserved herself to not talking to anyone.

"I'm well," Mac said. He had a high pitched voice, and a little bit of a lisp. "You must be the talented Abigail that I have heard so much about."

Abigail was taken aback. "How did you hear about me?"

"My sister was on a trip here a week back," Mac explained. "With her friends from school, and she heard you sing. I reached out to Pastor John about maybe coming to meet you, and he said that was okay. So I was actually wondering . . ." He furrowed his eyebrows together and grinned. "Do you think you could maybe sing to me? A little?"

"I don't know anything besides hymns," Abigail said, a little bit embarrassed. "That's probably not what you listen to where you're from."

"Whatever makes you happy!" Mac grinned. "Lucy said you were amazing at whatever you were doing, so I totally want to hear it."

Lucy. That was a more normal name. Abigail distinctly remembered the little blonde girl that was pointing to her when her and Jilly were singing the week before. That must have been Lucy.

Pastor John sat at the piano, and Jilly and Abigail circled around him. Abigail noticed her little sister had her back turned to Mac, and had a strong urge to tell her not to be rude, but she couldn't bring herself to do it.

Pastor John played the beginning chords to *In the Garden of Eden.* Abigail began to sing. Out of the corner of her eye she looked at Mac, who had his arms folded across his chest and a huge smile on his face.

His look made her feel more confident, and she smiled as she continued to sing.

When the hymn was over, Jilly crinkled her nose together. "I don't know if I like that one."

Pastor John didn't get a chance to reply; Mac began clapping as he walked over to the girls. "That was beautiful," he said. "Really. Beautiful. Abigail, you're amazing."

"Jilly too," Abigail said, because even though she wouldn't speak to this man, she knew her baby sister's feelings were hurt.

Mac nodded, a smile still on his face. "Jilly too."

"Is it everything you expected?" Abigail teased.

"Everything and more," Mac said, looking at Pastor John. "Which is why I am here. I am a music producer. I work for a predominantly Christian label in New York City."

New York City was a solid seven hours away from where Abigail's community was. She couldn't even imagine what it looked like; only that it was a huge city of the outside world. She heard they had buildings that reached the sky and trains underground. She would be swallowed in New York City.

"Label?" Abigail asked.

"Music label," Mac clarified. "And I think you might be our next solo artist. If you're up to it."

"Does my mamma and papa know you're here?" Jilly asked Mac, momentarily forgetting that she wasn't supposed to talk to him . . . technically.

Abigail looked at Pastor John. He looked guilty. Clearly he knew about Mac and his intentions, but did not bother to tell his brother. Abigail in turn felt a little guilty, but at the same time tried to imagine what could happen in a big city like New York. She would be able to sing for the label, and wouldn't be constricted to bonnets and shunning strangers.

And then she thought of Lucas . . .

"No," Mac finally answered Jilly. "But I would love to meet them."

"You can't come inside," Jilly said. "You could ruin our house."

"Let's not be too hasty," Abigail said, a little embarrassed at her sister's behavior. "Papa would most likely like to speak to you though," she continued, talking to Mac.

Mac looked at his watch on his wrist. "Well, I actually have to scoot today. I'm meeting with another Amish girl a little north of here, but yeah! Definitely tomorrow? How does that sound?"

Abigail looked at Pastor John. He nodded. "Sounds good," he said. "I'll talk to my brother tonight. Prepare him."

****

Abigail prayed Jilly wouldn't say anything over dinner about Mac. Fortunately, the little one seemed to know when she could tell things to her parents when she couldn't, so she stayed quiet. The entire time they were eating, Abigail's knees were shaking. She kept looking at her mother to see if she knew anything. Not that Pastor John had the chance to tell her, but sometimes Abigail was convinced her mother could read minds.

She wanted to move to New York City. She wanted to sing for Mac, and have fans, and be in the outside world. She was so excited, but so scared at the same time. She would be leaving her entire life behind, and she would not be able to come back. She looked at her brothers and sisters, and even her parents, and tried to imagine her life without them. She couldn't.

Yet at the same time, she imagined the outside world. She could do so much. She wouldn't be restricted to the tiny little community, and she could be with the modern times. She could wear pants. She could let her hair down and even cut it shorter if she wanted to. There were so many possibilities, yet she was so scared.

She kept yearning for Lucas. After dinner, once everyone was in bed, Abigail once again slipped out of the window and went to the barn. Miss Lavinia was there, along with Jedidiah. The baby looked exactly like his mother; cream colored with brown spots. He even had the same shape one covering his right eye. And right next to the calf, petting him on the head, was Lucas.

"Hey," he said.

"I got asked to record an album in New York City," Abigail blurted out, because she was scared if she held it in any longer she was going to explode.

Lucas stopped petting Jedidiah, and looked at Abigail. She couldn't tell what exactly he was thinking. "You . . .is this a joke?"

"Do I look like I'm joking?" she winced.

He looked back at Jedidiah, and began petting the little calf on his head. Abigail thought he may have been crying, but she wasn't too sure. The barn wasn't very well lit.

"You're leaving."

"I never said that," she replied.

"But you want to. Otherwise you never would have said anything to me."

Lucas looked up, and instantly Abigail felt heart broken. His eyes were swelling up with tears.

"I don't know," she said, and she began to break.

Before she knew it, he was kissing her. And she was kissing him back, pulling his hair and pressing her lips into his. How could she give this up? How could she move far away from him?

She didn't know what to do.

When he broke away, she was crying as well. Lucas wiped away his tears with his right thumb, his left hand still holding her face. "If you leave, you'll be shunned."

"I haven't been baptized yet," Abigail said. "Neither have you. We can come back. We don't have to leave forever."

"They'll never look at us the same."

"Your parents love you."

"That doesn't mean they'll support me." Lucas' hands fell away. "That doesn't mean they'll ever forgive me for putting their sheep and their livelihood in jeopardy."

"Maybe they'll have another baby?" Abigail offered, even though she acknowledged she was just being desperate. "A boy?"

"They can't control that."

Abigail understood that no matter what she said, she would not be able to make Lucas feel better. He left a few minutes later, and all she could do was try and figure out whether or not she was ready for this.

Before she could even try to say anything, the barn door opened. Lucas and Abigail sprung apart, and Abigail expected it to be either of her parents, and was surprised to see her brother Eli. He was eighteen, twins with Abigail's brother Aaron, and a hardworking man of Jesus.

"Eli . . ." she began. This was almost worse than being caught by her father.

He had a stern look on his face. "I came to check on Miss Lavinia," he said, and he looked at Lucas. "You should go."

Lucas left without any hesitation, leaving the two siblings alone. "This isn't what it looks like . . ." Abigail said.

"Were you having sex?" Eli asked.

Abigail shook her head. "Nothing like that." She bowed her head, ashamed. "I have been asked to leave the community, to sing for a music label. And I won't go unless Lucas comes with me. And he can't leave his farm because he is the only son. So I don't know what to do."

"You'll be shunned," Eli said.

"I know."

"Do you love him?"

That question caught her off guard. She looked up and stared her brother straight in the eye and said, "Yes."

****

The next morning, after Abigail and the four little ones milked the cows and got the eggs, they met inside their house for breakfast. Abigail helped her mother cook, while everyone else gathered around after doing their morning chores.

Her father had already been into town, and Abigail suspected he had talked to Pastor John. She was worried.

They all sat around the table, bowed their heads in prayer, and began to eat. The little girls began their usual chatter, and Abigail noticed her father kept looking at her. She could feel her stomach churning, but she could not ask him what he was thinking. That would be rude.

She also kept looking at Eli, expecting him to have cracked and told her parents what he had seen last night. Yet somehow, he was remaining cool.

Finally, her father said, "Ik denk dat je moet worden gedoopt, Abigail." *Abigail, I think you should be baptized.*

Abigail swallowed. He knew. She tried to remain calm when she said, "Maar vader, ik ben slechts zestien. Ik heb alles van mijn studie van de Bijbel niet gedaan. Ik ben nog jong." *But father, I am only sixteen. I have not done all my Bible study. I am still young.*

Her father waved his hand, dismissing the entire thing. "Je bent je moeder was dezelfde leeftijd," he said, looking at his wife.

He was right. She was the same age her mother was when she was baptized. Abigail felt that churning in her stomach.

"Lucas," she finally said.

"You're in love, aren't you?" Jilly asked.

"Jilly, uw ontbijten," their mother snapped.

"You know I don't speak Dutch," Jilly said, even though that was a lie. She went back to eating her breakfast like her mother told her to.

"I am not ready to get baptized," Abigail said, using English instead of Dutch. If she was going to be living in the outside world she had to get used to outside language. She also acknowledged that her and Lucas only spoke English to each other. Maybe he wanted to be as rebellious as she was.

She couldn't think about Lucas. Not then anyway. She ate her breakfast, and took in the silence at the table.

****

Later that day, Abigail snuck away. She found Pastor John in the church, sitting in a pew reading a Bible.

"Pastor John," she said. "May I talk to you?"

"Can I just say how relieved I am you asked me that in English?" He smiled warmly.

She sat next to him. Had he not been a man of faith she never would have put herself in the position with him. But most importantly, she needed to know what to do.

"I'm scared," she finally said.

"About Mac's offer?" he asked.

"That," she said. "And my parents now want me to get baptized. And there's Lucas . . ."

She stopped herself then, and felt her cheeks go red.

"Abigail," Pastor John said. "It is alright to fall in love."

"You don't fall in love here," she explained, feeling a little silly having so that that to a prominent member of the community. "You don't fall in love, you court someone your father approves and then you get married. You have sex with someone to reproduce according to what God had told you to do, you do not kiss them because it feels good."

She stopped herself again.

"Have you kissed Lucas?" he asked.

She nodded.

"That's okay," he said. "It is okay to fall in love. And more importantly your parents approve of you falling for him. The outside world is scary, and if you're going to go out there it'll be good for you to bring him with you."

"He won't go," she said, tears coming into her eyes. "He cannot leave the sheep. He is the only son in his family, and if he leaves they will be ruined. He can't do it, and I do not want to be angry with him for it, but I am. I am angry."

"Then you have a choice to make."

"I don't know what to choose. I don't want to be alone."

Pastor John sighed. "You know, in a different life, you would have called me Uncle John. You would have lived in the outside world. You would have been getting ready for your first prom right now, taking pictures with your friends . . . being a normal teenager."

"I always forget you're from out there," Abigail replied.

"You're father is too." Pastor John looked at her. "Your mother may not be able to understand, but he will. We left together and it was the right decision for us. But that doesn't mean you shouldn't be able to find the right decision for you."

"You really think my father will understand?" Abigail had a trace of hope in her voice.

Pastor John nodded. "I really do."

****

That night, Abigail sat with her parents, and Pastor John, and Mac, whom her parents had broken all of the rules and allowed him in the house. He wore a jacket and jeans, and he had tied his hair back into a ponytail. The other kids were away, outside doing chores or playing.

"You want to take my little girl into the city," Ethan said.

"I do," Mac nodded. "She's a talented singer and I believe her voice could be admired by those around the world."

"I grew up in the city," Ethan said. Abigail noticed her mother touch his arm. "I know what that world is like. It's cold and cruel, and here it is safe and nothing harmful will happen to her. If she is baptized, nothing will happen to her when she leaves this world either."

"I want to live, father," Abigail said. "I love you and mamma, and I love everyone here but I don't know what is outside of these walls and I want to learn. I know you think it is cruel and scary, and that life was hard for you when it was young, but why do so many people live out there instead of here? There must be something good there, and Mac can show me, and I can sing about Jesus. I don't want to be here and never know what I could have done. I would hate myself. I want to experience and if I don't like it . . ." She stopped herself.

"You would want to come back," Pastor John finished for her.

"I would want to come back." She nodded.

Before anyone could say anything, the door opened and Eli came in. He nodded, before going over to the bench next to the door to take off his boots. He was muddy; no doubt cleaning the stalls.

"What about Lucas?" It was her mother that asked the question this time.

Abigail felt tears well in her eyes, but she wouldn't dare shed them. "I would miss him terribly. So terribly."

"He could come with you," Mac offered. "I'm down with that."

"Down?" Abigail's mother questioned.

"Okay with that," Mac clarified. "If she wanted to bring him. He could come along."

"He can't leave his farm," Abigail said. "So that's that."

It was then that she noticed her mother was crying. She was dabbing her eyes with a handkerchief, and her nose was running. "Mamma . . ." Abigail began.

"I raised you to be a good Amish girl," her mother cried. "And I want what is best with you, and I feel like I have failed. I feel like I have not made you happy. I feel as though I have not given you a great life."

"Mamma . . ."

Breaking all the rules, Abigail stood up and walked over to her mother and hugged her. "I love you so much," she whispered. "And I'll come back to see you."

"Don't get baptized," her mother whispered back. "I don't want to shun my daughter."

"You don't have to shun me," Abigail said.

It was then that Abigail felt arms around her, and noticed her father was holding her as well. The three of them hugged, and Abigail almost felt completely at peace.

****

Mac had a car. Abigail had seen them before, but she had never ridden in one. This one was red, and it was small, but it looked like it would go fast. She thought of how her life was going to be surrounded by cars now, and she was nervous, but excited. The would be more predictable than horses, right?

Her entire family had gathered to say goodbye. Except Eli, but Abigail did not want to comment on that. Jilly looked annoyed, but her parents promised they would explain to her exactly what was going on. The other little girls looked sad. They had been crying all day.

All of her sisters hugged her goodbye, and her brothers shook her hand. Even her elder sisters, who were all married, had come to send her off with their children and spouses. Her nieces and nephews marveled at the car, and even tried to climb on top of it, before they were pulled away by their parents. Abigail's parents hugged her, and her mother whispered that she loved her in Dutch in her ear. Abigail prayed that she never forgot the language, even though she complained about it sometimes.

"Ready to go?" Mac asked her, and Pastor John. He had agreed to go with her for a week to make sure she settled in okay. That made her parents feel better. Abigail asked if he would be shunned, but since he was returning, it would be excused as a business adventure. He was off to hear about the Lord and he would be back.

Abigail was about to say yes, but down the path she saw two figures running towards them. It took a couple seconds, but she then realized it was Eli and . . .

"Lucas?" she whispered.

They were both out of breath when they reached them. Abigail noticed Lucas had a burlap bag in his hand. "Abigail," he panted.

"We made a deal," Eli explained, a little less out of breath than Lucas. His thick, black hair was sweat soaked, but his face was completely lit up. Abigail almost did not recognize her brother. "We made a deal, I talked to his father . . . I'm marrying Mary."

Mary . . . Lucas' sister . . .

"What?" Abigail asked.

"We've been courting," he explained. "In secret, we've been courting, and I asked her father if I could marry her and that way, I can get the farm and the sheep and Aaron . . . he could take over ours." He looked at his twin. "Is that okay with you?"

Aaron shrugged, and smiled. "I'll take it."

Eli looked at Ethan. "Is that okay with you, Pa?"

Ethan nodded, and then walked over to Lucas. He set his hand on his shoulder. "You take good care of my girl. It's a scary world out there. Don't hurt her. Don't cause her any pain."

Lucas nodded aggressively. "Definitely, sir. Definitely."

"And ask her if she wants you to come," Ethan continued.

Lucas looked at Abigail. "Does this plan work for you?"

Abigail could not imagine a better life. She hugged her father, and then her mother, and then Eli because she was simply out of words. She then got into the car with Mac, Lucas, and Pastor John, driving off to the outside world.

THE CRADLE

PHYLLIS ROGERS

THE CRADLE

The scent of white oak filled the tiny wood shed Samuel Fisher worked in. It was a pleasant herbal-like aroma with nutty overtones. He hand-cut each piece of wood and smoothed them with a wood planer his father and grandfather used before him. He used a lathe to form the spindles, which he fit into the sides of the cradle, one by one.

Samuel took off his black straw hat and wiped the sweat off of his head and face. It had been a grueling two months. It seemed as though the drought had settled and was there to stay. The farm work had become arduous, and between the long days of working in the fields with the blistering heat and taking care of his beloved wife, Hannah, the young man sometimes was overwhelmed. He paused and sighed, concerned. Hannah's pregnancy had proved to be a difficult one. It was the hottest summer on record.

The lack of air conditioning offered little respite for one in such a state. Hannah had lost their first child at only two months. She was much further along this time, and the doctor monitored Hannah and the baby carefully. He told her constantly to take it easy. Thankfully, Hannah's mother, Sarah, was able to help. She and Hannah's father, Jacob, were nearby in the main house, while Samuel and Hannah lived in the smaller cottage which had been built a few feet from the back door.

Samuel returned his attention to the wood. He had cut a white oak tree at the far side of the farm, which spanned seventy-five acres. The graying white bark had V-shaped patches and ridges. The characteristics of the wood blended well with the simple furniture he and his forebears had constructed.

Samuel intended the cradle as a surprise to Hannah. He devoted an hour each afternoon to working on the project and wanted it to be perfect.

There were times he questioned his competency as a husband and father. He had lost his own parents when he was young, and he wasn't really taught what it was to be a man. Hannah's father was the best example he had in that light. He deeply respected Hannah's father as did all the local Amish folk, however, Samuel often felt as though he lived in Jacob's shadow. Jacob seemed to do everything right. He was a loving pillar in their community and often thought of as a leader of sorts. Samuel wasn't sure if he could ever be the man Jacob was.

The cradle was an offering of love and devotion to his wife and unborn child. Samuel sanded the wood down to a smooth, soft finish and laid it carefully on his work table until the next day's work.

"*Liebchen*," Samuel whispered to Hannah as he went into their tiny cottage and kissed her on the forehead.

She was working on a quilt for the baby. The quilt had larger squares which had alternating white hearts at the centers, and every other square had smaller pastel squares sewn into an "X" shape. The colors used were yellow, blue, pink, and green. Whether Hannah had a baby girl or a baby boy, the quilt would be perfect. She placed the quilt she was piecing together on the table in front of her and turned her attention to Samuel.

"*Mann*. How did today go?" Hannah inquired.

"The heat is slowing us down," Samuel admitted. "All we can do is pray for rain and for fall to come quickly."

"Yah," Hannah agreed.

Samuel washed up and helped Hannah to her feet as they made their way to the main house for dinner.

"*Maemm*," the two said to Sarah as they found their way to the dining room table. Jacob joined his family and led them in prayer as they held hands in a circle around the table. They sat and prayed in silence until Jacob said, "Amen."

Sarah prepared a delicious meal, as always. They passed around the shepherd's pie and sauerkraut, while a peach pie awaited them for dessert. Though Sarah loved taking care of her family and preparing meals, it had become a more grueling task recently, given the lack of good, cool air.

The men didn't think about the heat during dinnertime. The long days of hard work kept their appetites going, and Hannah was always hungry these days. She was eating for two now.

***

Jacob arose at 4 a.m. as he often did and sat in his rocking chair as he read his Bible. He searched for answers to assure himself that things would improve, and that the drought would end soon. As head of the house, he felt responsible for his loved ones, but ultimately he knew it was all in God's hands. Still, everyone looked to him to be the calm and rational one in times of trouble. He sought comfort and strength through God in his daily Bible readings. As he finished reading the book of Jeremiah, he joined Sarah in the kitchen as she prepared breakfast.

"*Gute Mariye*," she greeted him with a smile.

Sarah felt total joy in each day. She arose each morning and saw them as new beginnings full of promise and hope.

"*Gute Mariye*," Jacob echoed as he hugged her gently, pressing his hollowed cheekbones over hers. His demeanor was always strong, yet gentle.

"Dr. Stotzfus will be coming today to check on our Hannah," Sarah informed Jacob.

"*Gut.*"

Jacob grabbed his hat from the peg near the front door, and rushed out after eating the breakfast Sarah had prepared for him. There was much to be done, and he wanted to make as much progress as possible before the stifling heat set in and slowed them down. He headed towards the barn to milk the cows. Samuel did most of the heavier work on the farm, while Jacob did lighter chores these days. Some days they worked together out in the fields.

It was only six in the morning, but the excess milk had to be delivered to the dumping station by 9 a.m. They kept only enough milk for the day and sold or gave away the rest. The few dollars they earned from the milk and eggs he collected were enough to keep them going, especially since the drought made the harvest so meager.

"That's a girl," he told the first cow as he pulled on its udders. They didn't have modern equipment to milk the cows as some of the locals did. Samuel hadn't given into the temptation to modernize. He gently patted the first cow before going on to the next. He steadfastly ignored the twinge he felt in his chest as he got up.

"It's just a little indigestion," he assured himself. He had eaten too much scrapple for breakfast, he thought as the pain passed. He had more work to do. The animals needed to be fed, and their pens needed to be cleaned.

Though some of the animals had to be sold from time to time, and some had been lost to the heat, there were a good many animals to care for on the farm. There were cows, goats, sheep, and chickens. The chickens laid fewer and fewer eggs during the oppressive heat, which almost didn't justify the cost on feed for them. Jacob remained optimistic and looked for better days. He had run the farm for a long time. He knew the drought would pass and better seasons would come.

***

Hannah arose and prepared for her visit with Dr. Stotzfus. She pulled her long auburn locks back away from her freckled face and fastened her hair into a bun at the back of her head. She then placed her white prayer cap over her head. She was anxious to see what the doctor had to say on his visit with her.

Dr. Stotzfus was a balding man of short stature, but a jovial fellow. He was raised Amish but had left the church to join the military and received his medical training there. When his career in the Army was over, he returned to serve the community as a doctor. He was one of the few in the area who had the modern conveniences of an automobile and a phone. He drove around to all of the homes in the community that needed his services. He faithfully kept watch over Hannah to help prevent another miscarriage.

He carefully examined Hannah and listened to both her and the baby's heartbeats. He took some of her blood with a syringe and did a couple of tests with some small machines he brought to the visit. His jolly demeanor turned to one of concern.

"I'm worried about your sugar levels and the amount of fluid your body is holding, Hannah."

He tried not to sound too alarmed, but Sarah could tell that he was.

"I'm going to check on you three times a week from now on, but in the meantime, I need for you to follow this diet," he said as he handed her a list. "And stay off your feet! You need to elevate your legs and rest."

He pulled Sarah aside and told him that Hannah had pre-gestational diabetes as well as signs of pre-eclampsia. Sarah was familiar with pre-eclampsia as she herself had lost a child due to having the condition. He told her that if Hannah were to get much worse, she'd probably need to be monitored closer to a hospital, so it was of utmost importance that she was taken care of appropriately. He knew Sarah did all of the cooking for Hannah, so he gave her special instructions - lots of meat, vegetables, minimum starches and sugar, and foods that had a lot of iron as Hannah was also anemic. He handed her a bottle of iron pills.

"*Denki*, doctor," Sarah said as she ushered Dr. Stotzfus to the door and handed him a couple of loaves of bread and some eggs. "Don't worry. I will take care of our Hannah."

Sarah returned to Hannah's side. Hannah grew weary of all the rest time, but she took the doctor's concerns to heart. She didn't want lose this baby too.

"Trust in God and lean not into thy own understanding," Sarah told her. "It will all be okay."

***

Samuel was back in his tiny woodshed working on the cradle. He had meticulously carved a hummingbird into the headboard. He knew Hannah loved hummingbirds, and it was a nice, added touch. He screwed the side panels of the cradle to the headboard and footboard. The bottom panel was secured by joints. He sanded the finish one more time and applied a coat of oil. He decided the color was perfect as it was. The cradle was finished. He looked at the cradle from side to side and top to bottom.

"*Gut*," he said to himself, satisfied with his work. His next project would be to build a frame swing that he could put the cradle on. He mopped the sweat from his brow.

"Another day," he said. "Another day."

Samuel whistled as he made his way out of the wood shed towards the house. He was happy with his surprise for Hannah. There weren't as many flowers along the path because of the lack of rain, but there was a huge mound of bright yellow Black Eyed Susan flowers. They had black centers and the flower heads were each about four inches across. Hannah had sowed the seeds herself along with many of the other garden flowers on the property. The Black Eyed Susan blooms didn't seem to mind the dry dust as much as the other flowers that had diminished.

Samuel paused to pick a few of the large yellow flowers for Hannah. He loved to make her happy, and there was so little to do that these days. The heat was hard on everyone, but especially hard on Hannah as the idleness proved difficult on her.

"*Liebchen*," he greeted Hannah as he pecked her dimpled cheek and handed her the flowers.

Hannah's face lit up.

"*Denki*."

Sarah decided to bring dinner to Hannah and Samuel, in an effort to minimize Hannah's walking. She prepared an iron-rich meal to help with Hannah's anemia – liver pudding, sauerkraut, and shoofly pie. The molasses pie had a lot of iron and would comfort and soothe Hannah's weary body. Hannah was not fond of liver pudding, however, and turned her nose up at the sight of it. She felt bad for doing so as Sarah worked so hard to help them, and Hannah quickly corrected herself.

"*Denki, Maemm*," Hannah said trying to sound more grateful as she restored her smile.

"I'll get the dishes in the morning," Sarah said on her way out of the cottage.

"You've been coming in a little later these days," Hannah quizzed Samuel.

"*Yah*," Samuel admitted. "There are a couple of smaller projects on the farm that I've been working on, but I'm almost done. You'll soon have more time to grow tired of me again," he said with a smile as he picked up their dinner plates.

"Never," Hannah said. "I don't know if that could ever happen."

Samuel brought the dishes to the kitchen, and Hannah started to join him. He motioned her back to elevate her legs as the doctor ordered, much to her disappointment.

"I'm so tired of just laying around," she exclaimed.

Hannah was accustomed to hard work. She was bored and restless.

"You won't be laying around for long, *liebchen*. You'll soon have plenty to do," Samuel promised as he kissed her forehead.

Samuel took the checkerboard from the table in the living area and brought it to Hannah so they could play a game. He was intent on distracting her from her boredom.

"I win again," she said.

"Ah, so you do."

"Perhaps you are letting me win so many games? Could that be, *Mann*?"

"Nope. You won fair and square."

There had been times Samuel purposefully put little effort out to score a victory, but this was not one of them. He normally gave Hannah a run for her money, but he was tired and ready for bed. He extinguished the oil lamp and lay down next to Hannah.

"*Guten Nacht*," Samuel said affectionately as he kissed Hannah on the forehead.

"*Guten Nacht.*"

***

Jacob lit the kerosene lamp as he made his way to his rocking chair. Though he had a full night's sleep, he was quite tired and felt somewhat under the weather. He held the Bible he had read from since he was a little boy and faithfully read from its pages. He had drawn strength from the Bible many times in his life, and he had learned the evening before from Sarah of the challenges faced by Hannah and her pregnancy. He had faith that God would see her through this. Everything seemed overwhelming at times – the drought and heat, the farm, Hannah's difficulties – but he knew it would all work out in the end, in God's timing.

It was a day that Samuel and Jacob were to work together in the fields. The fencing needed repair, as some of the animals had made their way out of the property. Sarah packed them a peanut butter sandwich lunch so they wouldn't have to make the long walk in the heat until they were finished for the day.

"*Gott* be with you," Sarah faithfully told him as she walked him to the door. She sighed as she lost sight of him, knowing the day would not be easy for him. They were not spring chickens anymore, and the heat did not help things. She pulled the crisp white curtains back to usher in the morning sun and went to check on Hannah.

The two men met each other in the pasture. Samuel had filled the wagon with fence posts, slats of wood, nails, hammers and other supplies. He pulled the wagon as they made their way through the farmland. The sun was rising and the widening crystal blue sky offered a panoramic view. The once fertile pasture was becoming more barren, and the cornstalks which grew the feed for the animals were more spindly and parched, but the farm was still a beautiful, peaceful place.

Jacob had worked the land all of his life. It was his gold and in his blood. He couldn't deny it was getting harder and harder. He was thankful to have the help of his son-in-law. He wouldn't have made those past few months without Samuel.

They pounded fence posts into the ground and drove nails where it was needed. There was a lot of fencing to cover. They worked relentlessly to get it all done.

As the day wore on, an orange haze cast itself over the farm and the fields. It was blistering hot in the afternoons. The men took a break under a large tree, which shaded them some from the heat.

"I'm really proud of the work you are doing on the farm," Jacob said to Samuel.

The compliment caught Samuel off guard. He looked up to Jacob and it meant a lot to him that Jacob noticed his efforts.

"*Denki*, sir," Samuel nodded.

"One day, this will be yours and Hannah's. You've earned it for sure."

Samuel had lost his parents to an accident when he was younger. They were in their buggy on the road when a truck hit them head-on. Samuel was the youngest, and his older siblings raised him with the help of an aunt and uncle who lived nearby. It was a logical choice to live with Hannah's parents on their farm when the invitation was extended as everyone else seemed to have a place, and Hannah's parents needed help on the farm.

The men drank from their thermos bottles and tried to save some water for the walk home. It would seem like a longer stretch since it was later and hotter, and they were more tired. As they made their way back, Jacob's breathing grew labored. He tried to convince himself that it was normal given the circumstances, and he pressed on. He paused a moment and rested his hands above his knees as he tried to catch his breath. His chest felt heavy, and he couldn't speak. He waved at Samuel as he grabbed his chest. Helplessly, Samuel watched Jacob crumble to the ground.

There was nothing Samuel could do. He was in shock. Hannah's father was gone. He felt the weight of the world on his shoulders. He didn't want to have to tell Hannah. This would crush her.

Samuel carried Jacob back home on the empty wagon from which he had dumped the remaining supplies. He tried to wipe the tears which flowed from his face. He needed to be strong for the women.

Sarah looked through the window and saw Samuel pulling the wagon with Jacob stretched across it. She let out a gasp and ran to them. Samuel explained what had happened in a low voice. Sarah allowed herself a moment of grief, but turned her attention to Hannah. How could she tell her in such a fragile state?

"We must be strong for Hannah," Sarah gently ordered Samuel.

He nodded in agreement, wiping away his tears.

***

Funerals were about the only time the small Amish communities stepped away from the tradition of wearing their simple, light colored clothing. The women wore black, and those closest to the family wore it for an extended period of time.

Hundreds of people from around the local Amish communities went to the farm for Jacob's funeral. Hannah's and Samuel's siblings had come out early to set up seating and food areas, from the barn to the house. Jacob's body was placed in a simple pine coffin, which rested in the middle of the living room of his and Sarah's home. People payed their respects and told many stories of Jacob, filled with their fond memories of him, then made their way out where guests visited and ate. A simple spread of cold cuts, cheeses, breads, vegetables, and pies lined the tables. Everyone pitched in and took the burden off of Sarah and Hannah. Hannah was allowed a break from bed rest for the day, but Samuel and Sarah monitored her closely to be sure she didn't overdo it.

When the time came to bury Jacob, a procession formed for the ride out to the nearby cemetery. Samuel helped Hannah and Sarah into their buggy as they led dozens of horses and buggies toward the burial ground. He suppressed his emotions, but Jacob's passing had rattled Samuel, bringing back strong memories of losing his own parents.

The cemetery was a beautiful spot and a weak breeze occasionally blew through the grounds, lending a scant respite from the heat. All of the headstones were plain, unmarked, white stones in keeping with the Amish tradition.

The minister spoke a little, and the ritual concluded with the funeral goers chanting the words to the hymn, "Nearer, My God, to thee":

"Or if, on joyful wing, cleaving the sky,
Sun, moon, and stars forgot, upward I fly,
Still all my song shall be,
Nearer, my God, to thee;
Nearer, my God, to thee, nearer to thee!"

***

Two weeks had passed since Jacob's burial. Sarah spoke to Samuel and Hannah during dinner concerning a decision she made.

"It is time for me to live in the cottage and for the two of you to move into the main home. It is as it should be, and your father would want the same thing. It's time for a new generation to make their home here."

It was also Sarah's way of trying to make Samuel feel more comfortable as the new head of the household. The young couple conceded to Sarah's request. There was not much to move as they lived a simple life and did not have many personal belongings. Samuel moved what little there was while Sarah visited with Hannah.

"*Maemm*, are you sure this is what you want?"

"Of course, my Hannah. This is as it should be. And I will be right at your back door should you need me," she offered with a smile as they held each other's hand.

Sarah was a pillar of strength and faith. She fully believed that everything happened had a reason, and she trusted in God's plan for all things.

After Samuel moved things from one house to the other, there was one last thing to bring into the main house. He felt it was the right time to surprise Hannah with the cradle he made for their baby.

"For you, my *liebchen*, and our baby."

Hannah's eyes filled with tears. The cradle was more beautiful than she would have hoped for. She realized this was probably what Samuel was doing all those evenings he returned home later than expected.

"It's beautiful. I love it. *Denki*."

Samuel placed the cradle in their new bedroom off to the side and noticed a chest that was left behind. As he started to carry it out to Sarah's new home, she stopped him.

"It is mostly heirlooms. Some were Hannah's when she was younger, including some clothes that will be perfect for the baby. Leave it here."

Samuel nodded and left the chest in its place. Everything was moved from one house to the other, and Sarah kissed them as she made her way back to her tiny new home, but not before reminding Hannah to rest.

"Remember to take it easy, my Hannah."

"I will, *Maemm*."

"And I will be sure she does," Samuel promised.

***

Time was getting closer to the baby's arrival. Dr. Stotzfus remained alarmed over a few things concerning Hannah and the baby, but things had not progressed as badly as he had feared. He was more hopeful than he had been that Hannah could safely deliver her child.

Samuel had neighboring helpers on certain days to help with the farm chores, but he handled much of the farm responsibilities on his own. It was Sarah's job to continue looking after Hannah until the baby arrived.

It was August, and there were not too many more hot days left for the Pennsylvania summer. Rain had fallen too infrequently and the crops continued to struggle. Samuel wondered if he should bother planting the winter crops. He was not as confident in his decision making as Jacob always seemed to be. Some of the wheels for the buggy needed to be replaced, the barn was in need of repair, a new well needed to be dug, and more. The canned goods in the cellar were depleted as there was less to preserve. There was so much that needed to be done and not very much money, time, or manpower. Expecting a baby added more to the urgency of it all. He felt responsible for his family and wanted to make the best decisions.

Samuel stopped the plow and grabbed his suspender as he looked out into the fields. Composing himself, he prayed silently:

"Make me the man you intend for me to be. Make me a man that Hannah can be proud of. Help me to be half the man Jacob was. Please look after Hannah and help all to go well with her and the baby. Amen."

He unleashed his burdens to God and felt somewhat better, as he continued plowing the fields. He made his way home, and he saw that Hannah going through the heirloom chest that her mother left behind for them.

"Hannah," he said. "Should you be out of bed?"

"It's only for a little while," she assured him. "I get so tired of doing nothing all day."

Samuel noticed the doll that Hannah was holding. It was a muslin doll with a blue dress and a white pinafore fashioned over the long sleeved underdress. The doll had a black bonnet and no eyes or lips. Hannah had received the doll one Christmas, and it was tucked away once she outgrew it.

She had once asked her father why the doll had no face? Jacob told her it was because everyone looked the same to God, and he loved everyone equally. Jacob had asked Sarah to sew a wooden button at the center of the pinafore, after he had carved an "H" at the center, which stood for "Hannah."

"I had almost forgotten about this doll all these years," Hannah told Samuel as tears flooded her face. Finding the doll had unleashed a wash of memories of her father's kindness and wisdom.

"Do you ever wish our faith allowed us to have photographs, Samuel?"

The question surprised Samuel.

"If we had photographs, it would be something we could remember our loved ones by," she reasoned. "Then I could see my father every day and you could see your parents."

"Perhaps," he told her. "But we can keep our memories of them in our hearts," he told Hannah as he lay his hand over her chest.

"*Yah*," she agreed as she placed the doll back in the chest.

***

Hannah woke just before daybreak with labor pains. It was not supposed to happen yet. The expected delivery date was still two to three weeks out.

"*Bobbel*," she yelled and awoke Samuel. "Baby is coming!"

Samuel leapt from the bed and assured Hannah that everything would be ok. He lit the kerosene lamp and told Hannah he was running to the cottage to get Sarah. Deep down, Samuel was frightened. He knew it was too early and with the difficulties she had experienced during the pregnancy, he knew Hannah would be too. He collected himself quickly, because he knew he had to be strong for the women and most especially, Hannah.

Sarah rushed to Hannah's side. Her water had not broken yet, and Hannah's contractions were still far enough apart to get help, Sarah hoped. Sarah had assisted in home births before, but she didn't want to take a chance with Hannah.

"Go, as fast as you can and get Dr. Stotzfus," she quietly told Samuel. "But first, put a pot of water boiling on the woodstove."

Dr. Stotzfus lived three miles away and whether Samuel ran or took the buggy, it would take him about a half hour to reach Dr. Stotzfus. At least with a car, it would only take Dr. Stotzfus five minutes to return.

Sarah's attention focused on Hannah. Hannah held her breath out of instinct, but Sarah told her to breathe.

"Slow, deep breaths, my Hannah," she gently ordered.

"I didn't know it could hurt so much, *Maemm*," Hannah said.

"Of course, it hurts, my Hannah. But when it's all over with, you will quickly forget the pain," Sarah promised.

Hannah was supine on the bed. Sarah had learned through many births this position was okay until the birth pains got closer. Then, Hannah would have to sit up.

The contractions soon grew closer, three minutes apart. Sarah figured Hannah was mostly dilated, but her water still had not broken. This worried Sarah. She knew the water should have broken by now. She hoped Samuel would soon arrive with Dr. Stotzfus.

Hannah's breathing quickened, and she panted furiously, while sweat poured from her face. Sarah grabbed a towel and dipped it in cool water, as she gently dabbed the damp towel over Hannah's face.

"You are doing well. You are doing well, my brave Hannah. Just try to slow your breathing down a little bit," Sarah requested.

At that moment, Hannah's water broke, and the labor pains were very close together. The baby began to crown, and Sarah knew it would not be long before the baby would be born.

"Slow, deep breath, then one big push," Sarah told Hannah.

Hannah pushed hard and let out a scream as the baby made its entrance into the world. Samuel and Dr. Dr. Stotzfus entered

the room just as it happened. They rushed to Hannah's side, and after a quick check, Dr. Stotzfus assured everyone that both Hannah and baby were okay.

"Looks like you two ladies didn't need me after all," Dr. Stotzfus chuckled.

"Hannah and Samuel – you have a little baby girl," Dr. Stotzfus announced as he wiped the baby clean and cut the umbilical cord. Sarah wrapped the baby in a blanket and handed her to Hannah.

"Now you will know what it's like to love someone more than anything else in the world," she told Hannah.

Samuel and Sarah sat on either side of Hannah, proudly smiling from ear to ear at the events of the morning. The sun was rising, the birds were trilling their songs, and a new life had come into the world.

"What shall we name her?" Samuel asked.

"How about Ruth?" Sarah nudged. "After your mother, Samuel."

Samuel had no words. He was twelve when he lost his mother, and he couldn't think of a more perfect way to honor her.

"Ruth, it is." Samuel and Hannah were both touched by Sarah's thoughtfulness.

Samuel went to the heirloom chest and retrieved the doll that was Hannah's when she was a little girl. Since they had a little girl, it was fitting for it to be handed down to baby Ruth. Hannah agreed and the doll would stay with baby Ruth in her cradle until she was old enough to play with it.

***

Baby Ruth was growing and healthy. Days were more normal at the Fisher farm. Hannah was able to help her mother with chores to help keep the homestead going, and Samuel was busy working the farm and planting crops. The days were getting cooler, but rain was still scarce and threatening production of the crops.

Hannah became more concerned that Samuel wasn't being decisive enough about the problems that plagued the farm. She worried more about things now that she was a mother.

"*Maemm*," she told her mom. "We have very few canned goods left, and I think Samuel could use help on the farm, but he insists on doing it all."

They always had a bounty of jars filling the cellar. They had canned most of their vegetables, and fruits from their trees, as well as some of the meat from their animals. They didn't have a freezer as some of the neighbors did. So they relied on the food they produced and preserved to survive, but the months of the drought affected their stock.

"Not to worry, Hannah," her mother told her. "God always provides."

"But *Daat* wouldn't have let things get to this place," Hannah responded.

Sarah raised her eyebrows in surprise. "Patience! It will all happen in good time. Your father had years of experience. Samuel is just learning to be his own man, and he didn't have always have a father to teach him. Give him time and trust your husband and God."

"I will try," Hannah agreed.

The women continued their Saturday work. It was the day of the week when they dusted all of the furniture and mopped all of the wood floors. It was a tradition they did together, both helping the other with their houses.

Later in the evening, Sarah told the young couple that they should devote time to each other alone, and she would watch baby Ruth. It had been a while since the young couple had spent some time together, and Sarah hoped the evening together would be good for them. She didn't mind the extra time with her granddaughter either.

Samuel had a surprise for Hannah. He had waited for a moment such as this. He lured her into the pasture, where he had nailed sheets between two trees. He parked the buggy out in front of the sheets, and there was a projector that he rigged to a car battery. He had found the items in a junk heap in the barn. He played Charlie Chaplin's film, "The Kid", over the projector and handed Hannah a paper bag filled with popcorn.

Hannah had only been to the picture show one time during Rumspringa when she was a teenager. During that time in her adolescence, she was permitted to spend the weekend at a cousin's house, whose family was part of a more liberal Mennonite community. There, she had watched "The Wizard of Oz." She had been amused, then, at the idea that Dorothy would laugh at the two men below in the boat as she was hurled into the tornado. She couldn't deny the movie was entertaining.

"Samuel, should we..." She was unsure of doing this. She was always taught to follow the Amish customs, and many didn't agree with the idea of watching films.

"I think it's okay. Don't worry," he told her.

Apprehension gave way to laughter as they watched the silent film star and his slapstick antics come alive on the makeshift screen.

The young parents settled into one another's arms as they watched the movie and ate popcorn. It was the most fun they had in a long time.

The next morning, Hannah went to get baby Ruth from Sarah, and Hannah reluctantly told her mom what happened the night before.

"I know *Daed* would be so disappointed, and we shouldn't have done that, *Maemm*, but..."

Sarah laughed and interrupted Hannah before she could finish.

"Where do you think all that stuff came from, dear? Your father did the same thing with me when we were about your age."

Then they both chuckled and made no mention of it again.

***

The holidays were coming up and Samuel continued to feel pressure about the lack of goods and funds for the homestead. He confided in Sarah about his worries. It was not a common thing for an Amish head of household to do, but Samuel felt comfortable speaking to Sarah about it.

"Jacob and I had the same trials and hardships when we were younger," Sarah shared with him.

"How did you get through it?" Samuel listened intently.

"Well, at times Jacob handled things without me knowing what he had done, but I do know that he sold trees off the property. It would tidy us over nicely."

Samuel had not thought of that. Suddenly, he felt a bit of hope for their situation.

He sold a few walnut trees at the far side of the property and received a generous sum. The wood made from the trees was in high demand and yielded a pretty good return. The loss of the trees hardly put a dent in the forested part of their land, and they were left with enough money to make necessary repairs around the farm, as well as fill their cellar until there were better times for the crops. Samuel also purchased a few things that made chores easier around the house and farm.

There was a good bit of money left, and Samuel wanted to bring the family to town to get things they needed. Hannah had gotten into quilting in a big way and decided she wanted to sell her creations, so she needed more supplies. Sarah gave them her blessing, and decided to stay home for the evening.

Samuel parked their horse and buggy along the path of the street as the family strolled the town. Baby Ruth was in a strolling carriage, and Hannah and Samuel pushed her as they enjoyed the sights of the town. It was nice to get away.

Hannah found her way into a shop that offered some beautiful fabric that she would enjoy fashioning some of their wardrobe items with as well as items that were perfect for quilting. She picked a few things out for Sarah as well.

Samuel enjoyed spoiling her that evening. They ended the day at a nice restaurant, which they had not done before as a new family. As they left the restaurant, they saw a flash of light from the corner of their eyes. It was a traveling photographer taking a photograph of a young family.

The flash of light jolted a memory from Hannah's mind. She remembered a time when as a young girl, about five or six, she and her father had come into town just as she had with her little family. She was drawn to the same kind of flash of light and asked her father about it.

He had allowed them to be photographed, and she remembered him placing the picture in a pocket that was on the dress of the muslin doll that had been Hannah's.

She remembered it all so vividly, yet wasn't sure if her memory was playing tricks on her. She picked up the muslin doll from Ruth's stroller where it rested, looking for a pocket.

There it was – a photo of Hannah and her dad. The photograph she once wished she had of her father when he passed away was near her all the while and now in her hands.

Hannah and Samuel smiled as they looked at the picture and read each other's minds. They had their photograph taken, along with baby Ruth, so that she would one day have a memento of their little family. Though they did not go so far as to display it, they could not believe that such a beautiful moment captured in time was truly part of the forbidden tree they had heard of their whole life.

9 798223 853480